LEADERS IN THE LABYRINTH

College Presidents and the Battleground of Creeds and Convictions

STEPHEN J. NELSON

AMERICAN COUNCIL ON EDUCATION
PRAEGER
Series on Higher Education

Library of Congress Cataloging-in-Publication Data

Nelson, Stephen James, 1947-
  Leaders in the labyrinth : college presidents and the battleground of
creeds and convictions / Stephen J. Nelson.
      p. cm. — (ACE/Praeger series on higher education)
  Includes bibliographical references and index.
  ISBN–13: 978–0–275–99792–2 (alk. paper)
  ISBN–10: 0–275–99792–8 (alk. paper)
  1. College presidents—Professional ethics—United States. 2. Education,
Higher—United States—Administration. 3. College presidents—
United States—Interviews. I. Title.
  LB2341.N3865 2007
  378.1'11—dc22   2007009380

British Library Cataloguing in Publication Data is available.

Library of Congress Catalog Card Number: 2007009380
ISBN–13: 978–0–275–99792–2
ISBN–10: 0–275–99792–8

First published in 2007

Praeger Publishers, 88 Post Road West, Westport, CT 06881
An imprint of Greenwood Publishing Group, Inc.
www.praeger.com

Printed in the United States of America

The paper used in this book complies with the
Permanent Paper Standard issued by the National
Information Standards Organization (Z39.48–1984).

10 9 8 7 6 5 4 3 2 1

To my loving wife, Janet
and
our inspiring and radiant son, Geoffrey

CONTENTS

ACKNOWLEDGMENTS

I t is an understatement to say that undertaking to research, write, and publish a book is tremendously complex, is fraught with ups and downs, and extracts extraordinary claims on patience, physical and mental resolve, and self-awareness and understanding (as well, certainly, as the patience and understanding, at the least, of others). More simply put, this task requires simple doggedness, though at the same time it is ultimately one of the most satisfying of life's endeavors. This book reflects all of that and more. Fortunate as I am that this is my second—and I trust not the last—opportunity to have a book appear in print, comparisons with the first are unavoidable and striking. However, going through the journey a subsequent time, I am repeatedly reminded about discipline and diligence.

I was struck last summer when Andre Agassi, having announced that the U.S. Open Tennis Tournament would be his last, began to reflect on the decision and the realities that gathered around him. He kept stressing the "process" involved, the fact that he had never faced the prospect of playing his last match, and that his evolution from unformed, ill-behaved, and mold-breaking teenage phenomenon to the seasoned, smart, senior professional athlete he had become was now in its last act. His insight about living in and through the process, about soaking it in because we all only rarely and only with the best of fortunes get to live such moments, is probably the best advice imaginable for any writer.

The tasks involved in producing a book are never easy. In fact, for this writer—and I am guessing surely for most, at least those whom it is my pleasure to know—the demands and the creative act of writing actually become more difficult. Nothing but the best will do. Even having been this way before and thus knowing much of what was entailed and would be demanded, I still found so many twists and turns and aspects of what is required in producing a book as to feel like beginning anew all over again. There are no shortcuts in writing, or for that matter in anything worth doing, and even foreknowledge of this reality proves to be of limited, though certainly not inconsequential, value.

Finally, and this dawned on me only as I began to write, this book is very different, crafted in a distinct way from *Leaders in the Crucible*, its predecessor. *Leaders in the Labyrinth* is a broader statement about the college presidency and the academy. I am grateful for having had this opportunity to extend my thinking and ideas about the presidency and the state of colleges and universities. Once again my perceptions and propositions are offered for public consumption and scrutiny. I take responsibility for the ideas, arguments, and thoughts contained in these pages. I hope that they contribute to our understandings of the college presidency and to the influence that these considerations might exert in shaping the future.

I am and continue to be indebted to numerous people. Once again, I am exceedingly grateful, and will be forever, for the counsel and wisdom of Professor William Jellema, professor emeritus at the University of Connecticut, my doctoral advisor there and my scholarly guide since then. Professor Jellema, in addition to his continued support and urgings to me to craft my inquiries in pursuit of ideas about the presidency, informed the pivotal focal point for my inquiry to the presidents who were interviewed and thus by extension for the unfolding story and the argument I make in this book. When I asked for his advice about the direction for the research, he responded that if it were he, the questions to the presidents would be: "What do (did) you grapple with most inside the gates of the academy, and what do (did) you grapple with most outside the gates?" These two questions formed the basis for the interviews with presidents, and thereby the narrative that unfolds here.

Second, I am extremely indebted to the Kellogg Foundation and Dr. Richard Foster, its program director. Rick enthusiastically endorsed my original proposal and pursued financial support from Kellogg without which I simply would not have been able to travel to interview the 15 presidents whose thoughtful analysis are the basis for this research and account. Funding support in the humanities is not easy to come by. The Kellogg Foundation's and Rick's investment and support for this endeavor were critical and essential.

Fifteen current and former college and university presidents were willing to share thoughts, ideas, and beliefs about the presidency, about the immediate and long-term challenges and issues that they regularly face, about the demands that influence the presidential office, and about the present and future shape of the academy. I selected this distinguished group for a couple of important reasons.

First, they are all prominent leaders of renowned colleges and universities in America. Thus their presidential "homes" are at institutions clearly on the radar screen, certainly to those who follow higher education but to casual observers as well. Second, these presidencies have all been publicly challenged for their responses to controversies, and for their decisions. In some instances these circumstances, realities, and decisions are relatively well known publicly. In others, the circumstances are less well known and require an insider view that informs a sense about what is on the record and about making reasoned choices in selection. Finally, this group is admittedly elite, not necessarily or maybe at all representative—other than my attempts to garner a reasonable mixture of individuals and their perspectives—of the full range of previous and contemporary presidents, and the widely varied types of colleges and universities around the land. However, it is my belief that they are not very different from presidents of any type of college or university. That is, despite the by and large high status they and their institutions represent, the major ideas, the issues, the ideals, and the leadership navigation and negotiation they engage, as well as the fundamental values and principles of the academy to which they adhere, are in a mainstream that is experienced universally or nearly so throughout American higher education and its presidencies.

The presidents and the institutions they serve that are featured in the pages that follow are as follows: Johnnetta Cole, Spelman and Bennett Colleges; Mary Sue Coleman, University of Michigan; John DiBiaggio, University of Connecticut, Michigan State University, and Tufts University; Theodore Hesburgh, Notre Dame; Donald Kennedy, Stanford University; Nannerl Keohane, Wellesley College and Duke University; James Laney, Emory University; Walter Massey, Morehouse College; Robert Oden, Kenyon, and Carleton Colleges; Frank Rhodes, Cornell University; Judith Rodin, University of Pennsylvania; Neil L. Rudenstine, Harvard University; John Sexton, New York University; Harold Shapiro, University of Michigan and Princeton University; and Stephen Trachtenberg, University of Hartford and George Washington University.

All presidents have staffs that make things tick. I was greatly assisted in my work by the professional staff members serving these presidents, sadly far too numerous to list by name, who were gracious and resourceful in scheduling the interviews, assisted in leading me to complementary speeches and writings, facilitated logistical arrangements, and otherwise provided great hospitality. These are fine people without whom these presidents would not be able to function as they do. I could not have done my work without their aid and guidance.

It goes without saying that presidents are extremely busy people, so even the dedication of an hour or so of their time to serve as cornerstones for this research project is a remarkable contribution and its own testimony to their leadership, style, and vision. These presidents shared their stories and their ideas. It is my task and opportunity to pass on their thoughts and perspectives as accurately as possible to you, the reader. You will and should judge the extent to which I have succeeded. However, I hope in no way will that judgment diminish what these presidents have to say, and the willingness and candor with which they said it.

Every book must have an editor, a critical influence and guide in the process. In this case, I wish to thank Susan Slesinger of Praeger Publishers for her support, guidance, investment in this work, and follow-through in bringing about the completed project. She is truly professional, gracious and honest, and works with the utmost capability, collaboration, and partnership. No author could ask for more. Susan enabled this book to see the light of day.

The Center for the Advancement of Research and Teaching (CART) at Bridgewater State College supported the last stage of preparations for the publication of this book through a small grant that enabled the employment of one of our graduate students to assist with the critical but time-consuming tasks of gaining necessary approvals and copyright permissions, as well as the copyediting, final preparation, and indexing of the manuscript. Thus I am thankful for Carla Blanchard, who also served during the present academic year (2006–7) as a graduate research assistant, for her capacities and enormous help in the final preparation stages, assisting me in meeting the necessary requirements and deadlines, and providing outstanding and dependable assistance. I was also assisted with research by Marc DeBush in the summer of 2003 under an undergraduate research and teaching assistant grant from Brown University.

I would be most remiss not to mention the debt I owe to my spouse and life-partner of over 35 years, Janet Cooper Nelson. Janet shares love without measure, and provides boundless support, especially in the ups and downs from the start to the completion of this book. She is an intellectual teammate in our many probing and passionate discussions driven by our mutual interest in the academy, its leadership, and its inspirations and aspirations. Janet is truly a strength, guide, and stay. But finally, but no less crucially, is our son Geoffrey, who continually inspires with his own emerging voice and writing style, and who is another teammate in ways that he probably knows only in part, but will come to know more fully as our lives unfold.

I am grateful for the opportunity to be able to research and write. It is a passion and a lifework. I have had the good fortune of many gifts throughout my life. That life is a blessing and a treasure. This book is a small portion of what I am able to give in return.

Stephen J. Nelson

Providence, RI
April 17, 2007

INTRODUCTION

This is a story about the college and university presidency at the dawning of the twenty-first century. Presidents and their leadership are directly connected to the institutions they serve; thus it is impossible to consider presidential leaders and their office absent considerations about the institution of the university. The voice of today's presidents tells much about the state of both the presidency and the university, linked in fortunes and misfortunes.

The premise of this book and its bird's-eye view of presidents is that the presidency has developed, in response to historical times and pressures, to the people aspiring to the office, and to the tradition of and changes in the university and college. Changes have not been planned in any global sense. Rather they occur as institutions address their discrete hopes and needs in different times and in their selection of leaders. Likewise, as an institution, the university has evolved more than been systematically engineered, its autonomy a glorious characteristic making higher education in America the envy of the world.

The problem is that there are fundamental values and principles underlying and undergirding the university, and presidents are expected to be protectors and defenders of that heritage and foundation. If the university is to remain the university as it has historically been known and has flourished, it will in large part be because of the duty and wisdom of presidents. This is where our story begins.

Presidents, especially those who oversee high-profile institutions, are visible public figures. Their every word and their daily actions are signals that regularly draw strong positive and negative reactions, which lead to caricatures of individual presidents and stereotypical characterizations of the office. One need only consider the early-term controversies of President Larry Summers at

Harvard about public utterances and assumptions about private conversations to understand the weight of these judgments on presidents and their institutions. The situation is amplified and often exaggerated in the climate of inquiry and skepticism characteristic of the academy.

The intention of this book is straightforward, but also complex. The hope is to reveal the voices of leaders, allowing them to speak about the challenges they face and about the future they envision for the presidency and for the academy. At the outset it is important to note three general assumptions about the college and university presidency underlying the problematic of this book.

First, there is an ongoing debate about historic changes to the presidency. Are those changes simply few and of minor consequence in the larger picture of the office? Or has change, especially in recent decades, been so extensive and dramatic as to alter the presidency significantly and irrevocably? Our sense about present leaders is frequently set against romanticized opinions and renderings of the college president "giants" of previous eras. Regardless of judgment about these changes, the presidency remains a highly significant and highly rewarding post. At the same time it is an enormously complex and demanding position with significant potential and realized influence on campus and in society. Presidents report workweeks that approach or exceed 12-hour days, six and seven days a week. Neil Rudenstine allegedly worked on the order of 120 hours per week early in his presidency at Harvard, prior to reducing that load when it became clear it was physically impossible to continue such a pace.

One belief is that over time there has been a major change in the length of tenure of presidents. Some lower estimates purport the average tenure to be in the range of three or so years, at first glance much shorter than in previous eras. However, if we look at the continuous service of today's "career presidents" and their multiple presidencies, service for 10 years and more as a president, whether at one or more than one place, is not an anomaly. Thus, many presidents continue the tenure tradition of the "giants," serving much, much longer than many contemporaries.

To name just a few: Stephen Trachtenberg, 25-plus years and counting at the University of Hartford and George Washington University; John DiBiaggio, three presidencies, at the University of Connecticut, Michigan State University, and Tufts University, spanning nearly 25 years; Gordon Gee, similarly 20-plus years at West Virginia University, the University of Colorado, Ohio State, Brown University, and Vanderbilt University; Nan Keohane's recently completed more than 20 years at the head of Wellesley College and Duke University; and John Silber's nearly 30-year tenure at Boston University. On balance, the presidency, at least in terms of long tenure on par with the "giants," may have changed much less than commonly assumed.

Second, in general anyone succeeding to a presidency must want to do the enormously strenuous work demanded in order to survive well in office and to fit the role. Surely, there are exceptions to this assumption. Some aspire to presidencies only to find that it is not a personal "fit." For example, President Heffner at Brown in the middle to late 1960s came to his post through a brief time as a provost at the University of Indiana, and appeared to have the proper preparation of an upward ladder to a presidency. Heffner's were tumultuous times for presidents, many being driven from office by protests, tensions, and the often no-win grind of mediating between warring factions. After four short years, Heffner concluded this was simply not for him. He was a Renaissance literature scholar, personally drawn to return to that life.

More recently there have been a number of similar instances of mismatch between the personal complexion of a president and the realities of the expectations of the position, including ever-present institutional political dynamics. Whenever there is such a "misfit," the preferable course is a change as soon as possible in the interest of both individuals and institutions.

Certainly there are occasional presidents who merely seek status and prominence, failing to embrace the work and the larger role and duty of the office to the future of the university writ large for its own sake. John DiBiaggio tells of attending one of the many annually held meetings of newly appointed presidents with already serving presidents.[1] An elevator conversation ran something like this. A "veteran" told a couple of new presidents how difficult, impossible, and really horrible the job was. He warned them that the high point was the appointment itself and everything would be downhill from there. DiBiaggio's experience had been quite the opposite, but he withheld comment at the time. However, he remains at a quizzical loss as to how or why someone would bother doing such a consuming job without a sense of its historical importance and potential. It will come as no surprise that the perspectives and opinions of presidents we will see here see the position and office certainly to be enormously demanding, but also highly and fully rewarding.

A last assumption, important in the present and for the future, is that inevitably and repeatedly we get what we look for in searches for presidential appointments. Presidents must wear many hats. Their primary responsibilities are often simply and somewhat cynically reduced to being politicians both on and off the campus, managing public relations, administering academic bureaucracies, and spending inordinate amounts of time fund-raising. Of these, the last draws great and regular attention.

Fund-raising is commonly believed, in stark contrast with their predecessors, to be *the* major priority bar none that current presidents must accomplish. Influential constituents, especially trustees and alumni, frequently want tangible results and stress money-raising above all else. Certainly developing the resources necessary to run colleges and universities is a chief responsibility. Mary Sue Coleman of the University of Michigan indicates that a foremost agenda item and expectation of her tenure as president is to engage a capital campaign, putting the university on a future footing like that enjoyed by private universities.[2] In short, even presidents of public universities, such as Coleman and her successors, will have to function more and more like private university presidents. Not only will this pressure not go away, but, if anything, it will expand and worsen in intensity and reach.

But if we reduce the criteria for a desirable college president to fund-raising and development alone, then that is surely what we will get. If all we seek are leaders capable of creating a public image for themselves and their institutions, then that is what we will get. I believe it critical to view the presidency more comprehensively. We have to understand both the office of president and the academy as institutions possessing fundamental and essential foundations. Presidents must embody these foundations as features of their office and visibly connect them to the values of the university. That requires presidents defined by more than being fund-raisers, managers of academic bureaucracies, and public-image spinners for their campuses.

The presidents featured in this volume point to these foundations and concerns about the office. In these presidents we see not simply fund-raisers, although they clearly understand the expectation and responsibility to raise money and do not shirk from this task. Rather they integrate these core duties into the presidential office. They define the role and prospects of the presidency, framing development and fund-raising in ways that do not diminish their public leadership and voice. These presidents show that the bully pulpit of office can be maintained, and that there is space to be a public intellectual.

Shifting from these assumptions, what then are the primary responsibilities and expectations that sketch the state of the college and university presidency at the beginning of the twenty-first century? What issues and concerns constitute the major challenges to presidents, to their office, and to the values and principles of the university?

One major responsibility today, though one also observable historically, is the need for presidents to identify, to create where necessary, and to preserve a common core and common understanding among the diverse constituents within and beyond the gates of the academy. Donald Kennedy, former president of Stanford, uses these lines from Yeats' poem, "The Second Coming," to underscore this challenge and what is at stake:

> Turning and turning in the widening gyre
> The falcon cannot hear the falconer;
> Things fall apart; the centre cannot hold;
> Mere anarchy is loosed upon the world,
> The blood-dimmed tide is loosed, and everywhere
> The ceremony of innocence is drowned;
> The best lack all convictions, while the worst
> Are full of passionate intensity.[3]

From the very beginnings of colleges and universities in America, presidents have been responsible for locating and protecting a "center" by defining a set of central values, beliefs, and premises within the saga of their institutions to which broad and diverse elements of their varied constituencies can adhere.

This task has evolved over time with changes especially notable in the decades beginning in the 1960s. Maintaining and holding the "center" has become even more critical, and one factor in making the job of president at the very least more complex, if not more difficult. The growth of diversity and the expansion of pluralism have forced presidents and their campuses to come face-to-face with the increasingly multifaceted constituencies comprising and complicating the power base of the academy, thus creating challenges for presidential leadership. These changes produce more dramatic and higher voltage interchanges and interactions within campus communities, as well as within the larger communities in which they reside. As a result, to be effective in making the center hold, presidents must focus much more energy and capital than their predecessors. In fact, presidents incapable of doing so or conveying insensitivity to the demands of a diverse cultural marketplace will likely have short-lived tenures.

Yeats raises not only the question of whether the center can hold, but concomitantly whether passions are loosed in such a way that his concluding thought obtains: "The best lack all convictions, while the worst are full of passionate intensity." Protests and unrest on many college campuses in the last 40-plus years have produced many moments when this has been the case, and with the dire consequences predicted. For example, Frank Rhodes, who took the helm as president of Cornell in the early 1970s, describes how he inherited an institution still reeling from the campus upheavals of the preceding decade.[4] We must also not forget the reality on some campuses and for college and university presidents in those days. Cornell's experience may be extreme—an armed student takeover of one building and other major disruptions—but protests associated with the Vietnam War and battles over racial issues and charges of racism within the ivory tower were a fairly regular occurrence for many colleges and universities. These times brought down many a president. To hold the center of Cornell, Rhodes invested leadership to rebuild the institutional confidence that was shattered by passions loosed during the previous decade and the near anarchy that had characterized campus life.

The ability of presidents to balance factions within campus communities, threatened and further complicated by external forces entering the fray from time to time, is a major determinant in whether the center is held. This is no easy task in the climate of the academy. Anything presidents do must inevitably pass muster with the core symbols of the academy: free thought, questioning, and inquiry, along with the standard fare of academic and scholarly, as well as pseudoscholarly and academic, positions and criticism. Academics are very passionate, as are students, about various social and political causes. Presidents must be masters at permitting, sometimes even encouraging, this debate and discourse. However, they must work to ensure that dialogue and discussion are characterized by the utmost civility, intelligence, and candor possible. Only then will "the best" have convictions and passion balanced by the ethos of intellectual and spirited communities of inquiry. This is a high bar, but the reality for presidents is that a university culture shaped in this fashion will have a center that holds.

Presidents face a second major responsibility connected in part, but by no means exclusively, to the challenge of making the center hold: the wise and judicious, reasoned and calculated use of the presidential pulpit. College and university presidents hold many assets, but none greater than the capital they possess to make public utterances about important issues. The dilemma faced is to use this power and influence in ways that enhance and do not diminish their voices and the stature of their office. This requires making wise choices and decisions about both the frequency and the content of matters they elect to address. These choices must be made in the face of constituency pressures varying from the reasonable and justified to nothing more than the grinding of axes and the scoring of political points. However, like all political figures, presidents neglect these unpleasant and taxing pressures at their peril.

In the contemporary ideological battleground, pressure to politicize the bully pulpit of the presidency creates critical problems for presidents.[5] Among other concerns, decisions about how and when to use the presidential platform have consequences not only for their office but also for the university itself. Kenneth Minogue's grave warning is that for the university to remain the university it cannot afford to succumb to the winds and fads of ideologies of whatever stripe.[6] His assumption is that the university is a unique social construct. If it willy-nilly becomes no different from dozens of other corporate and social institutions, the university's distinctiveness of purpose and raison d'être is irretrievably lost. The university has historically been this special and separate institution in society. Minogue's fear, not unfounded and in many ways underscored by events over the last 30 years, is that if the university becomes just one more social institution in society, driven by the political pressures of one faction or another, it simply ceases to be the university.

Presidents are the primary leaders with responsibility to prevent this fin de siècle becoming reality. Choices about the bully pulpit must be made in light of Minogue's belief about the sacred, above-the-fray position of the academy. This means preserving the university as ideologically nonpolitical and as untainted by social fads and forces as possible. As our story unfolds, we will hear much about choices of when and how to exert voice and to navigate the use of the presidential pulpit in the face of the challenges of diversity and diverse factions inside and outside the gates of the academy.

The use of the bully pulpit is not the only point at which presidents must consider the pressures of the ideological battleground on today's campuses and in society. Decisions are constantly made about critical issues in which ideological pressures are at stake. These include but are not limited to faculty hiring, affirmative action in admissions and personnel matters, the selection of who will speak on campus, and the relationships between and among students and their numerous group identities and interactions. Minogue's counsel applies to all these arenas, all the points at which capitulation to politicizing the university could have the consequences he fears and predicts. Considerations and choices about these decisions and about the use of the pulpit provide a pronounced way in which presidents stand up to the ideological pressures, some quite subtle, abounding and lurking in the halls of academe.

Another ready trap for presidents is the minefield of free speech and academic freedom.[7] These "freedoms" are embedded in the challenges generated by diversity on campus any time presidents try to identify and hold the "center." The necessary juggling act is to permit ideological individuals and groups the widest berth possible to express opinions, while at the same time preventing ideological domination of the university.

The terms "free speech" and "academic freedom" are not the same; thus it is critical to distinguish between them. As a working definition, free speech is a constitutional right as well as a responsibility. However, Richard Brodhead, president of Duke University, notes that free speech as a value in the academy precedes the affirmation of these protections in the Declaration of Independence and the Constitution.[8] The broad parameters of free speech include considerations such as one person's speech ending at the point where it impinges on someone else's; free speech does not extend to permit a person to yell "fire" in a crowded auditorium and cannot be used as an excuse to incite or urge the violent overthrow of the government. Most of the rights to free speech extend to life on the campus, although individuals may surrender some rights by voluntarily affiliating with an organization or community.

Academic freedom is theoretically the freedom to research, to pursue ideas and knowledge, and to speak about what one believes has been learned and can be contended from the standpoint and basis of academic endeavors, research, and scholarship. Academic freedom was at the center of the confrontation Diana Chapman Walsh, president of Wellesley College, had with one of her faculty members in the early 1990s. In this case, Walsh took the stand that academic freedom cannot be used to defend a professor publishing nonscholarly assertions, ad hominem attacks, and contentions lacking academic discipline, rigor, and knowledge without the professor's facing, at the very least, the consequences of reaction and reprimand.[9] Brodhead notes further the classical German tradition distinguishing the academic freedom of faculty from that of students: *Lehrfreiheit*, "the freedom of teachers in their teaching, the idea that faculty must be allowed the free exercise of their powers of inquiry," and *Lernfreiheit*, "the freedom of students in their learning."[10]

Presidents are vulnerable in free speech and academic freedom controversies because critics and supporters inside and outside academic communities correctly assume these to be fundamental principles in the academy. They are indicators that the university is doing its job of undergirding freedom of thought and critical expression, and that ideas and research are explored on the basis of academic rigor and demands. This is the holy of holies inside the gates of the college and university. Thus presidents must be careful and on guard about the criticism incurred if they appear (or worse, are) merely ideologically selective in applying discrimination with regard to free speech.

This does not mean presidents cannot discriminate among choices of response in controversies centered on free speech and academic freedom. Presidents frequently confront these matters and sometimes must react. Regardless of time for thought and reflection (and Walsh smartly used an expanded group of advisors including faculty to map strategy), presidents need to anchor, in principles and values, any territory they stake out. They cannot simply use discretion as a leader, but rather must rely on the engrained and fundamental values of the academy. Even when fundamental values are factored into decision making, debates about what constitute the core values of the campus will still remain. However, Walsh engaged that debate by consulting with key faculty members about bottom line concerns, gathered an agreed-upon, broad consensus, and thus was able to stand on a firm footing—embedded values about free speech and academic freedom in Wellesley's fundamental traditions—for her actions.

In the last decade or more, since the mid-1990s, the pendulum has swung significantly away from the in-vogue use, in the late 1970s and 1980s, of institutional speech codes designed to address speech and expression problems. This roughly 20-year period was a time when speech issues were a cause célèbre in the academy, although precursors could clearly be seen during the 1960s and in the McCarthy era of the 1950s. It could easily be argued that speech issues in the academy, while always with us, have been a leitmotif of sorts throughout the post–World War II era.

The genesis of the march toward speech codes, which some argue to be institutionalized infringements on freedom of speech and expression, is rooted in numerous episodes. However one moment stands out. At Dartmouth in the winter of 1979, two students masquerading in Native American attire and body paint skated on the arena ice between periods of a college hockey game. Many on campus were outraged and the students were prosecuted through the campus disciplinary system. One charge was that the student skaters had caused "emotional violence" to Native American students. Some behavior no doubt truly inflicts pain, maybe even emotional violence. But the slippery-slope problem is self-evident as campus speech codes advocates later came to find out. Who or which group will next contend to be victimized, suffering emotional violence caused by something considered offensive? Evangelical Christians, for example, could argue and have argued that the very presence of gay and lesbian students and their activities on campus constitute just such a problem. Similar complaints can be found at numerous campuses covering nearly the entire gamut of ideological and identity groups and politics. So speech codes looked, for a while, to be a solution.

But the story at Dartmouth does not end with the hockey skaters incident. As the college wrestled with these issues in the 1980s and beyond, it resisted instituting a speech code in spite of clamorings for one. All of this occurred despite continuing institutional battles with the *Dartmouth Review*, its highly conservative student newspaper.

Onto the stage marched President James Freedman. As a constitutional legal scholar, Freedman fought back, beginning in the early days of his tenure in 1987. Freedman finally had personally had enough of the *Review* after it used its stock-in-trade ad hominem attacks to demean him, and the Jewish people, for simply being Jewish. In an interesting twist on when and how to use the presidential pulpit, Freedman immediately elected to use the force of his presidency to confront the *Review*. In an impassioned address to over three thousand students, faculty, and other Dartmouth community members on the Main Green, Freedman assailed the *Review* for journalistic improprieties and outright failure to live by the dictates and decency of obligations under freedom of the press.[11]

Lines about what is offensive and who gets offended are thinly sliced and create legitimate slippery-slope problems that presidents must navigate. Freedman's handling of the *Dartmouth Review* is a bellwether in changes begun in the presidential and institutional handling of free speech in the early 1990s. Shortly after Freedman's outburst aimed at the *Dartmouth Review*, Harvard followed suit in its handling of a "free speech or expression" issue.

In a somewhat similar vein, in terms avoiding speech codes but reflecting a different style of leadership dictated in large part by different circumstances, Derek Bok, then president, and Harvard faced the issue of students displaying a Confederate flag from a Harvard House window. When black students predictably engaged the administration, demanding that it mandate the removal of the flag, Harvard administrators, one must assume with Bok's blessing, said no. They urged the students to discuss the matter rationally and civilly with their fellow students. The black students elected to display a Nazi swastika from another window on the quadrangle, knowing more than likely that this would bring protests from the Jewish community, and that together these incidents might lead to the forced removal of the Confederate flag. When the Jewish students not surprisingly and in turn similarly demanded the removal of the Nazi symbol, the administration still refused. Harvard's leaders reiterated that the students should engage each other in discussion about the propriety or impropriety, offensiveness or lack thereof, of such displays.

Within less than two weeks of the initial flying of the Confederate flag, both instigators removed their flag displays and the matter was over. Case closed. No speech code was needed, no disciplinary action was taken, and core values of the university were upheld, not eroded by some regrettable knee-jerk reaction.

Freedman's and Bok's leadership and actions served to embolden their presidential colleagues to shift course.[12] In contrast to the run on speech codes of the previous decade, a number of presidents since the mid-1990s have argued rhetorically, as well as in decisions and actions, for a hands-off, anti–speech code approach. Presidents are more inclined to use the pulpit to issue broad statements about the importance of dialogue, and about acceptance of the rights of others to free speech and expression, as long as it is done without intent to harm or to escalate and incite conflict beyond words. Presidents are thus relying on the values of their academic communities to wrestle with contentious, often strident, and always-difficult moments of hate speech and behavior. The strategy is to get these issues on the table for their communities to debate and to seek balance. In the words of a number of presidents, "The only way to combat hate speech is with more speech," or as George Rupp, former president of Columbia University, argues, "Our response to speech we find objectionable must be more speech, more responsible and civil exchanges, not enforced silence."[13]

Anyone who is aware of life on college campuses and the leadership of presidents knows that this rhetoric alone does not thwart "hate" or "harmful" speech and episodes. Presidents do not have the luxury to avoid these controversies when they occur. Presidents silent in the ivory tower quickly find these highly charged issues will rapidly produce accusations of cowardice or crumbling in the face of political pressure. As we shall see, Judith Rodin at Penn and John Sexton at New York University are just two exemplary contemporary presidential voices who approach issues of free speech and academic freedom in ways that bode well for the present and future.

There are numerous presidential pressure points of responsibility and accountability in the contemporary era. In this arena, presidents must craft and shape a civil and rational "center," choose how and when to use the bully pulpit, and navigate the tensions of free speech and academic freedom. This is not an exhaustive list of duties, or of the risks and threats to presidential tenures.

Whether presidential jobs are more difficult to do effectively today and to hold for any length of time than in previous eras remains open to conjecture. The argument here is intended to illuminate but is unlikely to resolve this issue. You, as the reader, are invited to develop your own perceptions and to draw widely divergent and competing conclusions about whether and how much the presidential office has indeed changed. Have historical changes in the presidency been most dramatic in the contemporary era, defined at least by the time period since World War II, if not just in the last couple of decades? Have changes been no greater during recent decades than during other times in the history of the office? Or have changes in the presidency, both historically and recently, not been as great or pronounced as many seem to think?

A former president whose successor had a relatively short-term tenure brings an interesting question to the fore.[14] Mark Edwards, president of St. Olaf College from 1994 to 2000, contends that the college presidency has arrived at a point where doing the job and being able to remain in office for very long is nearly, if not in fact, an impossibility. His point is telling, simple yet profound. Edwards believes today's presidency requires an enormous array of skills, each one of which must be possessed in significant strength. The reality is that it is impossible to possess the abilities demanded in the job at levels sufficient and comprehensive enough to stave off trouble. The inherent difficulty is that crucial and critical constituencies will inevitably assess a president as too weak in areas of performance expected to be met or exceeded. When the weaknesses are eventually exposed, as they surely will be with time, even a president's strengths cannot be an adequate counterweight, and the president's premature departure becomes a given.

In addition to these varied political and tactical pressures on presidents, there are many other obvious administrative responsibilities of managing the institutional and organizational components of today's college and university. Money must be raised. Public relations must be managed. The profile and visibility of campuses must be cast in a highly positive light to all manner of constituencies. Good or even the very best faculty and administrative leaders have to be recruited and hired. The human relations aspect of the presidency, not often mentioned, cannot be underestimated. The litany of responsibilities and duties goes on and on. Presidents rely on many players to make these things happen. However, no matter how many staff and people with great loyalty and dedication exist, still most of the responsibility, the duty, and the simple getting of things done rest on the shoulders of presidents.

Thus, Edwards's view is quite realistic, albeit a bit pessimistic, though not unfoundedly so. One solution to this seeming dead end is to narrow the field of presidential responsibilities to big-picture needs of the university, focused on tending to the foundational principles at the heart of the academy. Edwards's voice provokes a deeper look at the issues facing presidents and the ways expectations can be shaped by the office holders themselves.

A major assumption about college and university presidents thus becomes clear: the meaning and importance of the presidency is closely intertwined with that of the university itself. To a great extent, this is why so much rides on the shoulders of presidents. We tend to project on college presidents our expectations and aspirations for the university and its future, and we expect them to deliver, to build on the firmest foundations possible and to secure the future. Following his presidential tenure at Cornell, Frank Rhodes continued to be highly active about concerns facing higher education. He inspired and led a group of international higher education leaders to fashion the Glion Declaration, addressing the formation of the emerging university of the early twenty-first century.[15] Rhodes and the Glion Declaration stress that values are critical undergirding forces in the university. However, the problem is that the identifiable values in the contemporary university are no longer, as they once were, rooted in transcendent and universal principles of substance, which are both ideal and essential.

The perception that such universal principles are not commonly agreed to be at the foundation of the academy begs interesting questions about how a lack of substantial values at the heart of the university creates problems and challenges for presidents. If Rhodes and the Glion authors are correct, what should presidents stress and fashion as core values that reflect individual institutional sagas and fundamental ideals? Greater presidential reliance on tested values and traditions echoes Minogue's contention that colleges and universities must know who and what they are. Presidents exert the clarity essential to create and to sustain a foundation for the university. The quest for substantial values also offers clues as to why the job of president is so important but often is—the Edwards proposition—impossible, or nearly so, to do.

Whether presidents and their colleges and universities can locate more traditional values in more politically charged and diverse times, and if so, how, prompts a couple of suggestions, worthy of consideration, that complicate our exploration and understanding of the office. First, the university Minogue romantically invokes is historically grounded in root values and ideas. However, the university of old—pre-1960s or earlier depending how far the clock is turned back—was vastly less pluralistic and diverse than the colleges and universities of today's marketplace. Some argue that this "earlier" version of the university's primary roots, in a Judaeo-Christian mind-set and culture, suffocated the free flow of ideas and of academic and scholarly inquiry. The pre-1960s university systematically discriminated on the bases of gender, socioeconomic class, and race and ethnicity. For many if not most of today's universities and colleges, recreating some of the "old-time" core values would be impossible, functioning as they did for specific and historically time-bound times.

On the other hand, we must ask what kind of "university" we would have absent some set of agreed-upon and time-honored fundamental principles and core values, which is the concern of Rhodes and the Glion Declaration? If we believe that a set of beliefs and values must be established (or reestablished) at the heart of the "university," then the question still looms as to what those principles will be. The real battle is who will define and express them, and can the principles be defined sufficiently inclusively in times of increasingly diverse constituencies in the academy? The first problem then for presidents is not whether they will "voice" values, but whose values and what values will they voice? The simple contention here is that presidents are charged with, responsible for, and thus unavoidably at the center (even when they try ardently to avoid it) of this challenge and quest.

A second and connected consideration surrounds issues of orthodoxy, pluralism, and diversity and their effects on the academy.[16] These forces fashion continuing pressures and concerns for presidents. Harold Shapiro, former president of both the University of Michigan and Princeton University, is prominent in raising concerns about the contentious issues of pluralism and diversity in the university.[17] In the tradition of Tocqueville, Shapiro contends that a commonly agreed upon and accepted core of values and beliefs is essential for the coherence and formation of communities such as colleges and universities. He believes the principles of any common core must at its foundation be constituted of values, mores, morals, and ethics.

In short, Shapiro suggests that presidents must use their leadership to identify and articulate these (and this is his word) "transcendent" values and beliefs. In the process, presidents shape meanings that endure and are less subject to fads and the winds of change. In this role presidents could be viewed as theologians or priests, or at the least philosophers, of a civil religion of the academy. Some will argue that speaking about higher purposes and grander visions once was the major function of the presidency, and certainly any such conceptualization of the shape of the presidency in the face of pressures rooted in competing ideologies is itself fraught with hurdles.

How does a view of the presidency based on fundamental and "first" principles provide a response to Mark Edwards's realistic assessment? The argument worthy of consideration is that a sharpened definition of what the university qua the university is in turn provides a more specific set of presidential expectations, of capacities that should be possessed, and of ways to mount the presidential pulpit. Realistically, even reconceiving the office of president will not eliminate the wide range and array of responsibilities and duties presidents face. However, a reconception would sharpen the focus of the burdens on presidents and thereby concentrate their work on more primary and central functions. To gain a handle on how this might work, we will look at a capsule view of two presidents, Judith Rodin and John Sexton.

Rodin placed a personal stamp on the University of Pennsylvania that was rooted in the types of core values and principles envisioned by Shapiro. She articulated Penn's needs with a vision and plan based on the university's historical foundations, for example, making more visible the philosophy and thought of Ben Franklin, Penn's prime mover and founder. Thus, Rodin presented Penn today as rooted in its founding ideas, echoing, in consistent messages, these "old" but tested and applicable beliefs and values.

Sexton brings a highly focused leadership style to the presidency of New York University (NYU). His modus operandi is the daily use of the president's office to engage efforts that strengthen and raise the profile of the university. He is very clear and tactical about what he is doing. Like Rodin, early in his tenure (even in his previous position as Law School dean) Sexton believed the university had wandered from its historic saga. NYU's saga had morphed into something with far less gravitas than its true traditions. So, Sexton brought to the fore and underscored NYU's rich history, a heritage of providing education and of making contributions in a major urban context. This platform, rediscovered in a contemporary context, enables Sexton to embody, as president and for his constituencies, what the university means and what it should be doing. Unabashedly embracing this ambassadorial role on behalf of his institution, Sexton shapes his presidency to fulfill this purpose, and readily accepts any judgment about his definition of the office.

Narrowing the focus of a president's role and responsibilities to a few key priorities is beneficial because it produces clear expectations in the eyes of constituents, be they supporters or critics. However, there is a potential downside. What happens if presidents become so specifically focused on two or three major commitments that other institutional needs, not subsumed as part of that agenda, are shunted aside? Then the president could justifiably be accused of neglect. Suppose a president was so fixated on the intellectual life of students that concerns about basic issues at the core of the development and physical life of students were ignored. Ever-juggling these competing demands is a necessity of the office and their breadth can be narrowed only so far. No matter what might be done to shape and winnow their duties and expectations, presidents inevitably face challenges from every nook and cranny of the campus.

As we think about conceiving the office of president more comprehensively, we must also recognize that the best and most high-profile presidents and their reputations as leaders regularly produce calls to provide leadership on stages larger than those of their own campuses. Examples abound, but one need look no further in the not very distant past to John Kemeny, president of Dartmouth College, solicited (he would later say nearly having his arm twisted) to chair the Three Mile Island Commission following the near-disastrous meltdown at that power plant. Or more recently, Richard Levin, president of Yale, being called upon as a member of the highly important President's Commission on the Intelligence Capabilities of the United States Regarding Weapons of Mass Destruction in the wake of the September 11th attacks, the war in Iraq, and the prospects of a protracted battle against terrorists in America and abroad. Ted Hesburgh at Notre Dame is probably the "dean" of the presidents who have been called to leave this national and global imprint. Such presidents must judge what is sufficiently critical to draw time and attention from the immediate campus concerns (likely seeking the upfront support and approval of trustees). When they do so, they generally view these opportunities for service as an honor, and pragmatically delegate to others the running of the institution.

Where does this sketch of the contemporary presidency and its leadership leave us? The job of being president is, as we have seen and as most observers would agree, enormously complex. The demands on presidents are severe and unrelenting. The ideological battleground with its increasing diversity and pluralism can greatly constrain presidents in exercising leadership and vision. This is especially true if they cannot find the voice to confront ideologies with transcendent beliefs and values, and to place a common core in front of competing constituencies in an effort to create more united communities. The presidential bully pulpit is one way to exercise that responsibility. However, in today's critical and judgmental environment, the use of the pulpit must be even more wisely considered and the utterances from it made more judiciously chosen than in previous, more monochromatic eras. Presidents and those who observe them see the clear conundrum: a simultaneous search and hope for more character and courage in presidents as leaders of colleges and universities while acknowledging the need for practicality and pragmatism. What then might we look for as guiding forces in the presidential stories that follow?

A provisional foundation of our story is that presidents must seek balance. The contemporary era most definitively calls, some might say yearns, for this equilibrium. However, this should come as nothing wholly new. The desirability of equilibrium is a leadership expectation spanning all eras of the presidency and of America's colleges and universities. Presidents have always had to run these institutions by developing the foundations that make them work best. Successfully leading with equilibrium and balance always entails reliance on agreed-upon common values and beliefs. The best presidents know how to lead from the middle ground, even in the face of controversy and contention finding ways to bind communities together. The major difference today is that they must search for unifying transcendent values and beliefs. In bygone eras, transcendent purposes were generally, although not always without debate, more readily agreed upon and accepted.

Stephen Joel Trachtenberg, president of George Washington University, argues that the fact that presidents must be "balance wheels" for their institutions does not mean they are not able to lead and act with character and courage. As our story unfolds we will find they in fact can and must do both: that is, be mediators but also be preachers from their presidential pulpits. They must provide balance, equilibrium, lead in ways that locate and hold the center, and exert influence in wide-ranging ways based on their values and beliefs and those of their institutions. Balancing on one hand and leading with character and courage on the other are not mutually exclusive expectations of presidential leadership.

Whatever presidents do well, and however successful they appear, they function in a contemporary climate that yearns for moral leadership, leadership based on convictions, a willingness to take risks and to be seen as speaking out on the issues of the day. But it is a climate fraught with political correctness and ideological thinking, which simultaneously and regularly hems them in—especially if presidents do not battle against this pressure. The tendency of presidents to succumb to pressure creates the perception that the risks are simply too great for them to speak out on issues and concerns of the day.

What is the state of the modern presidency? What is the range of responsibilities and demands on these leaders? What are the major issues and concerns with which they find themselves grappling, both inside and outside the gates of the academy? Opinions abound and the real story is not an easy or simple one to develop. We turn then to the voices and thoughts of contemporary presidents and their contributions to an important and ongoing discussion about these vital and forceful leaders in American society: its college and university presidents.

NOTES

1. John DiBiaggio, former president, Tufts University, interview with author, August 12, 2003.

2. Mary Sue Coleman, president, University of Michigan, interview with author, July 23, 2003.

3. Donald Kennedy, *The Last of Your Springs* (Stanford, CA: Stanford Historical Society, 1998), p. 130.

4. Frank Rhodes, former president, Cornell University, interview with author, July 22, 2003.

5. This issue is discussed in detail in Stephen J. Nelson, *Leaders in the Crucible: The Moral Voice of College Presidents* (Westport, CT: Bergin and Garvey, 2000), pp. 157–76, esp. pp. 157–65.

6. Kenneth Minogue, *The Concept of the University* (Berkeley: University of California Press, 1973). Though Minogue's work is over three decades old and was significantly influenced by the protests of the 1960s in both the United States and his native England, it speaks across these historical eras. In many ways, Minogue's thinking about the importance of preserving the university as the institution it has been historically in society since

its founding is prescient in light of the pressure created by multicultural factions on one hand and now conservative commentators and groups, for example, the National Association of Scholars, seeking "balance" in the academy from their perspectives, on the other. Minogue, including his treatment in this book of the threats presented by ideologies in the academy, informs much of my thinking and work.

7. This issue is discussed in detail in Nelson, *Leaders in the Crucible*, pp. 91–106. Of note are the case examples of presidents addressing free speech and academic freedom from different institutional and issues perspectives.

8. Richard H. Brodhead, *The Good of This Place* (New Haven, CT: Yale University Press, 2004), p. 155.

9. Nelson, *Leaders in the Crucible*, pp. 97–100, provides a detailed account of President Walsh's handling of the Tony Martin affair.

10. Brodhead, *The Good of This Place*, p. 156. The specific "author" of the tradition that Brodhead cites is von Humboldt.

11. For a more detailed account, see, Nelson, *Leaders in the Crucible*, pp. 22–23. As is pointed out there, Freedman in a sense "stepped out of character," realizing only after his address how personal and impassioned the address was. But many, if not most, of those who heard it that day agree that it was still enormously "presidential." Thus, there are these rare occasions when decisions about using the pulpit of the college presidency are indeed occasions of very personal choice when the rhetoric used is equally personal.

12. This assessment is based on my doctoral dissertation research, concluding in Stephen J. Nelson, "A Study of the Moral Voice of the College President" (University of Connecticut, 1996), and the subsequent thinking in *Leaders in the Crucible*, as well as the research conducted as part of this Kellogg project and presented in these pages.

13. George Rupp, inaugural address, President's Office, Columbia University, October 4, 1993.

14. Mark Edwards, former president, St. Olaf College, personal communication, June 7, 2005.

15. Werner Zvi Hirsch and Luc E. Weber, *Challenges Facing Higher Education* (Phoenix, AZ: Oryx Press, 1999), p. 182.

16. Nelson, *Leaders in the Crucible*, pp. 188–92, concludes on this theme. I extended the argument in "College Presidents: Voices of Civic Virtue and the Common Good of Democracy," *Journal of Leadership Studies* 8, no. 3 (Winter 2002): pp. 11–28. There I contend that what may be required is the formation of a civil religion in the academy, based in the broad range of values and principles—religious, cultural, and political—as all civil religions are, that have been part of the university in America. This "religion" would not be unlike the national American civil religion (see p. 174, n. 6, of *Leaders in the Crucible* for a detailed account of this term). In effect the call I have made is that college and university presidents may need to function as architects, theologians of a sort, of this civil religion in the academy.

17. Harold Shapiro, *Tradition and Change: Perspectives on Education and Public Policy* (Ann Arbor: University of Michigan Press, 1987), pp. 63–71; and "American Higher Education: A Special Tradition Faces a Special Challenge," May 22, 1986, Shapiro Collection, Ann Arbor Commencements, Michigan Historical Collections, Bentley Historical Library, University of Michigan, Box 178; and "Ethics in America—Who Is Responsible?" *New York Times*, Presidential Forum, December 1, 1987.

PART ONE

Presidential Leadership: Navigating Climate and Challenges

From inside and outside the gates of the academy, the academic presidency has always been viewed as a most prestigious, valuable, and high-profile position. This is the case for all tiers and types of colleges and universities. Though not absolutely universal, there is strong commonality in the issues faced and the concerns with which college presidents grapple and battle. All of them regularly must choose how and when to make their voice visible and heard in the public square.

There are indeed many places to begin the story about the realities and choices embedded in the presidency. We will start by painting a broad picture of the leadership of presidents. This ethos and the "big picture" challenges of its climate for college and university presidents set the context for the expectations and responsibilities constituting today's presidency.

While by no means exhaustive, three critical large-scale issues emerge that define the climate with which presidents must grapple. The first is increasing criticism, maybe even hostility from some quarters, by citizens and society toward higher education. The second is fear about the role of governmental interference and reduced federal and state financial (and other) support. The last is the ongoing tension between the pressures of research and scholarship, and the ensuing debate, particularly about the effect of the research emphasis on undergraduate teaching and learning.

Donald Kennedy served as president of Stanford University from 1980 to 1992. More than a decade removed from his presidency, Kennedy still shows the robust sense of humor (often enormously self-deprecating) that many colleagues associated with him throughout his distinguished service to Stanford. His was an internal appointment, despite a major national search to fill the post when his predecessor, Richard Lyman, announced he was stepping down.[1]

When Kennedy first arrived on campus in the early 1960s, Stanford was almost exclusively known as a solid regional university but a relatively minor player in the larger world of American higher education. Kennedy's rising career as a young academic paralleled Stanford's growth and expansion in size, scope, and influence as an instutution. Serving as Lyman's provost afforded Kennedy the platform to be the next presidential choice of many in the Stanford community, including close senior cabinet colleagues with whom he worked and who enthusiastically supported his candidacy. Upon assuming the presidency, rather than seeking the typical fresh start with new-face administrators, Kennedy retained most of these senior leaders. This alone required some courage in the face of those who no doubt thought it too acquiescent in the status quo. However, Kennedy felt this group served the university admirably, were familiar with each other's strengths and weaknesses, and would more than likely continue working well as a team. From most reports he proved enormously prescient in this assessment.

I met Kennedy in the simply, almost sparingly appointed campus office he retains as a faculty member and emeritus president. Adorned with memorabilia and artifacts of his presidency, for the most part it looks like any faculty office. Its studied neatness is a testimony to his academic home in the sciences. Kennedy self-effacingly and cordially greeted me in an outer reception area serving the suite of offices shared with departmental colleagues. His office on an uppermost floor of a not very tall major building (the campus after all sits on the San Andreas Fault, tragically suffering major damage in the 1989 earthquake) overlooks a typically picturesque part of the Stanford campus. Visible in the distance is the baseball stadium. Reflecting his interest in sports in general and baseball in particular, Kennedy happily reports that only recently were lights installed for the first time thanks to a generous donor, and thus the university will in the future be able to host any NCAA tournament coming its way.

A characteristic of the contemporary climate confronting college presidents is change in public perceptions of higher education. This has in turn altered ideas about traits presumed desirable in presidents themselves. These changes have become amplified in the last decade or two, resulting from public cynicism about institutions in general—post-Watergate, post–Vietnam War, postmodern—and ebbing public trust in colleges and universities. Kennedy is gravely concerned about this "new" reality. As we will see in more detail later, his concern is largely due to the public wrath Kennedy experienced toward the end of his presidency because of investigations of Stanford's handling of federal grant funding.

With an eye on this episode, Kennedy compares the first and last years of the period of just over a decade in which he served as president. In the 1980s and early 1990s, Kennedy says, "I think the public view of universities became much more critical, much more negative, even in some quarters hostile. If you poll people, what you discover is that regard for all kinds of institutions fell."[2] Mimicking the rhetoric of higher education's critics, Kennedy muses: "Why don't you get more productive? Why don't you get more efficient? Why is tuition going up so fast? Why can't you keep intercollegiate athletic scandals under control? What about grade inflation, isn't that terrible?" This is an oft-heard litany that begs the question: what should higher education leaders do?

Ever quick with advice, Kennedy argues that "we are in an environment, for better or for worse, in which what we do as institutions [is] going to attract public criticism and we had better be prepared for controversy and willing to meet it head on." However, we know well that the pressure created by such public criticism can readily silence presidents. Against this, Kennedy contends that the big picture of what is at stake is too important. Universities cannot afford to "become too hesitant about getting their views out there about what they mean to society." Academic leadership must speak "for the better values in that society." Sitting on the sidelines in this realm of the university's impact on society and vice versa is untenable to Kennedy, who simply concludes that "it would be wrong to be hesitant about that."[3]

Kennedy's advice to colleague leaders, advice he lived as president, stems from his firm belief that in the ivory tower, silence is not an option. This means presidents vigorously standing up for and defending their institutions whenever criticisms and situations dictate. However, defensiveness alone will not do the job. More importantly, presidents must convince society about the highest values that colleges and universities can and should (and will) pursue. Increased citizen criticism and governmental scrutiny, combined with the reality that money talks, create demands for accountability and proper handling of the public trust. Presidents must respond to the realities of this contemporary context of criticism and work hard to offset a growing general public distrust.

Failure to counter a gathering negative view in society, a "perfect storm" of sorts, especially if allowed to perpetuate over time, can have lasting destructive consequences for colleges and universities. Nothing less than the ethos of the university is at stake. Kennedy's warning: a breakdown of presidential leadership in arguing the value and importance of a higher education to society readily compromises the academy's very foundation. Presidents must refute these erroneous and unfounded claims about the university, clearly and unalterably, and both as individual and collaborative leaders across institutions. Too frequently in higher education, as is almost universally true for corporate sector leadership, the value of developing collegial cooperation to produce a unified, more influential voice is neglected. This challenge of responding to unfair criticism is one of many where the voice of presidents is enormously critical.

The concerns Kennedy raises are not rhetorical. Robert Oden, president of Carleton College and formerly president at Kenyon College, reflects similar misgivings from a vantage point that might conventionally be viewed as more protected—a small liberal arts college. But indeed Oden, and such colleges, face the very same social contract and conscience. For decades Oden was a beloved and distinguished teacher of religion at Dartmouth College. His unique journey began as head of the Hotchkiss School, from which he jumped to presidencies first at

Kenyon and then at Carleton. Oden's office, located in one of Carleton's older buildings, rather like an "old Main," is simply appointed and not particularly large, divided into his working office and an adjoining room taken up almost entirely by a conference table. Oden carries the look and demeanor of his pro-fessional roots: tweed jacket, bow tie, and a quizzical, intellectual, though very personal conversation style. He greets me warmly, and very quickly but seamlessly shifts into the substance of the discussion about his presidential perspectives.

Oden believes there is a disconcerting trend of federal interference in the life of colleges and universities. This concern centers on the drift of the federal government, in part through the Department of Education, into the microman-agement of colleges and universities. He believes that colleagues in Minnesota and throughout the country who advocate for private higher education broadly share his view about governmental pressure on higher education.

Echoing Kennedy, Oden is gravely concerned about leaders in Washington, DC, homing in on how colleges and universities are run, particularly questioning efficiency, and accusing "higher education of being out of control in regards to costs."[4] With a great sense of irony, Oden connects the difficulty colleges con-front in managing costs in the face of escalating costs for health care premiums to governmental policies that exacerbate the problem. He views precipitously increasing insurance benefit expenses in the early years of the first decade of the twenty-first century as largely resulting from government inaction in controlling health care costs. On the other hand, he cites governmental intrusion in the affirmative action Supreme Court case, *Gratz v. Bollinger* (along with *Grutter v. Bollinger*) in which Carleton, at Oden's instigation, participated with a group of other liberal arts colleges in an amicus curiae brief in support of the University of Michigan. Despite the seeming isolation of Carleton, Oden views interference by government in the private, internal affairs of colleges and universities as a real and major threat to be contested.

Consideration of the relationship of the federal and state government to colleges and universities cannot be conducted absent the ironic recogni-tion of the reality that, as monitoring has become more aggressive, funding has been dramatically reduced. The public system of education in America is the envy of most of the rest of the world. Historically one of the grand character-istics of these diverse, uniquely American educational institutions—from local community colleges to major state system campuses, land grant and other large public research universities—is highly autonomous governance and leadership. At their beginnings, these institutions were exclusively publicly funded, with tuition significantly subsidized by state and federal budget support. However, recent state funding trends reveal continual reductions, to the point where many average citizens would be surprised to know that they no longer "own" the public institutions.

For example, Mary Sue Coleman, president of the University of Michigan, one of the premier public research universities in the country, reports that Michigan state funding accounts for only about 40 percent (and this figure is falling) of the institution's total annual revenue.[5] At the University of Rhode Island the figure is less than 25 percent. States and their publics want to reap 100 percent of the perceived valuable benefit of their major universities, when the reality of their support is quite different. This creates a paradox for leaders such as Coleman. She must raise money as though the University of Michigan were a private institution, ironically doing so in a public climate where state intrusion into university affairs, and thus into Coleman's leadership, is inversely proportionate to the state's financial support.

Battles over federal and state support and involvement constitute a major contemporary change in the life of the university. A second change concerns whether universities, and even many smaller colleges, have become overly bureaucratic and depersonalized. Frank Rhodes's tenure as president of Cornell, beginning in 1977 (and ending in 1995), overlapped with Kennedy's at Stanford. They contemporaneously experienced changes in the academic climate during the latter decades of the twentieth century. Rhodes questions whether the university retains the capacity to reach and relate to students and other members of its community in individually personal ways rather than simply as a large bureaucracy.

One form that this concern about the lives of students takes—an old but continuing tension—is pressure on the one hand to emphasize research and the quest for scholarly knowledge, with, on the other, the question of the capacity of a university to address the education of students, including all aspects of their development. In some ways the history and fears of this tension began nearly 150 years ago, when the German research university was imported to the American higher education landscape in the form of Johns Hopkins University. Rhodes and other presidents, at times while in office and at others following their tenure, have been compelled to venture into the murky territory of this dilemma. Its outline is often reduced to a forced choice of one over the other— pick research or pick an emphasis on undergraduate teaching and education, in and outside the classroom, but not both. As a source of questions about the core purpose of the university itself, this is a critical matter for presidential leadership to address, and it defines what the university is and will become.

Citing Cardinal John Henry Newman, Rhodes argues that Newman "offered the antidote to the depersonalized university. 'The university,' he declared, 'is not a foundry, or a mint, or a treadmill...but an *alma mater,* knowing her children one-by-one.'" Rhodes continues: "One-by-one, person-by-person, student by student: that is the basis for educational success. It is also the basis of a free society, and the secret of a great university. Universities will remain great only to the extent they are great student universities, as well as great centers for individual learning, discovery and outreach."[6] Rhodes still wants to have it both ways. Indeed there is no escape from the reality that major research universities, even those in the second tier, must emphasize capacity and dedication to research. But Rhodes argues for equal, if not greater, emphasis on students, especially undergraduates. He critiques the research university as being at risk of losing (or having lost) its way by overemphasizing research and scholarly pursuits, and in the process evolving to the point where personal concern for undergraduate students and their education is significantly jeopardized.

Rhodes and Kennedy are just two presidents at "big-name," high-profile universities, places with large faculties, heavily committed to the scholarly world and its research trappings. They clearly wonder whether something important is being lost, more than a century after the advent of the research university in America. Because of the tone-setting nature of their institutions, this message has to be taken seriously by all major research universities. It is also a warning to smaller, historically teaching-centered liberal arts colleges, which are not free from the pressures on faculty to be more accomplished in scholarship and research. This is a sound and reasonable goal, but one that simultaneously threatens the emphasis on students and their learning, something certainly at the core of both research universities and smaller colleges.

These four pressures, a more highly critical environment about higher education that challenges presidential leadership, governmental interference, reductions in federal and state support, and the need to maintain a personalized university with as little bureaucracy as possible, are among many others that create the climate in which presidents must navigate and function today. Shot through these forces is the underlying challenge for presidents to amass the resources to make these places work and survive, if not thrive. This responsibility, clear and important though it is, also complicates contemporary views of the presidency. Many critics contend that the nearly exclusive concentration on raising money distracts presidents and prevents them from embracing the heritage of voice and leadership long thought to be associated with their office. So, it is critical (and unavoidable) to wade into the territory of the involvement of presidents in fund-raising and development, examining the ways in which today's presidents conceive this responsibility. The nagging and unavoidable question at hand: can presidents exercise their fund-raising responsibility and duty without throwing overboard the high ideals and expectations historically associated with, and that many feel must remain embedded in, the presidency?

NOTES

1. Donald Kennedy, former president, Stanford University, interview by author, August 29, 2003. The personal information that follows was shared in the course of the interview.

2. Donald Kennedy, interview by Anne Flatte, http://becoming.stanford.edu/interview/donaldkennedy/html, p. 11.

3. Ibid.

4. Robert Oden, president, Carleton College, interview by author, August 26, 2003.

5. Mary Sue Coleman, president, University of Michigan, interview by author, July 23, 2003.

6. Frank Rhodes, "Thoughts on the American University at the Dawn of the Third Millennium," December 7, 1999, paper provided by the Office of the President Emeritus, Cornell University, p. 38.

CHAPTER 1

The Hunt for Dollars: Appealing to Constituents and Critics

Money may not run everything, but it runs a lot of things. On this front, the life of universities and the work of their presidents are no different. To many eyes, presidential devotion to fund-raising and development has evolved into a preeminent organizing principle, the modus operandi of the office. Frequently characterized as etched in stone, this assumption promotes a vast and growing mythology about presidents as ceaselessly engaged in development and fund-raising.[1] From the most scholarly to the most casual considerations about the presidency, there is a tendency to assume that raising money is the primary, if not the only, task of these leaders. If we are to have any hope of understanding the presidency more completely and precisely, addressing this hunt for dollars is a must because the perceptions and assumptions surrounding it are so unavoidable.

Contrived in a high-sounding manner, the search for financial support by colleges and universities from their constituencies is about educational philanthropy and about stewardship. Education is an expensive, cost-intensive business, and colleges and universities cannot survive absent donor and institutional wealth and stewardship. No one knows this responsibility and this calculus better than presidents. These leaders have no choice but to be concerned about institutional finances and financial management. There is an ever-present demand on their leadership to be front and center in the constant, arguably universally draining hunt for resources and dollars. Presidents must run their institutions, moving them as securely as possible into the future. Given these expectations, presidents also cannot avoid thinking about what it takes to secure their legacies.

Introducing this subject early in the telling of our story acknowledges the imperative to take head-on the implications of the hunt for money on college presidents. Raising money, euphemistically termed development work and donor cultivation, is a constant pressure on today's presidents. Demands exist on the fund-raising front itself, and in the closely connected dilemmas involved in cultivating constituencies critical to short- and long-term success in amassing wealth.

Two thoughts about this reality are important. The first and most obvious is the fashionable perceptions, well embedded in the common currency, that today's presidents are vastly more consumed by this task than their predecessors. A second and connected concern is the historical view, but also near-mythology, about those predecessors, the arguable "giants" of bygone eras.

Today's commonly accepted notion is that fund-raising is the only thing presidents are hired to do. This capacity is *the* prime prerequisite for consideration as a viable candidate for presidential appointment. Then once in office, raising money is really the only thing presidents have time to do, and that those to whom they are accountable want them to do. As with most perceptions, this one contains elements of truth. However, it is also well on its way to becoming an indelible contemporary myth about the office and about the university. Worse, this mythology clouds clarity in any attempts to develop depictions of and future forecasts about the college presidency.

One view is that the overriding need to raise money obliterates "old-style" visions of the presidency. In this rendition, the expectation to hunt dollars makes it impossible for today's presidents to uphold the fundamental values historically associated with their office. The assumption is that presidents can no longer afford to be intellectual and scholarly leaders, today's public intellectuals, let alone be moral, ethical, and spiritual leaders, inside and outside the gates of the campus and society. Thus they pale in comparison to the "giants." There is another view. While money matters indeed can affect what presidents say and when they say it, this practical and political reality does not mean presidents have no choice but to withdraw their voice from the public square.

Johnnetta Cole, having served with distinction as Spelman College's president, and serving now in another presidency at Bennett College, reacts using the oft-told description of the president: "I look at my colleagues all around the country, [and] I realize that indeed this business, as I describe the presidency, of living in a big house and begging for a living, is far, far too prominent in the role of the presidency." The reality is that Cole now, because of Bennett's fragile financial state and stability as a small, tuition-driven liberal arts college for black women, finds herself "spending so much time worrying about dollars." "I think I'm fairly good at fund-raising. It's really tough in this climate," but, Cole protests, "that's not what attracted me to this."[2] Though admitting the bind, Cole contends the best part of the president's role is as public intellectual, something she is certainly known to be. At Spelman, even while raising large sums, Cole was a prominent voice in political circles and on the national stage.[3]

She is by no means alone among presidents who know that they must be able to raise money, and do it well, while still being publicly audible voices in the public square. However, it is not an easy juggling act either.

Former Brown University president Vartan Gregorian comments, citing Lord Chesterfield, that "wisdom is like carrying a watch. Unless asked, you don't have to tell everybody what time it is."[4] Gregorian's is a warning that reacts to what many think: the emphasis on raising money compromises the force of presidents as public leaders, especially in moral and ethical controversies. Cole acknowledges that development work can make presidents "think twice" about what they might say.

That said, any number of presidential decisions and duties could cause presidents to be compromisers, hindering outspokenness and diminishing power and influence. Presidents are challenged by many daily distractions and intrusions as managers of academic bureaucracies, and raising money is certainly on the list. Size and scale of institution is a not a factor. Academic politics are easily as stifling and consuming at small colleges as at much larger universities. Ever-present pitfalls range from mishandling constituency concerns to making unwise decisions about using the bully pulpit. Any of these and uncounted other forces can result in squandering the presidential platform of public leadership and voice. But in large measure whenever presidents become silent, when their voices become compromised, blame cannot be affixed to any single issue or responsibility, be it fund-raising and development or anything else. Blame rests solely on themselves and their leadership.

Historical perspective is also critical in any comparison of the role of fund-raising today to perceived images of past presidents. There is a strong tendency to overromanticize the past, perpetuating the myth that presidents of earlier eras were distracted little if at all by the need to gather resources. This simply is not the case. The establishment of many colleges and universities was absolutely tied to the massive philanthropy of wealthy founding donors. Although usually with the best intentions and concern about education, these donors clearly wanted a quid pro quo: their imprint on the shape of these institutions in return for their largesse. Presidents often had to hunt for resources to match donations. On occasion, philanthropic founders and their heirs attempted to dictate institutional affairs, forcing presidents into the unenviable positions of trade-offs of money in the face of demands about policy and decision making. No further example is needed than the widow of Leland Stanford, who prevailed in pushing a professor out the door at Stanford because of personal disagreements with him.

In cases where there were no wealthy donors, founding leaders and presidents had to scrape together resources from wherever they could find them, often in economic times much less secure than today. For example, in October 1929, days before the stock market crash, Brown University inaugurated President Clarence Barbour. Barbour's short-lived presidency, marred by ill health no doubt caused by the pressure he faced, concluded with a farewell lament that his dreams for Brown simply could not be realized because of the economic climate and troubled times of his tenure. The Crash of 1929 was an unusual circumstance, but other difficult times, often of national crises, have marked the history of American colleges and universities: the Revolutionary War, the Civil War, and other times of war, especially World Wars I and II, when college student enrollments were decimated by the demands of national service. The protest era of the 1960s and its spillover effects of diminished institutional loyalty and diminished institutional self-confidence caused many presidents of "old" to fixate on resources and how they could be garnered. In short, the requirements and pressures of the money hunt in the presidency are by no means exclusive to the later twentieth and early twenty-first century.

History also reveals episodes of pressure on presidents about the finances of their institutions as connected to difficult leadership and even moral decisions related to money. The extraordinary story of Horace Bumstead, president of Atlanta University in the era of Reconstruction, is just one example.

Bumstead refused to continue taking an annual injection of State of Georgia funding because the legislative mandate tied to accepting these monies would force the university to choose to segregate itself as either black or white, a step that would have compromised its very mission to provide equally accessible education to blacks and whites alike in the post–Civil War South.[5] The funds turned down were not insignificant. The yearly $8,000 was roughly one-third of what Bumstead was annually forced to raise by barnstorming, primarily through churches in New England and the Northeast, just to keep the doors of his institution open. The university's precise budget at that time is not known; thus it is possible only to make a ballpark guess about what the figure would be today. A reasonable assertion is that in constant dollars Bumstead's annual additional fund-raising task to replace the state funding he "voluntarily" rejected would easily be in the million dollar range or more, a significant challenge for Atlanta or any university. Bumstead refused easy, guaranteed money to defend principles and his university's core mission, a telling story in his or any era.

Nonetheless, hotly contested debate about whether today's presidents are more trapped by financial snares than their predecessors continues. Voices persist in urging presidents to do nothing other than raise money. That contemporary presidents and those of the future will be responsible for raising large sums of money is beyond doubt. However, having said that, what can be learned about college and university fund-raising and about the expectations that appear to have grown in the role of presidents over time? Among those who hold office today, are there models, especially for those concerned about the money quest, that might reveal ways in which the development work of presidents can be reconceptualized?

There are as many approaches to fund-raising as there are presidents. There are as many different circumstances and ways to amass resources as there are institutions. Public and private colleges and universities have morphed together, with pressure now on public universities to mimic the fund-raising traditionally associated with private higher education, especially in major capital campaigns. Mary Sue Coleman, president of the University of Michigan, forthrightly asserts that, contrasted even with her immediate predecessor, the demand to fashion fund-raising in a manner similar to that of private universities has ratcheted up dramatically. Reaching its current high point in a 30-year trend, the reality is that Coleman "can't rely on just revenue from the state or from tuition," an evolution in her eight years as president, first at Iowa and now at Michigan. On the fund-raising front she has had to become "more like a private university president."[6]

Another aspect of the hunt-for-dollars game is that many private institutions, absent the luxury of massive endowments, rely primarily on tuition dollars, and annual gifts and other revenue. For example, Stephen Joel Trachtenberg, president of George Washington University, labels his school as operating on a "momentum model," and he has much more company than many in this category would want to acknowledge. "We succeed because we succeed because we succeed. And in order for us to succeed, we have to keep the momentum rolling, going up a sharp incline from plateau to plateau. To the extent that we stumble," and herein is the extreme danger and challenge, "we can slide back down that incline a lot faster than we came up."[7]

A "momentum model" is the only hope for the many colleges and universities lacking significant endowments. Annual budgetary expenses have to be offset by raising revenue because they have no ability to fall back on the shock-absorbing and momentum-generating effects of generous endowments. Presidents like Trachtenberg regularly make long-term commitments in areas such as faculty tenure (an investment likened to a lifetime annuity of millions of dollars for each professor), and buildings and infrastructure, without assets firmly in hand or any assurance of the financial wherewithal down the road to back up the commitments.

The year in, year out gathering of resources is much easier in good than in hard economic times. So the leaders of "momentum model" institutions are at the mercy of the nation's economy and its inevitable swings. Institutions without massive endowments have to be creative in attempts to build them. However, no matter how ingenious and risk-taking the strategies, these colleges and universities are forever in a catch-up game as they try to gain a viable edge in an enormously competitive game. The only exceptions are moments when by design or luck a major donor instantly transforms an institution's endowment status through a major gift. (I will elaborate on the good fortune James Laney crafted through the Woodruff gift at Emory.) Whether working to maintain the "momentum model" or hitting the jackpot of major donor largesse, judgment about success in bringing in the dollars rests squarely on the shoulders of presidents appointed for their ability to fulfill this vital role.

With this premium placed on the time presidents must dedicate to fund-raising, what can be learned from the ways they conceptualize this obligation? How do they frame this aspect of presidential duties and responsibilities within the overall conduct of the office? Is it possible to do so in ways that preserve the core heritage of the office? In short, can presidents, despite the time that must be invested in the money hunt, still be players as voices of intellect and persuasion in the public square within and beyond the gates? Can assumptions about fund-raising as a centerpiece of the presidential office be de-mythologized to a point at which they are viewed with some clarity in a different light? The assumptions made about presidents may after all be a grand self-fulfilling prophecy for these leaders, those to whom they are most accountable, and their institutions. If we presume presidents can and must concentrate the bulk of their attention on cultivating donors and on playing the correct political game to make sure no major source of largesse is offended, then it should come as no shock that they spend vast amounts of time meeting these commitments.

James Laney served as president of Emory University from 1977 to 1993. Judged by most observers, Laney's impact on the university compares favorably with the presumed type of footprint of the "giants" among presidents.[8] During Laney's almost two decades at the helm, Emory was transformed from a reasonably noted regional university in the South to a university of national and global renown and reputation. Laney's path to the presidency was meteoric. Because of his theological education and background, Laney is a throwback to the "older" notion of minister-presidents. He served as a faculty member and dean at Emory, left for a time to return to Yale University where he had been an undergraduate and divinity student, and then returned to Emory as president (having been approached to throw his hat in the ring when the presidency was previously open and his predecessor was selected).

I interviewed Laney at the Yale Club in New York City where he was staying for a Yale alumni awards event. He greeted me warmly. His demeanor is jovial yet serious, and very engaging. Our conversation was over breakfast in an open, airy room on one of the upper floors of the club. Laney, dressed in a professorial-looking tweed jacket, seemed to know almost everyone wandering in and out of the room throughout the couple of hours of our discussion.

Reflecting on money-raising as president, Laney began at the beginning with his relationship with Robert Woodruff, who, at the time, had recently retired as chairman of Coca-Cola. Laney describes Woodruff as the "beneficent angel of Atlanta in the best sense. Not only did he have money, but he wanted Atlanta to be a good city and he really worked at that and gave in support of that. So from that standpoint there was a coincidence of interest," Laney continues with typical enthusiasm, "because I was interested in a city where the races lived together, not just harmoniously, but with mutual benefit.... And through that relationship with him, we've received a considerable amount of support, which made a lot of our work and development possible."[9] The story behind Laney's relationship with Woodruff and the seminal "Coca-Cola" gift Emory received early in Laney's presidency is emblematic of his leadership and style. The legacy of the story and the gift reveals Laney's intellectual prowess and will in the business of development, showing how much the craft of fund-raising truly is an "art."

Like many presidents, Laney entered office facing the pressing need to develop and successfully carry out a major capital campaign. Whether this was definitively in the mind of the trustees at the time of his hiring is not clear. What is clear is that during the search process Laney put on the table that if appointed president his first major commitment would be to the goal of rapidly raising the university's profile. Laney knew this required a push to raise funds on a scale more aggressive and unprecedented than anything Emory had previously undertaken. But equally this was the only ticket to transform Emory from a sleepy, almost hidden, regional school to a major research university of worldwide acclaim. A larger endowment was essential and this rested on launching a bold campaign.

During the planning stage of the campaign, what is now known as the "silent" phase—setting the goal and seeking the bulk of the major gifts committed in advance of any public announcement—Laney knew *the* key question: "Was Mr. Woodruff going to be a supporter and at what level?"[10] The $160-million campaign goal was divided into two portions, as is often the case, part for buildings and part going into the endowment. Laney continues: "That was the strategy. And I put it all neatly on one page. It was very simple. It wasn't a complicated thing at all." It was now time for Laney to meet with Woodruff to seal the deal.

The plot thickens, as Laney recounts: "So I took it over to Mr. Woodruff. I had the two categories, construction and endowment. Mr. Woodruff looked at it. It was a long time before he began shaking his head. He said, 'Dr. Laney, I understand construction and all, but,' he said, 'I don't believe in endowment.' He said, 'I'm never for higher endowment.' I didn't know what to say. . . . I couldn't argue with him. I thought, 'our campaign's dead in the water. This is bad news.' I didn't know what to do. I was really heartsick.'" It is easy to imagine the despair in Laney's mind. Here is a new, fairly young, very "green" president, facing his first major "ask." This is an essential component to a critical campaign, and judgment about Laney's leadership (probably about him personally, as well), his presidency, and Emory depended on his ability to cash in on Woodruff's largesse.

Following this seemingly ill-fated meeting, Laney says: "I left. He could have blown me away. A sleepless night. The campaign's dead. I can't get Mr. Woodruff." A few days later, Laney begins thinking and develops a new angle: "Mr. Woodruff thinks endowment is" just putting money away. "But what it is, is that this is what you use to do the job. So I changed the categories." Displaying a mixture of genius and desperation, on a piece of paper Laney "put construction and 'working capital' instead of 'endowment.'" About a week later "I took this piece (I was a nervous wreck. 'If this doesn't work, I guess I'll just resign') [parentheses mine]. I gave it to him. He looked it over a long time and said, 'Dr. Laney, every institution needs enough working capital. This is a good idea.'"

Laney indefatigably and literally used legerdemain and chutzpah to get a commitment from a badly needed major donor. Woodruff was ready to be in Emory's orbit, but like any donor he needed to be convinced. Emory's need, as Laney first presented the campaign boilerplate, using the two major categories of "construction" and "endowment," was not attractive to Woodruff. Maybe because of his corporate background or simply his personal philosophy, Woodruff did not like the idea of endowment. To him it appeared to be just amassing wealth, certainly with some small percentage on an annual basis being used as part of the operating budget of the university. But to give of his largesse, Woodruff wanted to see it working in one way or another, to be utilized and realized tangibly, not sat on. So, Laney altered the conceptualization of the campaign's goals by simply changing the nomenclature. A small creative step enabled him to seal the deal with Woodruff on the more attractive basis of "working capital."

Laney got $105 million from Woodruff, the largest single gift at that time to any college or university. The Woodruff gift, which became known as the "Coca-Cola money," in a single stroke increased Emory's endowment from $175 to $280 million. After receiving this donation, Laney's next move was to ensure Emory handled the Woodruff gift well. Turning to theological and church notions of stewardship, he convinced the trustees and his senior leadership group to make a university commitment to place the Woodruff $105 million in a set-aside, separate fund. Laney conceived of this "almost like an in-house foundation" within the Emory endowment, not to be touched at all for at least the first three years.[11] To pursue the agenda they envisioned for the future, Laney and his trustees needed "working capital" well beyond the means of the university's "other," regular endowment. Ensuring the realization of their vision meant delayed gratification while the Woodruff gift grew.

Laney's decision to follow a strategy to delay a payoff caused colleagues to grumble and press to use the funds more in the shorter term. However, delaying the use of the Woodruff gift enabled it quickly to reach the point of generating $25–30 million dollars annually. Only then did Emory began to use it, as new "working capital"—Laney's understanding with Woodruff—in the way that other endowments support buildings, faculty appointments and salaries, new programs, and other initiatives. By late 1997, with the good fortune of a steeply climbing stock market, the Woodruff Fund had grown to a net worth of $2 billion.[12] Woodruff's philanthropic generosity coupled with Laney's smart stewardship enabled him to begin meeting the challenge of pushing Emory to a heightened profile and reputation.

Laney's story underscores the fact that the development game for colleges and universities is a high-stakes affair. It is a game of inflated egos of presidents and donors and ambitions of trustees and alumni for their alma maters. Fund-raising is an example of the business *realpolitik* of the presidency. But Laney shows how fund-raising is also part of the grand scheme of educational values as it also meets institutional needs.

John DiBiaggio elaborates on Laney's framework. I met President DiBiaggio in the lobby of a hotel where he was staying during a visit to New England from "retirement" in Colorado. He served in three presidencies, two in the public sector—the University of Connecticut and Michigan State University—and one in the private sector, Tufts University. DiBiaggio is plain spoken, personally engaging, and quite at ease socially. Justly proud of his heritage as the first college and university graduate in his family, DiBiaggio feels this "blue collar," common-man background positively shaped his identity and character. He is enormously personable, clearly someone who has enjoyed life in education. As he tells stories of his "best" presidential moments, the major personal characteristic rising to the surface is his sheer pleasure at dealing with students and an embrace of "teachable moments" as president.

DiBiaggio views the "issue of financing" and managing resources well as a responsibility presidents must address because of its direct connection to the rising "cost" of education. His bottom line is quite simple: presidents must be able to justify the cost of students' education in terms of their value to them. To DiBiaggio this means "constantly to be concerned about generating adequate resources," and using the institution's financial levers "to assure that an environment exists where the faculty can teach and investigate and the students can learn, as well as protecting academic freedom and re-assuring that there are no intrusions on the prerogatives of the institution."[13] The presidential role in fund-raising and gathering financial support connects directly to the core purposes of the institution: faculty research and teaching, and student learning.

DiBiaggio links fund-raising not only to institutional purpose but also and especially to how it positively affects the cost of the education. When thinking about money, the overriding consideration for presidents and trustees to keep uppermost in mind is what we want and need to use the money for.[14] He asks rhetorically, if we cannot show that colleges and universities exist to expand knowledge, to seek "truths," and to stimulate inquiry and learning and argue this rationale satisfactorily, then why are we doing what we are doing? This is the critical distinction setting colleges and universities apart as institutions, especially when hunting money. It is what makes the academy different from other corporate entities, whether of the "for profit" or " nonprofit" variety.

Neil Rudenstine, president of Harvard University from 1991 to 2001, also believes in the vital connection between the purposes of the university and its worldly need to raise money (some might argue even to amass wealth). Like an increasing (all for the better) number of today's presidents, Rudenstine brought a scholarly background in Renaissance literature to his tenure at Harvard. Also, like many contemporary presidents, Rudenstine was clearly moving on the presidential track for many years prior to assuming the helm in Cambridge.

I interviewed Rudenstine in New York City at his office at the Mellon Foundation, where he went following his presidency. He greeted me on the first floor of the foundation's headquarters in a converted brownstone and we walked three floors up the narrow stairs to his office. Rudenstine is a tall, distinguished-looking man, but very much the professor in his demeanor and style. He was dressed casually and throughout the interview sat comfortably but always reflectively as we pursued our conversation. When he was president at Harvard, one characteristic associated with his leadership was his commitment to collaboration and dialogue. A personal meeting confirms this perception, in both the style and the substance of Rudenstine's persona. His take on the presidency is shot through with a leadership approach based on belief in collegiality, collaboration, and consensus.

As did Laney, Rudenstine came into the presidency with a major capital campaign on deck as a given. Kicking off the campaign and using his love of literature, Rudenstine turns to a Robert Frost poem to capture the essence of this massive capital campaign and its goal, subsequently met and exceeded, of over a billion dollars. The talk is a clarion call to the Harvard forces that will raise the monies for the campaign. Rudenstine suggests to his audience a litany of the "motives and reasons that led so many of us to Harvard in the first place."[15] "We came because we wanted to test ourselves against the best, and to learn all that we could possibly learn: not simply about particular subjects or disciplines, but also about other people and their points of view." Tapping the educational vein in the Harvard experience, Rudenstine continues: "We wanted to learn not only what individuals (often the world's greatest authorities) actually knew, but also what they did not know; and where their knowledge began to dissolve into uncertainty, and then slip suddenly into ignorance. We wanted, in addition, to discover how individuals and great institutions coped with uncertainty and ignorance, because that too was a central part of human experience and reality."[16]

But Rudenstine also pushes beyond the mere saga of Harvard to the university writ large: "This passionate pursuit—this desire to find out what lies just beyond the ideas we have barely understood, beyond the discovery we have just made; this desire to marshal the evidence, tighten the argument, polish the stanza, design exactly the right experiment, and convert ideas into effective actions—this is the primordial energy and motive force of the university, in all its many forms and purposes."[17] At this point Rudenstine uses Frost's poem, "The Star-Splitter," to bring home his conclusion: "Finally, there are the difficult, unanswerable questions at the end. How useful is the knowledge we have gained? Do we know any better where we are, or how things stand between ourselves and the surrounding outer darkness? The questions are real, but they do not erase what has been learned and experienced: the sense of having pressed further, and having seen infinitely more than what we had ever seen before. That is what universities are created to do."[18]

As long as there are presidents and as long as there are colleges and universities, money is going to be raised. Presidents are obligated and expected to do this. Rudenstine shows how to charge up troops to raise the money, while maintaining attention to the roots of the educational experience. These are ideals of the university, what it is and what it means to individuals and to society. The contemporary reality of fund-raising as presidential duty also reveals the creative integration of this obligation into the fundamental purposes of the university itself.

Rob Oden served in two presidential and one independent (private) school head leadership positions, respectively, at two highly reputed liberal arts colleges—first Kenyon and now Carleton—and at the Hotchkiss School, a private boarding school. At all three, Oden faced significant fund-raising demands and challenges despite the elite and reasonably well-established nature of these schools. From this experience he crafts an interesting take on fund-raising. Oden's tone and style as an administrator reflects his professorial "first" life as a scholar of religion and Near Eastern languages. However, behind the academic exterior is a strong-willed, self-admitted competitor confessing his love of fund-raising, not brashly but in an almost understated manner. This trait is at the fore of his fund-raising philosophy. It is an approach that belies the horn-rimmed glasses, bow tie, tweed jacket look of the academic, the intellectual, the professor.

As with most colleges and universities, the external world of Carleton and Kenyon is significantly centered on alumni and parents as critical constituencies to be served. With these groups, as well as in general, "the chief obligation and chief time devotion is fund-raising," Oden acknowledges. He continues: "[I]n my case, since I particularly like that, it doesn't feel like a pressure or a sore point or a demand on my time. I think—and I said this in front of an alumni group two weeks ago—fund-raising is the most fun you can have standing up. It's something that is really important to me."[19] Oden cites Fay Vincent, former commissioner of major league baseball, to underscore the *realpolitik* of fund-raising for colleges. Oden recounts a conversation with Vincent: "We were talking about raising colleges to the next level, and he said, 'You know, Rob, don't make it too complicated. It's simple. It's all about endowment.' Now I said, 'Well, you know you're right.' You can look at the top 10 colleges by anybody's list, and they would be the top 10 endowments. So, you raise money to make possible what you want to do in human terms and educational terms and curricular terms."[20]

As the "Vincent principle" reveals, fund-raising is directly connected to reputation and stature. But presidents readily know that resources translate into grander standing only to the extent that they "buy" higher quality faculty and students. Oden repeatedly stresses the major responsibility to bring together the best possible faculty and the best students, and to let the interaction and learning between them run where it will. Presidents are the architects of the intellectual and academic culture, and Oden directly links his philosophy of fund-raising to success in building the intellectual culture of a learning community. Arguably such an esoteric view is what is normally expected of elite institutions, and is not at all reflective of the mainstream of American higher education. However, this approach to fundraising certainly could and should be applied to lesser "ranked" institutions, including community colleges. Otherwise how are they too going to be able to improve their standing in terms of these basic ingredients of quality that transcend institutional stature?

In an array of presidential conceptions of fund-raising, John Sexton's is one of the more provocative views of the relationship of development work to the presidential office. Like others, he embraces the same core connection between the university's fundamental purposes and the fund-raising quest. But he goes a step beyond, to the assumption that building the core mission means the dollars will follow.

The interview with Sexton was scheduled late on the day of his return from a combined business and pleasure trip to Europe. He landed in New York and came directly to the office, and our conversation was the first appointment on his calendar that afternoon. Sexton is enormously outgoing, a very tall man with a clearly commanding but very family-style approach to his office staff. This became evident from the bags of gifts he had for various members of the staff and the air of holiday celebration generated as he greeted everyone, giving out presents. The staff appeared pleased he was back in town, and though this was only a snapshot from one afternoon, the scene was extraordinarily authentic. After making these welcome-home rounds he immediately led me into his office. Given that it was already mid-evening in the European time zone where he had begun his day, our conversation continued much longer than I thought possible, having enormously underestimated Sexton's energy. Even though he was headed to a Yankees' game after our appointment, he was quite focused and generous in the time he made for our discussion.

Sexton reports that New York University must raise nearly a million dollars every day—to be more precise, about three hundred million per year—in noncapital campaign years. For many colleges and universities, large-scale, year in year out fund-raising efforts are now nearly rolling campaigns, each major one flowing immediately into the next. Addressing his strategy for bringing in resources, Sexton claims to avoid—he would argue refuses—engaging directly in fund-raising. Rather, conceptually and in the reality of handling the job, Sexton uses all the president's office levers to raise the university's profile and prestige— one might say in true "development" work—thereby gathering support from all quarters and the many varied constituencies of NYU.[21]

Sexton's way of raising money might appear fantastic, particularly in light of popular conceptions (though these are more misconceptions) about college and university presidents. How can the presidents of universities in the modern era not be instrumentally and practically involved in the fund-raising work of their university? Is this not a key part, if not the major part, of the job? But Sexton's way is counterintuitive and he aligns NYU's development work to its core mission and to his vision of the president's office and duties. When Sexton took the university's helm in 2001 he confronted a major task: to "reorient" the financial picture of New York University.[22] For a number of years, the university had been running, and was increasing, a "fairly substantial structural deficit." As he learned more about the long-term consequences of this trend for the institution, Sexton knew he had to change the situation.[23]

Employing a focus on the central principles of the university, Sexton contends that "in the last three years, we've had our three most successful years [of fund-raising], and we've had it notwithstanding the fact that we've said that we will only accept gifts that survive a [screen of] substantive impact on the campus. They are really our focus," Sexton confirms, alluding to the "core" he is articulating for NYU, that "people say how much of your time do you spend fund-raising to raise almost a million dollars a day?" Sexton's unique response is: "I say

I don't experience myself spending any time." Getting to the heart of the way he conceptualizes the task, Sexton adds: "For me what I drive constantly and that in which I participate constantly is a conversation about the university and what it is we are going to do of value and how we operationalize that. And, particularly, how we operationalize it in terms of specific faculty and programs. And that goes on constantly and there's a testing of that in two highly sophisticated markets. One is the philanthropic market and another is the faculty recruitment market. But those markets are essentially responding to the same thing."[24]

The center point of Sexton's idea is "conversation about the university." He promotes that conversation within and beyond the confines of New York University through occasional essays crafted to engage dialogue about the university. In these tracts, Sexton tackles big-picture ideas that colleges and universities face today as well as historically, and the change the universities and their leaders must manage in an enormously complex society and world. Sexton tests positions based on ideas about his philosophies of leadership, the university, education, and faculty and student inquiry. He combines these ruminations into core understandings of the academy for which he garners support.

Sexton would certainly agree that like all presidents he is engaged in this development work daily, maybe even hourly. Trying to make New York University a leading educational center not only in New York City but also around the world is no small task. However, the major difference in his approach is that development results from regular involvement in "conversation" about where the university is and where it needs to go with all constituents, from key staff members to the broader circle that surrounds NYU. Development, garnering resources, is a byproduct of the "conversation," and of Sexton singing the praises of NYU. Sexton's position is that presidents should want to speak not merely to raise money qua raising money, but rather to discuss and define NYU or any university in the context of the academy's ideals. From this base Sexton is convinced that the dollars will follow.

The hunt for dollars, then, must be tied to the concept of the university itself, to the university writ large, and to the unique character of these distinctive institutions. Institutional support and development are cultivated best by connecting the minds and hearts of constituents and their philanthropy to the core educational mission of the college or university. If presidents do this they reinvent the business of development and fund-raising in ways that complement the higher calling and broader role of the presidency.

Additionally, presidents can and should be concerned about more than money as they perform the duties of office. It was not so long ago, just less than 30 years ago, in the late 1970s, that during a major campaign at Dartmouth College, President John Kemeny accepted national leadership as head of the commission on the nuclear power plant accident at Three Mile Island. He did so because he understood that college and university presidents must, among other burdens and responsibilities, assume leadership and public visibility beyond their campuses, at times on the national stage. While Kemeny accepted the challenge of leading the commission, money for the Campaign for Dartmouth continued to come in, and shortly afterward, the goal was reached and exceeded.

Money, as Oden, like Faye Vincent, acknowledges, dictates the position and health of these schools—not only elite colleges and universities, but all of them, regardless of perceived status. Therefore, it is essential that presidents fund-raise, and do it well. Historically, this has been the case since the founding of the Colonial colleges. Contemporary mythology portrays fund-raising as *the* only, or by far the major, duty of the presidency, eclipsing all other responsibilities of the office; but this is simply nothing more than a myth. Fund-raising does not have to prevent presidents from embracing long-standing traditions of what we believe college and university presidents should be—voices in society and leaders speaking from a bully pulpit about critical issues of the time. Their deliberation about these other responsibilities—especially their public voice and leadership—can be done even as they tend to the undeniably important development quest and the hunt for dollars.

NOTES

1. For example, to mention only one such contention, a very fine student of higher education and writer, David L. Kirp, in his acclaimed book, *Shakespeare, Einstein, and the Bottom Line* (Cambridge, MA: Harvard University Press, 2003), makes this unsubstantiated claim early in his book: "Strong leadership used to be regarded as crucial in the making of great universities, but nowadays presidents are consumed with the never-ending task of raising money" (p. 4). Certainly, as I point out in this discussion, the perception and reality of the amount of time presidents spend in raising money is not inconsequential. But to say that it is the only thing or even that on which they spend inordinate time today in comparison with bygone eras (maybe they do spend more time, but it is not clear how much more) is not supported by evidence.

2. Johnnetta Cole, president, Bennett College and former president, interview by author, Spelman College, June 2, 2003.

3. In the interview, she notes that her success at Spelman was due in large measure to a major donation, at the very beginning of her tenure, of $20 million by Bill and Camille Cosby, adding to Spelman's endowment of just over $40 million. Cole's major capital campaign raised $113.8 million, the largest amount ever raised at that point by a historically black college or university, and Spelman's endowment shortly after her departure reached $200 million, making it the wealthiest historically black college or university in the nation.

4. William H. Honan, "At the Top of the Ivory Tower the Watchword Is Silence," *New York Times,* July 24, 1994, sec. 4, p. 5. Note the comment about this citation in Nelson, *Leaders in the Crucible,* p. 14, n. 8.

5. For a full account of this episode, see Nelson, *Leaders in the Crucible,* pp. 42–44.

6. Mary Sue Coleman, interview by author.

7. Stephen Joel Trachtenberg, president, George Washington University, interview by author, May 7, 2003.

8. I draw on a number of sources for the material about President Laney, among them the work of Stuart Gulley noted below (n. 16) and a video documentary, *Leading Out,*

produced by James Ault (James Ault Productions, Northampton, MA, 1994). In the Ault video, a number of Laney's upper level administrators, senior faculty, recent alumni, and trustees are interviewed for their perspectives about his leadership. The growth and change at Emory during Laney's tenure is dramatically portrayed and appears clear. Some comments about the change from the "old" Emory to the "new" reflect criticism from some quarters that were upset about the evolution of the university. However, this type of critique in reaction to changes as dramatic as those occurring at Emory during the decades of Laney's presidency is to be expected, and even those making it also applaud Laney's leadership.

9. James Laney, former president, Emory University, interview with author, April 27, 2003.

10. I am indebted to Stuart Gulley for sharing with me transcripts of interviews he conducted with President Laney during the research for his doctoral dissertation and subsequent book, Stuart F. Gulley, *The Academic President as Moral Leader* (Macon, GA: Mercer University Press, 2001). The material that follows is taken from an interview conducted by Gulley, June 23, 1998, pp. 14–15. Gulley's book is a definitive and thorough overview of Laney as a leader and president.

11. Gulley interview transcript, November 11, 1997.

12. Ibid.

13. John DiBiaggio, former president, Tufts University, interview with author, August 12, 2003.

14. Ibid. DiBiaggio expands on his contentions about fund-raising and resource acquisition in both the public and private university settings. He connects it to the responsibility of presidents and their institutions to show that the financial support is directed to and concretely enabling a change in the lives of students, that there is some "value added." He believes this is especially crucial, and can be most dramatically shown for students "at the margin" when their level of performance is greatly enhanced by the opportunity a college education affords. He relates this to the needed financial support and the ways in which the monetary support actually makes a difference. He also cites this capacity to connect education to its personal impact on students as something that the historically black colleges have traditionally done well. His implicit and explicit question about elite institutions where the tuition fees are yet higher is that their challenge is to show they too make a real difference for students in order to justify the need for monetary support.

15. Neil Rudenstine, *Pointing Our Thoughts* (Cambridge, MA: Harvard University, 2001), p. 251. The title of this book of presidential speeches is taken from the campaign kickoff talk, "Pointing Our Thoughts."

16. Ibid., pp. 251–52.

17. Ibid., p. 252.

18. Ibid., p. 254.

19. Robert Oden, interview with author.

20. Ibid.

21. John Sexton, president, New York University, interview with author, June 29, 2004.

22. Ibid. The material that follows is taken and the quotations are excerpted from this interview.

23. While it would be difficult to sketch the full details of this fiscal and budgetary situation, suffice it to say that it included the university being significantly tuition driven, deferring maintenance at a rate with dire future consequences (Sexton estimates for a physical plant of their size, the industry standard is about $30 million a year and they

were spending $8 million, that is, maybe a quarter of what was needed), borrowing money (again he estimates over a decade in the 1990s to the early years of the twenty-first century, a billion and a half dollars), and not building sufficient space or hiring sufficient faculty members for a rapidly increasing student enrollment (8,000 more students from 1992 to 2002).

24. John Sexton, interview with author.

CHAPTER

Presidential Engagements and Entanglements: The University Tackles the Wider World

Colleges and universities have always had unavoidable relations and interactions with the cities and communities of which they are a part, with government and its agencies, and with a marketplace interested in their resources and services.[1] The contemporary era is no different, except for the fact that these relationships occur in a faster paced global environment with its more complex entanglements.

Some of these relationships are "town-gown," but more and more the academy goes beyond the confines of this old-style notion of college-town and student–local citizen contact. From major universities like Harvard, Boston University, and the Massachusetts Institute of Technology, ever encroaching on the communities of Cambridge, Allston-Brighton, and Boston, to other large-scale and smaller higher education institutions in both cities and towns, questions about the value and social good of colleges and universities persist and must be answered to the satisfaction of external constituencies and citizens.

Presidents speak for their campuses and are the personae of the university to this wider world. How do presidents handle these relationships? What is their nature and what external force do these connections create for presidential leadership? What do presidents face in addressing the often tense and difficult issues arising from the university's association with the wider world?

The University of Pennsylvania under the leadership of Judith Rodin, in the 1990s and the early years of the twenty-first century, is a prime example of a major university tackling long-standing issues in relationship to its community setting. When we met, Rodin had only recently stepped down after a distinguished

11-year tenure at the helm of Penn, one of the oldest universities in the nation. When Rodin, who shortly thereafter assumed leadership at the Ford Foundation, left the presidency, by choice she moved to a simple office buried in the bowels of a massive building serving as the plant operations and long-term planning "brain" of the Penn campus. Rodin wanted her emerita office located there as a reflection of the commitments made to long-range thinking and planning throughout her presidency. Her office was almost spare, just one room leading out to a corridor with pods of office support staff for the various administrators, including Rodin, located just across the hall outside. We sat at a round table and were joined by her presidential executive assistant.

Rodin hails from Philadelphia, having been born and raised in the city and an adjoining town. Upon becoming president, Rodin was immediately involved in one major issue: Penn's standing with the city. As a former resident and alumna, she knows well the neighborhood situation surrounding the university and its direct and sometimes negative impact on the campus (though community activists would argue this is never a one-way street). Though Rodin risked a great deal of presidential capital on the goal of city improvement, the commitments she made and the leverage of Penn's investments to transform large neighborhoods of Philadelphia are a story of committed leadership.

Penn's transformation as a university was based on the hope that initiatives directed at the city would sow seeds of change. Early in her tenure, Rodin "got the trustees to give us a two million dollar fund" as a risk capital investment in housing and urban development. The goal was that "we wouldn't gentrify the neighborhood, we would really allow it to be very, very diverse, and multiethnic, multiracial, multicultural. And that started a housing boom," one that increased the residential stock for citizens "in West Philadelphia."[2] Rodin is matter-of-fact, but by no means arrogant, recounting how she convinced Penn's board to be aggressive and to take financial risks. For Rodin this strategy was about taking a stand, a stand she felt essential to the long-term interest of the university and its relationship with the city. Penn would make "a social and political statement both internally and externally that we were not some ivory tower. We were not separate from the city, we were of and we wanted to be part of the urban landscape."

The institutional saga plays a role in the perceptions of presidents, the shape of their leadership, and the transformation of the history and sense about the future for their campuses.[3] Rodin characterizes changes and commitments at Penn as "part of the saga that we were going to the best urban university in America. We were going to look that way, we were going to feel that way, we were going to think of ourselves that way. We worked very hard then to articulate to the community very clearly and very deliberately what our internal physical plans were, where we intended to put things and why." This meant that Rodin needed to make "a public commitment to the community early on that Penn would not expand further into West Philadelphia ever again. We created a neighborhood initiative," and to make this work effectively "a trustees' committee which had never existed before, and gave it standing, not an ad hoc committee, so that everything that we did that had a neighborhood focus... would really have both the approval and [have people] buy in at the highest levels internally."[4] Penn needed to change the way it related to the local communities surrounding the campus and to the City of Philadelphia as a whole.

Changing the climate of relations and the relationship of a college or major university with its local community is fraught with challenges. But another external arena in which presidents must lead is relationships with the federal government. These associations have become ever more crucial in recent years, marked by increasingly complex and consistent scrutiny by federal authorities and agencies. Clark Kerr first identified this era of increased governmental influence as creating a significant shift and challenge for higher education and its leadership. It is the era characterized by the GI Bill, increasing federal government support for student financial aid, and subsequent investment in research and development and in physical plant expansion. Federal support was instrumental in the growth of community colleges and of the major state branch campuses affiliated with state university systems, and the continuing development of flagship public universities. These so-called state institutions constitute the system of American higher education that Stephen Joel Trachtenberg aptly calls the "University of the United States," a constellation that is the envy of the world.[5]

The increasingly close connection of universities to federal agencies and their support delivered through state bureaucracies requires presidents and their administrations to possess new navigating and negotiating skills, to pay more attention to audits and reports, and to engage in public defense of both their campuses and of all higher education. Practically speaking, this demands the time of presidents, placing enlarged burdens upon them as compared to the simpler days of their predecessors. However, with the bad comes some good: heightened governmental interference and control has evolved hand and glove with enormous federal and state largesse, expanding student enrollment and enriching faculty development through research grants and facilities. Even though layers of administrative support staff and insulation aid them, presidents still solely set the strategy and tone for managing matters with the government, its agencies and personnel.

From a public relations standpoint, carrying out these responsibilities can have a significant impact on the reputations of presidents and their institutions, the experience of President Donald Kennedy at Stanford being a prime case in point. Kennedy spent nearly his entire faculty and administrative career at Stanford, reaching a pinnacle as president. Four issues concerning governmental policy and oversight controls of higher education plunged Kennedy into public positions and visibility.

The first was pressure on campus research and freedom of inquiry in the 1980s, sparked by the Cold War and Ronald Reagan's characterization of the Soviet Union as an "Evil Empire." Similar reverberations are felt today as a result of George W. Bush's "war on terror." While President, Kennedy cochaired the Department of Defense "Universities Forum" during "a time that the Reagan administration was doing some questionable interferences with academic science. And Richard Perle was assistant secretary of defense [Kennedy rolling his eyes that Perle is still involved in defense and foreign policy today]. And he and this undersecretary for R[esearch] and E[ngineering], Dick DeLauer, who is one of our alumni, were struggling over how much, how many strictures to compose on academic research using either the international traffic and arms regulation or other regulations."[6] The fear was that foreign scientists would gain training and knowledge and "export" what they knew as enemies of the United States. Kennedy led the academy's fight back on grounds of academic freedom and free inquiry.

With pride at the outcome, Kennedy depicts this as a "very interesting contest and we won it, but it was a very hard struggle. And eventually an Academy of Sciences committee made a recommendation and Reagan signed an executive order." However, the same struggle and battle continues in a post–September 11 world, Kennedy noting that "Condoleeza Rice just reinforced [the Reagan order] a few months ago, essentially saying the government would use only the classification process and no proxy use of adjunct regulations in order to manage access to university research."[7]

The autonomy of academic institutions is visibly at stake in such moments, though they often pass by an unsuspecting public without much notice. Kennedy vehemently defends university prerogatives concerning research as absolutely fundamental and believes the good news is that the battle won two decades ago still applies in the "war on terror" world. But he warns that vigilance is essential if the university is to remain protected from the use and abuse of national security and defense as cards to trump the autonomy of research.

Kennedy also pushed back against both a threatened reduction in federal Pell grant financial support to low-income students and government intrusion into the institutional allocation of student financial aid. Reagan's tax policy changes reduced federal revenue, requiring spending reductions in social programs including Pell grants, the major source supporting higher education for needy students. Kennedy advocated broadly and aggressively about the need for student financial aid, especially from the federal government.[8] He and Derek Bok, president of Harvard, led a national campaign, including writing columns in major newspapers and testifying in Washington to save the Pell grant program. Twenty years later, continuing clashes are being waged with regard to federal commitment to student financial aid and successor presidents are once again at the forefront, arguing against government fiscal policies.

Kennedy and Stanford also supported President Charles Vest of the Massachusetts Institute of Technology (MIT) when they became embroiled in a tendentious legal struggle with the federal government. MIT was one of more than a dozen schools, the seven Ivy League institutions along with a number of other elite universities, in what was called the Overlap Group. These schools competed regularly for many of the same students and their financial aid needs. But out of mutual and enlightened self-interest, the group set and offered commonly agreed aid packages. The federal government challenged this activity as monopolistic, impinging on the right of students to negotiate their financial need individually with these schools. Lengthy legal struggles and wrangling between the Overlap Group and the government led all except MIT to withdraw from the suit, agreeing no longer to engage in their previous practices.

Stanford was not part of the group, but its administrators were well aware, through their counterparts, of the controversy. Kennedy thought that withdrawal of the suit was a mistake and that the schools had legitimate arguments with the government. He sided with Vest, publicly supporting his courageous action in pursuit of MIT's legal case, which they eventually won. Kennedy lauds Vest as a hero for his stand, pushing back at the federal government to preserve institutional autonomy and collaboration.[9]

The last of the four public issues that enmeshed Kennedy (and Stanford) in problems with the government was by far the biggest and most notorious. In the early 1990s, the "grant audit affair" entangled Stanford with federal authorities in an episode that led to public hearings, examinations and audits of procedures and documents, the release of institutional information normally kept very closely guarded, and a major dent in the university's much-vaunted reputation. Stanford's experience is instructive about presidential leadership and its limits, as well as about how elite academic institutions can readily become easy targets for public scrutiny. Kennedy has consistently been extraordinarily open both about what happened, and thus much is known both from the public record and his comments.[10] Candor is one of Kennedy's strong suits, for better and worse. Among the lessons of this case, his reflections are shot through with the allegation that the audit affair is exemplary of the worst aspects of public and governmental scrutiny and interference.

Kennedy does not deny personal culpability, and accepts responsibility for the fact that his handling of the affair made his presidency and the university the butt of public ridicule and criticism. Certainly his version of events is based on 20-20 hindsight and is crafted to blunt negative judgments about him and Stanford. However, one clear lesson of the affair is that much of the bad press and sullying of reputation resulted from Stanford's perceived posture as being beyond reproach, as well as from Kennedy's public statements and congressional testimony that were read by many as a mixture of high-handedness and nonchalance. Nonetheless, his side of the story illuminates the dynamics embedded in such controversies.

This episode is also referred to as the "indirect cost controversy." Indirect costs, basic in most grants, are part of the business, normally specified as a percentage of the overall budgeted grant expense.[11] The focal point of the struggle at Stanford involved standard Memoranda of Understanding (MOUs) that define the permissible levels of indirect costs and types of institutional expense understood to be legitimate overheads. "That's where the big financial liability was," Kennedy acknowledges, and "we knew there was a financial liability that we couldn't avoid, which is that they were going to politically insist on lowering indirect costs for government." But what Kennedy and Stanford sought to do was to be certain that "we had defended the principle that the MOUs were binding. And so I felt obliged in the [congressional] hearing to undertake and explain what the MOUs were, why they were reasonable, what the cost and allocation principles were."[12]

The story became a public affair when a disgruntled Stanford employee whistle-blew, leaking information to contacts at a local newspaper. The paper's story led Congressman John Dingell, chair of the Subcommittee on Oversight and Investigations of the House Commerce Committee, to push, Kennedy is convinced for no reason other than political grandstanding, for a General Accounting Office audit of Stanford's indirect costs and overhead practices. Investigators focused on a yacht that Stanford had been given and that inadvertently "popped up in a pool no one had thought to examine, one including depreciation charges on a group of physical assets."[13]

When this came to their attention, Stanford's administrative leaders immediately wrote a letter of apology to the committee. The letter was almost simultaneously leaked to the local paper and shortly "it became established as media lore that the vessel was used to entertain administrators and that the taxpayers had actually paid for maintenance. None of us [Kennedy and his fellow administrators] had ever seen it [the yacht], and we insisted—as was true—that nothing more than an accounting error was involved."[14]

The tale quickly took on a life of its own, and Kennedy and Stanford were forced into an extreme defensive posture. Kennedy was caricatured in the media as arrogant and brazen. But there is, as always, another side to the story.

Kennedy's counsel about what happened is critical in an era of media scrutiny and frenzy that complicates leadership and public perceptions: "We had some difficult decisions to make in preparing for our appearance [before Dingell's committee]. Many Washington-wise advisers told us that appeasement was the only course—the chairman needed an abject mea culpa. We rejected that strategy, choosing instead to emphasize the important issues—the importance of basic university research, and our adherence to the government's own rules about indirect cost recovery—accompanied by a forthright admission that our accounting systems needed improvement."

Even though in the end it backfired, Stanford had (it believed) a thoughtful strategy for its committee appearance. More importantly, Kennedy continues, "I defended Stanford's people because I knew they had followed the rules. And I wanted to be sure that we insisted both on the validity of our agreements with the government and on the faithfulness with which we had tried to follow them." Revealing a grasp of *realpolitik*, Kennedy concludes: "We knew that eventually our case might reach the courts, and that any giveaways at this point were likely to hurt us later."[15] Ironically, though stubborn by any estimation, Kennedy is exemplary for leadership that upheld and defended core university values. He also maintained another principle as the case played out. That is, he protected colleague administrators from being made mere scapegoats, a step that would have made the controversy go away vastly more quickly and quietly, and thus would have been an understandably reasonable thing to do. But he resisted that temptation and as a result took more of a hit to his own role and reputation.

Despite the best intentions, Kennedy and Stanford took a severe beating in the press, other media, and the public eye. Though continuing to assert that many of "the most serious elements in the case against the university were both wrong and unfair," Kennedy acknowledges that "Not all the charges against Stanford were wrong, and we had some things to apologize for: some sloppy accounting, failure to examine the appropriateness of costs that were technically 'allowable,' and a certain reflex defensiveness in the early going." Kennedy believes lessons were learned, and from the experience he provides counsel to others who might face similar charges and allegations, noting simply that "the way in which they become so firmly implanted and so damaging is a cautionary tale worth telling."[16]

In his annual commencement remarks, as the dust settles on the controversy in spring 1991, Kennedy speaks personally about the travails of the year. He offers advice about handling "adverse public attention," and underscores the "loyalty of those who know us best" in trying times. In such painful lessons, dignity is often at stake, and Kennedy concludes that "no one can take your dignity away from you, but you can lose it. It is very much worth keeping." Finally, he urges students not to draw from his "experience any negative conclusions about the perils of leadership. Leadership...entails risks. But it also brings joy and satisfaction."[17]

Kennedy paid a price beyond the personal caricatures and the assault on his reputation. His tenure rapidly concluded, Kennedy openly admits that the controversy "led a year later to my turning it over because it had gotten pretty difficult to do things."[18] However, by the time he stepped down from the presidency, Kennedy had already served 12 years, longer than many of his colleagues of this era. Thus even without the audit affair it is unlikely he would have continued many years longer.[19]

The need for sensible caution can be drawn from the experience of Stanford and Kennedy. However, care should be taken not to read into this saga a message that presidents should refuse to enter the fray in the face of government pressure and intrusion. In fact, the opposite is the case when fundamental values and prerogatives of the academy are under attack. The question and the problem is how best to do this. Kennedy does not argue his and Stanford's response as a model to be precisely imitated: far from it. But their strategy was reasonable and understandable, and should not be ignored simply because of the problems that ensued.

It would be simple to subscribe to the view that Kennedy's big "mistake" was being both too arrogant and too naïve, guilty merely of assuming unrealistically that he and Stanford were somehow invulnerable. However, the message of this tale is not so one-dimensional. First, errors, large ones, of judgment concerning the ways this issue would play out were clearly made. Stanford learned the hard way about better grant accounting, providing hard-earned advice for other colleges and universities (more than a few "but for the grace of God, go we" sighs of relief were no doubt uttered in the process). Second, it would be inaccurate to conclude that presidents should remain silent in such episodes. Even if he became a sacrificial lamb, Kennedy's intuition, that he should stand up in defense of his institution, was correct, especially countering distorted images in public circulation. Finally and crucially, Kennedy used his presidency to stand up for principles firmly believed to be important: resisting government intrusion and interference in the internal affairs of the academy.

Governmental interference is not exclusively the concern of major research universities. A recent change proposed by the United States Department of Education to legislation regulating the release of student records information raises broad questions for the higher education community. Katherine Haley Will, president of Gettysburg College, a small liberal arts college, expresses fears undoubtedly shared by many colleagues about expansion of government control and access to information in a post–September 11th world. Will opposes invasions of student privacy and confidentiality, easily breached by these intrusions. She argues that such legislation would force colleges and universities "to report all their students' Social Security numbers and other information about each individual—including credits earned, degree plan, race and ethnicity, and grants and loans received—to a national databank."[20]

Will's concern is twofold. First, "The government will record every student, regardless of whether he or she receives federal aid, in the databank," a massive increase in the information the government currently routinely possesses. Second, "The threat to our students' privacy is of grave concern, and the government has not satisfactorily explained why it wants to collect individual information." "The potential for abuse of power and violation of civil liberties is immense. The database would begin with 15 million-plus records of students in the first year and grow. These student records would be held by the federal government for at least the life of the student," Will concludes.[21]

Whether or not this proposed legislation becomes law, it reveals an assault on the exterior walls of the academy that must be repelled. Presidents are on the line but have power to respond based in their right and duty to speak out.

Another challenge colleges and universities face when engaging the world around them is how they communicate the value of higher education. This is not as simple a task as it first appears. Presidents and their institutions cannot assume that citizens innately comprehend the role and significance of higher education, so they must be on the offense to explain the social, scientific, and humanitarian importance of the university. A failure to convey and argue where necessary about the value and impact of the university to society can create gaps in public understanding and perception. (As only one among many constant threats, consider the recurrent municipal propositions around the country to remove the tax-free status of campuses.) While this need for public communication is true for both public and private schools, public presidents have to juggle more players— elected and other officials backed by taxpaying citizens—as constituents concerned about expenditures and directly holding purse strings. However, private college presidents ignore political leaders and citizens at their peril.

Stephen Joel Trachtenberg of George Washington University knows well the university-in-the-world arena. I met Trachtenberg in a conference room in the President's Office at George Washington. It was a gorgeous spring day shortly after the university's commencement exercises. Trachtenberg, dressed in a tweedish-looking, spring-weight jacket and cowboy boots, entered carrying a shopping bag and a canvas bag apparently being used in place of a briefcase as a satchel for paperwork. He greeted me warmly, almost as if I was a long-lost relative, and we immediately began to converse. Trachtenberg is very sociable and outgoing, and he makes frequent use of gestures to drive home points. He has a great sense of humor, much of which is the self-deprecating sort. Exuding great energy and enthusiasm, Trachtenberg conveys a love and passion for his work.

Regarding the academy's image in the public eye, Trachtenberg captures the irony that "Very few people in the general public comprehend the complexity of what it takes to run institutions of higher education, even though a remarkably large percentage of the nation's population have a college degree or have taken some courses or have spent some time on a campus."[22] Unsurprisingly this creates a disconnect between the values of the university and college, and the public's perception and understanding of those values.

Trachtenberg's assessment warns about the relationship of universities and their leaders with various external constituencies, especially that portion of the populace with little or no connection to higher education and paltry knowledge of higher education's mission and purpose. Public sector schools must pay great attention to those in positions as popularly elected trustees and other officials with oversight responsibilities. But for both public and private institutions, even "internal" constituents, such as alumni, must comprehend fully the dilemmas and difficulties colleges and universities face and the inherent challenges in exhibiting their value to the public. Alumni, in particular, can hold dearly to overly romanticized perspectives born of bygone undergraduate memories of conditions that simply no longer obtain in today's world. In order to keep alumni fully in the fold and up-to-speed with the challenges universities face, from time to time they need to be disabused of these old-style assumptions that are rooted in a past that does not translate to today's complex times.

Even with regard to constituents inside the gates, Trachtenberg notes that often "in the academy itself, I am astounded at how narrowly focused various constituencies—professors, administrators, even deans—are about the operation of the university. Very few individuals use a wide-angle lens to view the institution." Maintaining a broad picture and keeping abreast of trends and issues in higher education in order to educate both internal and external constituents requires information. For Trachtenberg, this means the daily reading of a variety of sources to gauge the pulse of higher education, including the perspective of students, from a selection of college newspapers and other publications about higher education. With self-deprecating humor he adds that of course this leaves things in the hands of the president, who "understands, in his or her wisdom—everything!"[23] More seriously, Trachtenberg contends, "one of the primary goals of the university's president is to see the whole, to have an institutionally wide perspective."[24]

Harold Shapiro's presidencies at the University of Michigan and Princeton overlapped with both Kennedy's and Trachtenberg's. I met Shapiro in his emeritus office at Princeton University, where he maintains a status as a teaching member of the faculty, and continues to speak and write about higher education and the university. His office is furnished in a modern but simple style. Open on his desk is the working manuscript of lectures he had delivered at Berkeley University in honor of Clark Kerr (who was still alive at the time), lectures that he was editing for a then forthcoming book.[25]

The University of Michigan is arguably one of the most high profile and outstanding public universities in the country and its constituent pressures are significant. While its president, Shapiro routinely exercised the balance essential at public universities between the needs of the state and its citizenry with the purposes and intentions of the university and its constituents, especially its faculty.[26] He believes a major challenge for presidents in such settings is to get constituencies outside the gates to understand the points of overlap of their needs and concerns with those of the university. Any gap in information about and understanding of universities and colleges in the mind of the populace feeds and stirs contentions, sometimes even suspicions, that in turn can produce often-hostile political and public perceptions about higher education. Presidents cannot afford to take these dynamics lightly. They cannot merely sit on the sidelines thinking changes in administrations in Washington, DC, and in political fortunes will improve their situation. Rather, presidents must argue in the public square using the platform of the bully pulpit for advocacy of the public image of the academy.

At Michigan, Shapiro walked this line, navigating complicated political waters. The external pressures are magnified when the core principles and values of the university become unavoidably at stake in the discourse of a public and political marketplace. "The most difficult issue which required the most tenacious holding on to principle in the face of difficulty," Shapiro contends, "was to convince the major political actors in the state—whether that is the state legislature, the teachers' union, the automobile manufacturers' association, other unions, and so on, who were the major political forces in the state—that there in fact was some overlap between their interests and the university's interests."[27]

But this is only the surface negotiating and advocacy in which Shapiro engaged. The other part of the equation is "that the university had an independent set of interests, in addition to the interests of serving their needs." By his description, "this was a daily task—that's probably exaggerating. Some days we probably didn't worry about that or even think about it or didn't work on it, but it was an ever-present reality." For presidents, attention to this political dynamic and leadership responsibility is crucial because "to avoid being swept along by a set of interests and values that weren't central or not completely central to the university's own interests and values took (1) a capacity to articulate that, and (2) the courage to stick with it in the face of the much easier solution, namely to try to convince people that their interests were our interests and we would serve them, which would, politically, have been a much easier task."[28]

In debates about institutional mission and purpose, especially in the public university setting, it is essential for presidents to display balance and courage. Considering the numbers of people involved—to an extent the entire citizenry of a state in the case of public universities—and the fiscal pressures and investment at stake, the inevitable conflicting, often mutually exclusive, views at the fore should come as no surprise. The educational task for presidents is thus paramount. However, educating stakeholders with rational arguments alone will unfortunately not bridge the gulf or carry the day. Shapiro acknowledges the reality of an (always) easier, political avenue, that is, that the citizenry be permitted simply to dictate the agenda and the university "willingly" accept it. This course is a line of least resistance and is indeed very seductive. However, it will not prove helpful or productive in the long run.[29]

These tensions do not obtain only in the public university sphere. Private colleges and universities feature nearly identical or analogous battles over ideology and politics. Advocates on the margins of the ideological spectrum promote decisions and initiatives that they believe are critical to the success of the university. However, these ideas and platforms hatched to sustain ideological beliefs frequently stand in opposition or contradiction to the values of the university. In the face of these challenges, the question at stake for both public and private presidents remains: do they have the courage to stick to the fundamental principles of the academy when these values are under assault by external or internal forces?

As an example, Shapiro suggests the counterintuitive thinking often required to reach desired ends. At first glance Shapiro appears to divert from his presumed goal of fighting for the needs of the university, not capitulating to the perceived agenda and priorities of the "outside" world. In fact, he underscores how presidents must maintain a focus on "first principles" even as they unfold strategies that may on the surface appear to cave in to the agendas of those outside the gates of the academy.[30]

Early in his presidency at Michigan, Shapiro developed a strategy to address assumptions about the resources available and about what it would take to maintain or expand funding for the university. In order to reach the important goal of developing the traditionally assumed core of the university—the arts and sciences for undergraduates—Shapiro began by strengthening "the periphery and work[ing] into the core."[31] The "periphery" in this case was graduate and professional programs, assets Shapiro knew to be heavily associated with the profile of the university in public currency and thus crucial to attracting resources. The political and financial reality was that "the state legislature was willing to allow us considerable freedom on tuition in the graduate and professional area." Predictably the arts and sciences faculty rebelled when they learned Shapiro was emphasizing the graduate and professional components of the university. But Shapiro stuck with this strategy, what he calls "an outside, in" strategy, willing first to build what for him was the periphery until he could get the allocations of resources needed to support the more important core.

During Shapiro's Michigan tenure two things happened. First, to maintain the university's core values and purposes, he had to attract support from its broad constituent base by initially educating about the realities of what a university is. This convinced the citizenry of the ways their needs were in fact being served and met. In the process Shapiro had to avoid being "swept along by a set of interests and values that weren't central or not completely central to the university's own interests and values."[32]

Second, tactically Shapiro responds to the prejudice of Michigan's, like any state's, market—its citizens, legislators, and other stakeholders—that sees "value" only in the practical outcomes of graduate and professional education. Political leaders and citizens holding the purse strings for universities believe they exist to emphasize science, business, law, and technology, and to prepare people for careers and for practical, applied research. Shapiro addresses these desires by expanding graduate and professional education while still reaching a goal he feels is truly more important and significant to the overall health of the university: strengthening the arts and sciences core for undergraduates. He shows how to strike a fine balance between confronting external (as well as internal) forces, making the pragmatic adjustments and accommodations necessary, while refusing to capitulate to the dictates of the demands without any chance of compromise.

Trachtenberg is likewise a realist, but goes a step further, taking on the "purists" (mentioning Derek Bok by name) who believe the university does not need to alter course in the face of external pressure. He argues that changes in course for the university do not inexorably have to sacrifice previously held principles. The challenge is to ensure that the sacrifice of core purpose is not the unintended consequence of adaptation and change. Thus, Trachtenberg unapologetically believes universities must keep up with the times, and "sell" services of interest and demand to society. His argument, based in the realities of less well-endowed institutions, is that universities cannot afford to stand still: "[U]niversities have always been entrepreneurial—responding to the marketplace. If GW [George Washington] had stayed true to its origins as Columbian College, a Baptist school founded in 1821," he asserts, "we would be teaching theology and preaching, but not anthropology or particle physics. Universities, despite the predilection some of them have for Gothic or Georgian architecture, need to respond to their times—that is to say, they exist in a marketplace and need to respond to its contemporary pressure."[33] Sensitivity to external market pressure is different for more highly endowed than for less well-endowed colleges and universities. In the former, presidents and institutions are more insulated by their financial wherewithal, thus having little problem maintaining core values in reacting to market pressures. They are able to make decisions out of choice, not necessity. The latter, less well-endowed institutions do not have the luxury of as much of a cushion against market pressure, and are thus easily lured to increase financial and other strengths by appealing to marketplace interests. Certainly Harvard, and similar elite institutions, have established many centers, institutes, and other programs designed unquestionably in response to perceived and real "market" needs, and to generate revenue. But they have the luxury of maintaining a focus on their core mission even when electing to provide more peripheral services and resources.

Morehouse College faces an interesting array of these external pressures of practicality versus principle and purpose. I traveled to Atlanta and to the campus to meet President Walter Massey at the president's house, the most convenient location for him as he had flown into town briefly that morning and was to leave again that afternoon. His wife greeted me and gave me a tour of the house. Upon his appointment to the presidency, Massey had persuaded the trustees to build a president's residence (the college's recent presidents had owned their own homes off campus). In a smart tactical and symbolic move, he mandated that the design plans for the house incorporate a separate conference-style facility to be used for all types of college functions, not just those handled or sponsored by the President's Office. The result is that the ground floor of the house is a fully appointed conference area, heavily used for college-wide functions.

Massey was very welcoming and gracious, despite the obviously tight schedule of the day. He exudes personal vigor and a warm hospitality, and based on his roots as a college alumnus, he projects Morehouse as an institution with a sense of "place" about it. We sat for our conversation in the living room around a small coffee table.

Morehouse is a long-standing, prestigious, historically black liberal arts college with a superb history and tradition. The education it provides young black men is unparalleled nationally, and Massey proudly points out the astounding statistic that the college graduates more black males than any other college or university in the nation.[34]

However, notwithstanding great strengths, Morehouse faces delicate market pressures specific to the college, what it stands for and the function it serves. Despite its elite status, Morehouse caters to prospective students largely from families in which they are the first generation to go to college. Thus, the college must be responsive to parent expectations regarding the career and economic value of a Morehouse education. For Massey and his faculty, this creates a delicate balancing act between retaining a strong commitment to maintain their liberal arts heritage and foundation, and conveying convincing evidence about the "value" of a Morehouse degree to parents and students. In fact, Morehouse is by no means alone: many, if not most, liberal arts colleges face this challenge in similarly critical ways.

Massey indicates that many Morehouse students, whether from the first generation or not, "come from families who view education as a pathway to a career and they see that and they want to see it by way of connection to a career." Because they are looking for a Morehouse education to pay off, "one of our challenges is how do we shape a curriculum that really is faithful to our goal to give students a liberal education while meeting the demands or desires of our constituents who want their young sons to emerge with a career." Massey believes that can be done, but it is an "ongoing concern and an issue that we have to struggle with," and he adds that his faculty is "in the middle of revising our core curriculum to try to shape it so that it meets the needs of what an education should be."[35]

This task rests in the hands of the faculty, but as president, Massey shapes and is committed to the vision that the core of the Morehouse curriculum will not be pushed away from its liberal arts foundation, even if some contemporary skills or areas of study are incorporated. The reality for Morehouse and other liberal arts colleges is a constant and not easily abated pressure from students and parents, joined by other external constituents, for courses of academic study leading to careers. Like a canary in a coalmine, Massey transparently acknowledges these marketplace pressures and challenges and is urging his colleagues to counter them.

This discussion of external and market pressures on college and university presidents and their institutions would not be complete without attention to Shapiro's concerns about the co-opting of faculty due to the nature of their research and especially its funding. He believes this threat to be universal and worsening across academe—major research universities as well as smaller colleges and universities—and counsels that this problem fits within a realm of greater potential danger: broader commercialization of the academy, or as Shapiro labels the issue, the "relentless force for the commercialization of the key university products."[36]

Commercialization as Shapiro describes it threatens education in two ways. The first is in the recruitment and admission of students and the lures used to attract them, including the perceived value of the college degree. Shapiro highlights recent growth in the business path that colleges and universities have taken: heightened competition with each other requiring enormous investment of financial resources in recruitment, in student support services and facilities, and in non-need-based, that is, merit, scholarships and financial aid.[37] This competition is a "keep up with the Joneses" dynamic. Who would dare to be the first to withdraw from the contest?

However, it is on the second problem, commercialization's profound impact on faculty and their research, that Shapiro concentrates his primary focus. On the surface this looks to be exclusively a research university problem. However, the money at stake and the potential financial compromises equally confront almost all colleges, many vastly smaller in scale. In Shapiro's view, any college in which faculty research and support is expected, in which it is emphasized and blessed, and in which external funding sources are heavily relied on is susceptible to the corrosive effect of commercial pressures.

Shapiro's "commercialization" is the interaction of the university with "private markets." A realist about both the sources of pressure and their very obvious upsides, he asserts, "There's no end to the amount of resources people need and you have no idea when you have enough. And so, therefore, the incentives to engage in the private market in the short run are huge, and there may be a lot of positives." But there are undeniably simultaneous threats to the heart of the academy. Shapiro believes administrative and faculty leaders are inattentive to this threat, contending that "there's no one thinking about the possible costs of doing that [ignoring market forces] and what it means to protecting those special values of the university—intellectual values, educational values, and so on—that form the university [but] can easily be missed and sort of slowly slip away on you, as you become more and more engaged with private markets."[38]

Shapiro argues that the linkage and loyalty of faculty to outside forces directly herald the prospect of the university becoming "commodified." The very real danger is that faculty and the university are being co-opted. Shapiro believes, as with any slippery slope, the beginnings are benign or unconscious, because "one doesn't think about it and doesn't care about it in the short run," and when we do look at it, we are "just not thinking carefully about it." This lack of attention and vigilance results from what Shapiro views as a "fallacy of competition."[39] That is, in the academy the assumption is that competition is a good thing. Thus, faculty and administrators do not think ahead about the implications of large numbers of individual faculty members developing strong outside ties and relationships to support their work.

Pointing to where this slippery slope potentially leads, Shapiro suggests: "For an individual faculty member to join with a biotech firm for all the good reasons—they're going to produce an anticancer drug or something like that—there's almost nothing at stake. There are benefits, and resources come in, the research goes ahead, the society gets a new knowledge. It's all benefits, and for an individual faculty member, there's very little downside. They feel they can control the [situation]." But Shapiro does not think the situation is being controlled at all. The problem is that when faculty, society, and those helped or cured by a research discovery or breakthrough benefit, who is going to be sufficiently bold to question where the financial support came from or the possibility that it has compromised the faculty member, the university, or both?

However, to Shapiro the problem goes beyond a simple ethical concern about how research is conducted or the possibility that results could be compromised because of who holds the funding purse strings. The deeper concern is the influence on university governance when individual faculty largesse is garnered from external funding.

Here the slope gets more slippery, because "we're all doing this individually, and before you know it, we're enmeshed in a web of these things, with a hugely exploding set of conflicts of interests, and it's not a single faculty [member] anymore, it's the whole faculty." Shapiro fears for the cumulative effect of individual faculty member relationships that are external to and in many ways autonomous and independent of their university responsibilities and thus independent of the faculty as a whole in its decision making and policy roles.[40] The bottom-line concern for Shapiro is the playing out of this scenario in which truly independent, uncompromised faculty decisions about policy, protocols, and decisions—governance issues over which faculty members, as they should, have power and purview—may no longer be possible, becoming a thing of the past. This in turn would significantly hinder the university's capacity to keep its ship righted in terms of its core values, principles, and independence.

If that is not enough, there is yet another layer to this complex web: conflict of interest and divided loyalty problems that create even larger predicaments for the university. The danger is captured in a fundamental, albeit rhetorical, question at the heart of the university's role and purpose: "Who is it that stands in our society for an independent source of knowledge?" Shapiro's rhetorical reply is as follows: "Supposing you wanted an independent source of knowledge in the most impacted area [of the foregoing problem], which is the biosciences, you would be hard put to find a faculty member who didn't have a relationship with some private enterprise."[41] At one level these issues combine under the broader umbrella of "intellectual property," an issue with which universities and colleges have become increasingly concerned. This is a legitimate, but Shapiro thinks far from resolved, battle over the matter of the ownership of ideas and patents. However, Shapiro again returns to a central concern: the faculty's right over and responsibility for governance and oversight of the academic affairs of the university. For faculty members, "their benefits have a direct conflict of interest here. You want the university faculty to set policy, but how do they do that when everybody says they have a prima facie conflict of interest?"[42]

Shapiro believes presidents and other leaders, primarily among the faculty, inevitably must address these core governance issues in order to preserve the autonomy and integrity of the way affairs are conducted within the academy's walls. The unmistakable message: leaders must make certain the worst case prophecy—faculty with primary loyalty and allegiance, already strained in an era of the internet and other global academic connections, outside the university, and with compromised integrity and independence—does not become the predominant governing principle and ethos of the university.

If this were the eventuality (and some argue it already is), then the intellectual and educational values that are Shapiro's starting point about what the academy stands for would be put at severe risk. Further, the university would be "governed" (again some would argue it already is) to a greater degree by the sources of faculty research money, and the faculty would be reduced more to roles as independent contractors than is even currently the case. Shapiro's recommendation is that presidents should ally with the faculty in pressing a resolution, "because they are the ones where the real action takes place at the university, but sometimes you just have to face up to it."[43]

The genie may be out of the bottle, but Shapiro's voice must be heeded if the tide of external influence is to be stemmed or reversed. Each college and university has to confront and address its particular issues driven by external pressures and needs. But at least two crucial issues in these battles are broadly at stake.

First, attention must be paid to Trachtenberg's assumption about misunderstandings, misperceptions, and outright lack of knowledge in the land about the fundamental purpose and values of the university and college. Closing this perception gap is a challenge for leaders of all higher education institutions—presidents, for sure, but also trustees and governing boards, faculty, and alumni. Each must, for the greater good and for the cause of the university, advocate, educate, and communicate about the values of colleges and universities, particularly stressing what they give back to society and the world. In facing these external pressures, colleges and universities would greatly assist each other by responding less as "every boat on its own bottom," and more with a unified voice to educate society about their commonly shared values and purposes.

Second, presidents must navigate and negotiate external pressures, especially those rooted in economic bottom-line thinking, in ways designed to prevent Shapiro's greater danger: colleges and universities simply becoming commodified. All institutions engage in some give and take with their external environment, and none is able to remain absolutely changeless. Colleges and universities—even the Harvards of the world—are no different. Presidents are guardians at the gates to ensure that the core values and principles of the academy are maintained and strengthened. They must not watch powerlessly while those foundations erode and founder.

This task calls for courage, not mere political expediency. Kenneth Minogue's concern becomes even more relevant in moments of dealing with and addressing external constituents: The university must remain the university. If not, then the university becomes nothing more than simply another social institution. If the university is to be the university, presidents must exert primary and critical influence, especially in resisting and turning back external forces that could readily conspire to change the future university for the worse.

NOTES

1. See Kirp, *Shakespeare, Einstein, and the Bottom Line*, for a critical discussion and depiction of the ways in which higher education institutions have been more and more, Kirp would argue inexorably, drawn into the mentality and strategies of the "marketplace" in order to promote themselves and their wares.

2. Judith Rodin, former president, University of Pennsylvania, interview by author, August 16, 2004.

3. The term "saga" is used as first coined by Burton Clark, *The Distinctive College: Antioch, Reed, and Swarthmore* (Chicago: Aldine, 1970).

4. Judith Rodin, interview by author. The components of the planning and strategy that Rodin and Penn unfolded initially and over time are too lengthy to detail here. They were contained in a five-point strategic plan that included such things as Clean and Safe—a program for lighting, neighborhood improvements, security coverage—the founding of a K-8 public school, rebuilding and starting public libraries, collaboration with minority contractors and business owners, the use of university expertise such as that of architecture students to design new and rehabilitated buildings and structures, the development of retail space and public gardens. The major element structurally in place and holding promise for the future is the development of block associations that now assume responsibility for continuing efforts and changes throughout the neighborhoods surrounding the Penn campus.

5. Stephen Joel Trachtenberg, *Reflections on Higher Education* (Westport, CT: Oryx Press, 2002), p. 91. This book is a compilation of Trachtenberg's speeches and writings. The chapter from which the concept of the "University of the United States" is taken, "Going Bipolar in the Groves of Academe," is a reprint of a speech to the Educational

Testing Service/SUOA Summit, "U.S. Leadership in International Education: The Lost Edge?" September 24, 1998.

6. Donald Kennedy, former president, Stanford University, interview by author, August 29, 2003.

7. Ibid.

8. Kennedy, *The Last of Your Springs*, pp. 88–89 and 105.

9. Donald Kennedy, interview by author.

10. Kennedy recounts this episode at length in both *The Last of Your Springs*, pp. 188–97 and 200–202, and *Academic Duty* (Cambridge, MA: Harvard University Press, 1997), pp. 210–39.

11. Kennedy provides a thorough definition of indirect costs in *The Last of Your Springs*, pp. 190–91.

12. Donald Kennedy, interview by author.

13. Kennedy, *The Last of your Springs*, p. 191. The account contained here parallels and in many cases is nearly identical to that found in *Academic Duty*.

14. Ibid.

15. Ibid., p. 192.

16. Ibid., p. 189.

17. Ibid., pp. 201–2.

18. Donald Kennedy, interview with author.

19. Though this is by no means a scientific assessment, since the late 1960s, approximately a decade prior to Kennedy's presidency, to the present, the presidential tenures at Brown University, Dartmouth College, and Harvard University have averaged about 10 years.

20. Katherine Haley Will, "Alma Mater as Big Brother," *Washington Post*, March 29, 2005, p. A15.

21. Ibid.

22. Stephen Joel Trachtenberg, president, George Washington University, interview by author, May 7, 2003.

23. Ibid. Trachtenberg's tone is not one of condescension, but rather one of matter-of-fact thought that this is the way it often is. That is because of faculty members' focus on research and other professional concerns and desire to let administrators do the administrative work of the university faculty, which places faculty members outside the loop and means they tend to acquire less and less understanding of the practical affairs and demands of running the institution.

24. Ibid.

25. Harold Shapiro, *A Larger Sense of Purpose: Higher Education and Society* (Princeton, NJ: Princeton University Press, 2005).

26. For example, Shapiro spoke in his inaugural address at the University of Michigan of the role of the university as both "critic" and "servant." One of the "deans" of American higher education, Clark Kerr, in his classic, *The Uses of the University*, 5th ed (Cambridge, MA: Harvard University Press, 2001), and Jaroslav Pelikan, in his "conversation" with Cardinal Newman commemorating the centennial of his "idea of the university" in *The Idea of the University: A Reexamination* (New Haven, CT: Yale University Press, 1992), echo this approach.

27. Harold Shapiro, former president, University of Michigan and Princeton University, interview by author, July 8, 2003.

28. Ibid.

29. For an account of how difficult these issues can be and the way they played out for Shapiro's successor, James Duderstadt, see Nelson, *Leaders in the Crucible*, pp. 161–62 and 179.

30. John Henry Newman uses this term in his classic work, *The Idea of the University*, edited with introduction and notes by I. T. Ker (Oxford: Clarendon Press, 1976).

31. Harold Shapiro, interview with author.

32. Ibid.

33. Stephen Joel Trachtenberg, "President's Preoccupations," address provided by President's Office, George Washington University, pp. 12–13.

34. Walter Massey, president, Morehouse College, interview by author, May 25, 2004. Based on Morehouse's enrollment, the actual figure is approximately 650 undergraduates per year. This exceeds by far the number of black male undergraduates at even the largest universities. The figure is doubly important at a time when black male entry to college remains very low as a percentage of the demographic of high school black male students and when black males are regularly at greater risk for retention failure as college students.

35. Ibid.

36. Harold Shapiro, interview by author.

37. Again, this is the major thesis of Kirp's book, *Shakespeare, Einstein, and the Bottom Line*. Kirp goes even farther than Shapiro (though Shapiro is certainly not ignorant of this threat) in raising concern and giving examples of where ethical boundaries are being crossed in order to "win" in this competition.

38. Harold Shapiro, interview with author.

39. Ibid.

40. Ibid.

41. Ibid.

42. Ibid.

43. Ibid. In addition to his thoughts about strategy, Shapiro also shared ideas about possible solutions to this problem. He believes that the "generation of ideas" by faculty should be conceived "as a social product." This nomenclature fits Shapiro's philosophy of the university as "servant" of society as well as "critic." In this way, then, decisions could be made, theoretically at least, about how the interest in that product would be shared, some going to the faculty member, some to the partner, and some to the university. He believes that the right sharing arrangement should be negotiated, obviously with faculty input, but that something like this is needed to reduce or eliminate existing conflicts of interest.

CHAPTER 3

Inheriting the Wind: Institutional Stories and the Shoulders of Predecessors

Presidents serve colleges and universities at given points in their histories and in "times" that are not static, but rather replete with stories and sagas that fluctuate with the ebb and flow of good and bad fortune. Across presidencies there is no universal consistency to the style, substance, and ability critical for leading these communities and their constituents. Despite the best efforts of those who select them and of the presidents themselves, circumstances and contexts doom some presidencies, marginalize others, and create mismatches of talent and intention with institutional demands and needs. Even the most successful presidents sit firmly on the shoulders of their predecessors, inheriting the institutional saga of their campus.

No slate is completely clean. Each word a president utters and adds to a college's story is inevitably judged in light of the history of people and places that have gone before. How creatively and how well presidents navigate these inherited histories is a major determinant in how they are judged in the present and by history.

It is a beautiful early June evening, warm but not hot, when I arrive on the Bennett College campus to interview President Johnnetta Cole. Because I am a bit ahead of schedule, I have time to stroll around the campus. I walk past a row of buildings, coming to the chapel located at the top of a long quadrangle that stretches down a slight slope to one of the main streets bordering the campus. The chapel is built of brick, predominant by its size and position among most of the buildings, with white-framed windows. It is a simple but classic-looking structure bedecked with a tall steeple, further distinguishing it from the adjoining buildings. I pause, thinking about the story the chapel could tell if it could speak.

What events and services has it seen? What is its role in the life of the college? I complete my brief walking tour at the president's house, another brick, colonial-looking, but much more recent, structure across the street from the quadrangle to meet President Cole for our interview.

Johnnetta Cole has a distinguished, almost stately, persona, her ramrod straight posture contrasting with an enormously cordial and hospitable demeanor. On the road for a couple of days, she had arrived home earlier that evening. Cole's career stretches from beginnings as a scholar and faculty member to the presidency of Spelman College and numerous assignments in the public sphere, including social and educational policy service on Bill Clinton's presidential transition team. Following her highly successful career at Spelman, she returned to the scholarly and teaching world at Emory University as a president emerita. Now out of presidential "retirement," Cole has returned as a college leader to assume Bennett's helm at a very difficult time in the institution's history.[1] We take seats in the spacious living room, with a large bay window opening to a sizable backyard that she points out was the site of numerous trustee and commencement activities during the recent graduation weekend exercises. Cole sits on a couch, comfortable and, though tired from her travels, still extremely energetic and focused.

As the conversation progresses, Cole begins speaking about Bennett's first African American woman president, Willa Player, a predecessor of more than four decades earlier. A great supporter of black women's leadership, Cole cites Player to underscore the long history, of nearly a hundred years, before this women's college had its first black woman president. She then turns to the story of a significant moment in Player's tenure.

Player served during the tense civil rights era of the 1950s and early 1960s, a time when Greensboro, North Carolina, where Bennett is located, was a center of racial protests and of the tragic and hostile conflicts between blacks and whites. Cole recalls a planned visit to Greensboro by the Reverend Martin Luther King Jr. in 1958. King "was to come to Greensboro to speak under the sponsorship of the NAACP. And the very, very conservative—in fact, I would use the term reactionary—forces said," Cole injecting, staccato, "'No, no, no, no, no, he will never speak to you. Communist, rabble-rouser. No, no, no, no, no.'" In Cole's words, Player's response was simple: "This is the academy. He will speak at Bennett."[2]

Player's refusal to yield to opponents and her effort to make clear the invitation paved the way for King to come to the city. He delivered a speech in the college chapel (one of the tales it holds within its walls), a sanctuary Player felt to be the safest and most appropriate setting for the campus and surrounding community to hear this, at the time, nearly unknown black minister and civil rights leader. Cole asserts that Player's stand "is the best of the academy. Not that Willa B. Player had to agree with any or everything that Martin Luther King, Jr. said. [But t]here must be a place for the saying of it."[3]

Every college and university has a story. Burton Clark believes that "an organizational legend (or saga), located between ideology and religion, partakes [of] an appealing logic on one hand and sentiments similar to the spiritual on the other."[4] The saga is the history of a college, its traditions, ethos, mottoes, transforming and moral moments that shape the campus and from which it derives meaning. The stories form the catalogue of the seminal events describing the texture of the college or university. They shape the culture of the place—its character, its compass, its aspirations, and its most important values. The saga is intertwined with the leadership of presidents because of their large role in creating the way the story is told and publicly conveying it.

King's speech is part of Bennett's saga. Player's courage in creating space, the college's chapel, for King to speak is a moment of meaning in Bennett's history. Cole grabs this story as the tale of a predecessor's moral posture and its meaning for her as the college's present day leader. Cole's awareness of this moment in Bennett's history, and her readiness to underscore it as emblematic of the institution and her predecessor's tenure, confirms its lasting significance in the college's story.

A couple of weeks later, I visit the University of Michigan campus to interview President Mary Sue Coleman. Other than that Bennett and Michigan are both institutions of higher education and are led by women, there is little similarity between them. One is a struggling, small (700–800 students), historically black, women's college. The other is a mammoth research university, essentially a small city unto itself, what one of Coleman's predecessors, James Duderstadt, called an "international conglomerate."[5] But Bennett and Michigan share universal likeness in the institutional stories that shape who they are, moments in their foundations that create a fundamental "sense of place."

Recently completing her first academic year at the university's helm, Coleman greets me in the reception area outside her office and escorts me in. We sit down at a small round conference table. Her style is professional but friendly, conveying the welcome associated with Midwestern hospitality. Located on one of the upper floors of an architecturally plain office building housing much of the university's administration, the office is very orderly, maybe a reflection of Coleman's extensive background in science and public health. The space is bright, functional and nicely appointed, but not at all fancy or ostentatious, and almost understated for a university of Michigan's size and scale. It is toward the end of the afternoon, and this is the last "official" appointment of the day. But Coleman is generous with her time, before heading to an evening of commitments and probably of plowing through a president's usual irreducible load of office work.

On Coleman's plate at the beginning of her presidency some 10 months earlier, through no fault of her predecessors, were three large issues begun on their watches: a planned national conference on the Israeli-Palestinian conflict to be hosted by the university; the final stages, to be played out, of the Supreme Court case on affirmative action; and a continuing athletic scandal hatched from the discovery of illegal payments to a number of Michigan basketball players nearly a decade earlier. This issue featured prominently and was covered extensively in the national news. But Coleman's "inside" view presents nuances contrasting with media portrayals and offers lessons for higher education about leadership in such (sadly frequent) crises.

A U.S. Attorney brought a case focusing on Chris Webber, one of the "Fab Five" (a highly touted starting group of Michigan freshmen basketball players from the early 1990s), and the payments he allegedly (an allegation that was later proved to be true) received from Ed Martin, a Michigan basketball supporter. The university had attempted under Coleman's predecessors, James Duderstadt and Lee Bollinger, now president of Columbia, to discover information about what had happened. Coleman indicates that the university hoped an investigation would enable them to identify and to correct the problems. However, because the lawyers for Webber, Martin, and others involved were telling (more likely ordering) their clients to plead the Fifth in court and to say nothing to anyone in or outside the legal proceedings, Michigan had made little progress getting to the bottom of the matter.

On taking the helm, Coleman met with her director of athletics and coaches (none of whom had been in their respective positions at the time of the alleged events). They concluded that the university was on the right path but had to push deeper and develop additional approaches, if it was to get to the full story. The episode is interesting in that the university could easily have stood on the sidelines and probably come out with nothing other than further, probably minor, damage to its name, but no other sanctions or penalties, with most of the sanctions and penalties directed at the principals as individuals. To Michigan's credit, guided by Coleman's leadership, its willingness actively to seek the truth of this tangled legal web and to deal with the consequences is a testament to the university's sense of self and public ethic.

Coleman's position (and this was the university's new strategy) is that if Michigan "hadn't pushed it, the NCAA could never have done anything to us because there was no evidence. Nobody would talk to us." However, in a courageous step, "we made a deal with the U.S. Attorney that we wanted to know when they offered a plea bargain to Ed Martin, who was the person who had given these lines [about remaining silent] to the basketball players; we wanted to be able to give him questions so that we could find out the truth. So we did that." Michigan initiated this approach within the legal framework because, as Coleman emphasizes, "none of the players would talk to us and we don't have subpoena power."[6]

The upshot of this activity was that in November 2002, just a couple of months into her presidency, the university learned definitively of its institutional complicity in the sordid episode—there were, not surprisingly, violations of NCAA rules—and took compensatory action.

Following these revelations, Coleman made a clear, simple, and direct public statement that, given Michigan's high public profile, received extensive national coverage. "There is no excuse for what happened. It was," she admitted, "wrong, plain and simple. We have let down all who believe that the University of Michigan should stand for the best in college athletics. We have disappointed our students, our faculty, our alumni and our fans. This is a day of great shame for the University."[7] She staked out the promise "that nothing like this will ever happen again at Michigan. Today we will submit our report to the NCAA. In it we have listed the penalties we will impose on ourselves in order to make up for what happened. These sanctions are strong medicine."[8]

Finally, Coleman outlined the precise actions Michigan would take. The university would forfeit basketball games including Final Four appearances in 1992 and 1993, the entirety of the 1992–93 seasons, and the seasons from 1995 to 1999. In addition, she confirmed that "we took down the four championship banners" displayed in the university arena and would repay money from postseason play in the amount of $450,000 to the NCAA. Lest the message be lost, she concluded: "Let me say once again, loud and clear: Integrity is Michigan's top priority."[9]

Subsequently, in the spring of 2003, the university incurred additional sanctions from the NCAA. Though Coleman agreed with the substance of those sanctions she felt a ban on postseason appearances beyond the university's self-imposed one-year ban for 2002–3 went unnecessarily far, arguing that it "has the effect of further punishing our current, uninvolved student-athletes. This contradicts one of the core principles of NCAA enforcement."[10]

Coleman navigated this lengthy, litigious episode to a reasonable conclusion. However, it was only one of the previously mentioned three staring her in the face at the beginning of her presidency.

The second was the combination of great public notoriety along with substantial acclaim that the university gained resulting from the national affirmative action debate over Michigan's two pending Supreme Court cases. The legal actions that ended up before the Supreme Court were sparked by university admissions programs and policies rooted in President James Duderstadt's major platform, the "Michigan Mandate," established to address racial issues and affirmative action, and initiated on the occasion of his inauguration in 1988.[11]

Commitment to equality and equity are historically consistent in Michigan's heritage. In 1870, for example, President James Angell advocated and inaugurated the admission of women students, long before such a step was even a consideration at the university's Ivy League and other competitors in the East. Angell's diversity and equity slogan for Michigan was "an uncommon education for the common man," an education that clearly included women.

This avant-garde stand early in its history, a step not really fashionable, yet one on which Angell willingly expended political capital, raises interesting questions about Michigan, its ethos and saga. What in its foundation produces convictions and commitments to principles of equality? What values are rooted in its heritage of presidential leadership, and in its fundamental creed in fulfilling a role as a public university? Are there core Michigan values that are traceable and lead to its twenty-first-century stands?

Coleman's take on Michigan's story begins with the recent experience of the Supreme Court case. Affirming that "the University of Michigan has a very proud history," she notes that as the affirmative action case played out, there were alumni who expressed disagreement with the university's policies. However, at the same time they viewed the university's stand as a "point of pride that the university has defended itself on principle and [on] something that it felt was really important." This affection for the school transcended personal and inevitably narrower views, and is, in Coleman's estimation, "the best kind of characterization of the university." Similarly, the regents, even though representative of a wide and divergent range of political views, remained united, believing that bringing the case was "the right thing to do and we should keep together."

Probing the ethos of Michigan further, Coleman contends that an important aspect of its tradition of standing on principles and "doing the right thing" is supported and encouraged by a tradition of stimulating "discussion on troublesome issues in this society." Michigan's saga is established by the university as a place of intellectual ferment grounded in its faculty, and rooted in what Coleman views as "mechanisms across the institution" that are part of the "long tradition of this deep, intellectual engagement here."[12]

Two themes embedded in the value of the institutional saga stand out in these examples of Bennett and Michigan. First, for both, is the leitmotif that the academy is a place where ideas can and should be fairly explored and exchanged. Presidents and their leadership colleagues can find essential support in the firm establishment of this platform. Willa Player felt the walls of Bennett should be open to the voice Martin Luther King would bring to Greensboro and throughout the South. Battling those who wanted nothing less than to squelch him, Player offered the pulpit of Bennett's chapel so that supporters and opponents alike would hear King speak. She relied on and furthered fundamental values about free expression in the academy by her actions.

The roots of Michigan's tradition of doing the right thing, of standing on principles, and of accountability for its own mistakes is grounded in a fearlessness in the face of troublesome and difficult problems, and based in an intellectual climate, shaped by faculty, of ferment and engagement of ideas. This is aided and abetted by a strong attachment to values of meritocracy and basic tenets of human equality.

Second, both Michigan as a public university and Bennett as a small private college forthrightly engage an agenda featuring issues of social concern and the education of the public. To do this, universities and colleges require a definitive and inherent sense of institutional strength and purpose, coupled with presidents ready to make utterances in the public square. Such institutions possess an earned, sometimes hard-won, stature that undergirds a platform for their leadership. This foundation supports leaders, enabling them to present and argue positions to a public that regardless of agreement or disagreement about specific policies and decisions at least understands the overall mission of the academy.

In a contrast of institutional context, colleges and universities with religion and religious affiliation embedded in their heritage possess values and commitments based on faith and beliefs. A religious grounding can stand institutions and presidents in good stead but can also complicate decisions and actions, especially in the diverse contemporary climate. The ways presidents address the challenges of translating religious traditions and beliefs in an increasingly complex world with multifaceted constituencies are instructive about leadership and about the imprint of leaders on the saga. Nan Keohane at Duke and James Laney at Emory are presidents who led major religious (in both cases Methodist) universities in the South at the end of the twentieth century and the beginning of the twenty-first century.

At the time of our interview, President Keohane was entering the last of her 11 years at Duke's helm, service that followed her equally successful and almost identical tenure as president of Wellesley College, from 1981 to 1993. The President's Office at Duke is situated on one of the main quadrangles of the campus. Keohane's staff reflected her style in their welcoming and considerate attention to the arrangements for the visit. President Keohane greets me in a living room–style waiting area and escorts me into her office. We sit in a couple of high-backed chairs on either side of a small table and around a coffee table. Across the office, a large conference table is situated next to a wall of bookcases. The president, though businesslike in manner and approach, is quite relaxed and unhesitatingly engaging.

Keohane acknowledges a big-picture challenge in leading Duke, a task clearly complicated by its religious heritage: translating the traditional and deeply held meaning of its Methodist founding principles and beliefs to the secular and less parochial-thinking world both inside and outside the gates of the campus. If this heritage were articulated in precise Christian terms, it would be "hard for people who are not Christian to hear." Capturing the challenge, Keohane indicates on one hand that "I do feel the understanding of the relevance of the Christian faith that the founders of this institution had is a very generous and broad one." However, on the other hand it still "can be interpreted in enough ways that it's not exclusive."[13] This required communicating Duke's religious legacy in ways that were not off-putting to multicultural and even more tricky—because of their greater religious sensitivities—multireligious and multifaith groups and contexts.

In this quest, Keohane identified a "center" that had "to be a nuance of under-standing of the condition of that particular institution and the effort to draw from it whatever moral truths seem most relevant to the problems at hand."[14] Reminiscent of the old saw about whether it is better to have some religion than no religion, she quickly adds that "if you're leading an institution that doesn't have any moral tradition, then you're in bad shape." In actuality, Keohane believes few higher education institutions have no moral tradition at all, so even though Duke and similar religious colleges and universities possess a religious bent as a starting point, it is still overall a good thing. Regarding Duke's moral tradition in contemporary times, Keohane claims that "it's the Methodist heri-tage, it's the commitment to the people of our region, it's the faith and the vision of the founders when the university became a university less than a hundred years ago," adding that "this is our common ground."[15] However, she makes clear that when interpreting the university's foundation, it is necessary to "pick and choose" the ways the fundamental Methodist values in Duke's saga are presented to both internal and external audiences.

Creatively, Keohane applies Duke's religious foundation to "describe the ways in which it offers lessons for the current dilemmas" and to "draw it uniquely and deliberately into focus for the current world." Ever the political scientist, she views this process as "not a conservative strategy in the sense that you're just trying to sustain something that would have been relevant in 1924, but a kind of constitutional strategy saying," in the vein of a court justice interpreting the law, "'This is the way our forbears saw these truths.' *Eruditio et Religio* is still our motto. So, you want to think about that as a guide for saying, 'We cannot simply abscond from any responsibility or thinking about moral issues or taking some stance on them as a university without any effects.' But doing it in the way that refers directly to the institution."[16]

Keohane has a pragmatic tactic to address this basic conundrum of how a "Christian" college or university can maintain its history while still being relevant in a much less simple and certainly less homogenous age than that of its founders. The strategic problem for presidents leading religious institutions is to find and develop threads that link, by artful translation, the values inherent in founding purposes and intents in ways that speak to today's problems and dilemmas. However, conversely, these presidents cannot and must not operate without regard to sincere institutional principles that are valued by core constituents who must be courted and satisfied that the institution is not straying, or at least not far, from its founding landscape.

Laney's reshaping of Emory's saga as a Methodist institution paralleled that of Keohane at Duke, their presidencies barely overlapping, Laney serving from 1977 to 1993 and concluding his presidency just as Keohane was beginning hers at Duke.[17] As an essential starting point in his translation of Emory to the contemporary world, Laney cites its founding principle of "Truth as wide and as free as God's creation."[18] In a way similar to *Eruditio et Religio* at Duke, Laney uses this institutional heritage as a theme lending itself to broad interpretation. In navigating the Methodist religious beliefs inside and outside Emory, Laney had one card to play that Keohane did not enjoy: his ordained Methodist clergy status.

Laney employed this persona in reassuring potential critics that he would not take the school away from the church. Assuming that his churchly status would make more constituents trust him, he proceeded to use Emory's founding statement to develop a broader "moral thread and ethical thread" that enabled the creation of a new and more up-to-date interpretation of the university's mission. In this way he gave "both the intellectual articulation and the social articulation [of the university] broader, nonregional connotations because it wasn't just the church" in relation to the campus that had to be addressed, but also in that era (and maybe still today) the "provincialism of the south."[19]

Simultaneously with the push for Emory to come out of its regional, provincial, heavily church-related cocoon, Laney made another significant imprint on Emory's saga, one more indelible in his presidential legacy: connecting the emergence and future of Emory to that of Atlanta as a leading city in the "New South" of the 1970s. Strategically this was a stroke of genius on Laney's part, one that today might appear to be an obvious step. However, at the time the prospect of mutual benefit from the linkage of Emory to Atlanta's aspirations was not nearly so evident. In addition, there were risks, not least the pressure this would put on Emory by committing the institution to the movement afoot in Atlanta to do more than merely pay lip service to racial justice and equality. Laney was leading Emory to places where it might have to put up or shut up.

In actuality, Laney exploited to his advantage the fear that Emory might resist entering this new world by challenging Emory to keep pace with the progress stirring in Atlanta and establishing it as a major urban center. By pushing closer ties and a closer relationship and engagement with the surrounding community, Laney raised the moral expectations for Emory and for its leadership. It would no longer be an institution hiding behind the veneer of a mere regional university. Laney changed Emory's story line, not by abandoning its heritage and fundamental values, but by building and extending them. His leadership, certainly complemented by the times, produced this transformation for the future of the university.[20]

But, Laney was able to foresee the value in drawing "on the strength of Atlanta, which was so progressive in contrast to all the rest of the South in terms of both race relations and their sense of destiny and all. And that was a very happy kind of coincidence of interest. The aspirations and ambitions of Atlanta were a nice context for the ambitions and interests of Emory. And they went hand in hand."[21]

This became Laney's mantra both in the local community and with his colleagues at the university. He acknowledges that "in many cases when I couldn't make headway on any other kind of moral appeal, I appealed to the interests of Atlanta. They needed a university like this [Emory]. They needed a good university that's national and international in scope." Then offering the rhetorical question in his mind when discussing Emory's future with trustees and other influential decision makers: "'We're an international city, now why are we going to have a provincial university?'... I would point out the incongruity and... the appeal carried the day."[22]

Presidents make a difference at their colleges and universities for all manner of different reasons. Clark views the saga of a college or university as born out of traditions, key historical turning points and the ways they shape the institution. Often the saga is formed in moments of campus crisis.[23] Occasionally, if not in outright crisis, many presidents begin their tenure facing pivotal moments in their campus history. Presidents are figures who are relied on and who expect to lead through such times of institutional trial and doubt. Clark argues that one person as leader has the potential to make a difference. He calls this the "long shadow of a man," in today's parlance, a man or a woman.

Frank Rhodes began his presidency at Cornell at a time of crisis in institutional confidence in 1977. Rhodes inherited a campus still reeling from the events of a little less than a decade earlier, the turbulence in the middle to late 1960s and early 1970s at Cornell (as at so many other campuses during this time). While other campuses witnessed protests beginning with the "free speech" movement at Berkeley in the mid-1960s, Cornell gained major notoriety because of the militancy accompanying events on campus, including a building takeover by armed students. The nationally publicized pictures of their exit, guns raised, remain to this day striking images almost frozen in time.

No shots were fired and no one was hurt, but Cornell's image suffered a severe blow. Rhodes recounts that the student body of the 1960s had been "at loggerheads with the faculty and the administration. That had left a very deep scar on the campus—really an erosion of trust, a sense of distrust, and especially amongst the alumni, a sense of a deep suspicion. So that was something that had to be dealt with—the re-creation of trust and civility and respect."[24] Rhodes contends that "the university that I found had somehow lost confidence in itself."[25] The crisis of confidence and its connection to this distrust and alumni disaffection was producing an undeniable and grave impact on fund-raising and the university's financial health.

Normally colleges and universities try to avoid presidential leadership transitions in the middle of capital campaigns. For Rhodes, this was not the case. When he arrived, "Cornell was two years into a fund-raising campaign," so in addition to a need to address existing and growing distrust, and clearly connected to it, "the second issue was [that] the giving during those two years had actually gone down from the previous period. So, there was a real crisis in terms of financial support—external financial support. And we had to change that into a successful campaign, which worked out in the end. But in just the next three years, we had to turn what had been two negative years into three positive ones. We came out ahead of the target."[26]

This "solved" some of the problems Rhodes faced. But Cornell had been running budget deficits for half a decade or more, using, as well-endowed institutions are able, though at their peril if they prolong the practice, their endowment to cover the red ink. As is often the case, connected to this endowment drawdown problem was the deferred maintenance of facilities (a term many college business officials consider an oxymoron, that is, deferred maintenance is no maintenance at all).

The Cornell situation Rhodes inherited was not as full-blown a crisis as some institutions face. The university was not in danger of collapse; its short-term future was reasonably secure. Many colleges and universities get much closer to or even over the edge of financial disaster. Bennett College has a far smaller endowment "cushion" than Cornell. Thus, Cole faces greater pressure than Rhodes to perform urgent fund-raising miracles, and to stabilize and improve budget and financial planning in order to reduce the problems besetting Bennett prior to her arrival.

However, Cornell under Rhodes, largely because as its leader he was not about to settle for such a minimalist approach, did not have the luxury of simply returning to business as usual, expecting time to heal the distrust and lack of confidence it had suffered. Rhodes knew that without a change in course these corrosive characteristics could well become deeply embedded in Cornell's saga to the detriment of its health and future. In addition, for even the most well-off institutions, dipping into their discretionary endowment (the only part that is truly "expendable") cannot be continued for long.[27] For Cornell and schools like it and in similar financial straits, even "cushions" have limits, though the temptation to rely on them is always seductive.

Institutional self-confidence is very real, though rarely talked about in the academy in terms of who has it and who does not. Rhodes altered Cornell's saga in response to a crisis of confidence by presenting "Cornell not as something close to Harvard or Berkeley, but as something in its own right that was distinctive and that had a certain quality and a certain ethos." Like a cheerleader, Rhodes worked "to share that sense of confidence and pride with other people on campus." Justifiably boasting, Rhodes contends that as a result, "over the years people felt that they could take the world on and win on their own terms, and I think that's an important role of leadership."[28] Coincidentally this cultural phenomenon for colleges and universities (as for any corporate organization) develops from the degree to which core constituents come to believe, often affirmed by the views of outsiders, that their institution is in the elite class.

George Washington University under Trachtenberg's presidency is a case in point. Trachtenberg firmly believes that changes in George Washington's self-image in recent years have directly shaped the story that the university is able to tell and that it can legitimately expect others to believe.

The image and reputation of George Washington, Cornell, or any higher education institution is more fragile than at first glance it appears. Colleges and universities are promoted to internal and external constituencies as strong and influential institutions. However, once a myth and image become associated with a school, they can be hard to shake. In some instances only sustained efforts over time can alter these views, however fairly or unfairly conceived. In the battle to shape the saga of a college or university, these public images are critical to the institution's story, what the story tells, and how the story is shared inside and outside the campus community.[29]

Regarding George Washington's institutional self-confidence, Trachtenberg suggests that the university is "only now, after 180-plus years, starting to feel comfortable in its own skin and its own location. Like Boston University, which always cast covetous eyes across the river at MIT and Harvard, GW suffered for a long time by people comparing it to Georgetown, which was older and more sharply focused and better endowed—and generally conceded to be almost an Ivy League institution," and all this while, shifting to a biblical image, "GW was a light covered by a bushel basket."[30] Acknowledging the investments of those on whose shoulders he stands, Trachtenberg notes, "I believe that my various predecessors have brought GW to a reasonable posture. I didn't arrive here and discover an empty wheat field. But what I discovered, I thought, was an under-appreciated institution that needed an articulation of its mission and its place and its contributions." The source of "that underappreciation," Trachtenberg asserts, "interestingly enough, was from those within and those without."[31]

Historically, George Washington has had difficulty avoiding a loss of its iden-tity in the public's eye because of the proximity and prominence of its major sister competitor, Georgetown. With his trademark sense of humor, Trachten-berg notes that "when I came here, people regularly introduced me as the new president of Georgetown, a name that came tripping off the lips in a way that GW or George Washington didn't. The other day, for the first time, I heard somebody who was a Georgetown professor introduced as a professor at George Washington University. And I thought, 'Well it's taken me 15 years, but maybe the worm is starting to turn.'" Positively, this means George Washington has "arrived as an institution that has its own place within the higher education arena; its own location in the city of Washington."[32] Presidential footprints are critical in creating changes in image, especially in how a school "feels" about itself. In Trachtenberg's case, patience has also been required.

New York University (NYU) is another major urban university with an inter-esting story and a contemporarily evolving saga. As Trachtenberg leads George Washington University to "get comfortable in its skin," President John Sexton is refashioning NYU as a major city university—its historical heritage—but now re-created and rearticulated for the twenty-first century.

Formally announced as president in March 2001, Sexton gradually took over the reins in a transition until the following March, though in reality he began full time at the helm to stabilize NYU and map its future, shaken that year in the wake of the September 11th tragedy and the crisis created for the campus and the communities nearest the Trade Towers destruction. When he came to the presidency, the university had been riding what was referred to inside and outside its gates as "the Miracle of Washington Square," a nickname referring to the institution's monumental progress in prestige and visibility during the 1980s and 1990s.[33] The "miracle" provided Sexton and NYU a very desirable position, and is in many ways the tale of a great run of success. But it also had a downside that Sexton describes as "inherently denigrating of a previous period. It didn't connect to the roots. And in many ways it wasn't substantive."[34]

Sexton does not downplay the value of the "miracle" era, acknowledging it as a time when the university's financial situation was systematically stabi-lized and radically improved. Rather he asserts the need for a longer view, one signaling the university's saga with connections to and reflections of its rich history. Sexton wants NYU's story to be framed not as something it managed to pull off as a "miracle," something easily deemed as fleeting, accidental, and lucky. Sexton wants a substantive saga, a story that would "connect into the ratio studiorum of the place." To write and shape that story requires plumbing NYU's history more fully.[35]

Sexton mines the fact that NYU's founder, Albert Gallatin, served Presidents Jefferson and Madison and in the 1820s, and used his high profile appointments to begin conversations about universities with friends in both New York and London. These discussions led Gallatin to envision a university on a model different from the already established American colleges that later became known as the Ivy League and also different from the great British universities, Oxford and Cambridge. His idea, to "create a different paradigm...a university that's accessible to all and that is in and of the city," led to NYU's founding in 1831. Using those seminal founding conversations as a starting point, Sexton contends that "if we are going to be in and of this city as you move into the twenty-first century there is," further underscoring NYU's place in the city, "an enormous locational advantage." "There's no saga that's better than a founding story that works today," and for Sexton, this translates to "a university that is self-conscious of the fact that at this moment in history the city in which it is, is the first microcosm of the world.... It is the first "glocal" city, [a] word [combining] global and local simultaneously."[36]

Sexton continues: "So as we enter the twenty-first century, where one great, if not the great, issue of the century is going to be how do you build in a world where suddenly diversity is of an enormity we didn't realize existed.... This century is going to be a century where that diversity is unavoidable, it's palpable, it's far more enormous than we expected, which is the glory of the creation, but [the question is] how do we create community and communication, without creating homogenization?"[37]

Sexton argues that NYU is, in his mind prominently, among the institutions capable of educating people for a global, diverse, vastly more multicultural world than we had ever imagined. Sexton uses the image of a diverse globe "where New York City is the first experiment," and argues that NYU is a "university that takes seriously its interaction with that reality, as opposed to being withdrawn." Thus it is also a "university that simultaneously is perhaps the last best hope, with serious nuances in the conversation which people enter...not just desirous of trumping or winning but being in dialog."[38] Such rhetoric reshapes the university's saga in relationship to New York City and beyond, and more importantly fashions a narrative of greater substance than that based on the simple luck of a "miracle."

Burton Clark coined the term "long shadow" to describe the footprint presidents make as leaders. Often the "long shadow" of college presidents is cast in ways not clearly apparent at the time, but ways that subsequently become more evident and are woven into the institutional saga. In some cases it is later presidents, sometimes many years removed, who fashion and make integral to the school's story their predecessor's strong imprint. Rob Oden has created a profile at Carleton College that is in this tradition, and he believes that the "long shadow" is a hallmark of at least one of his predecessors.

In making the transition to Carleton's presidency, Oden immersed himself in the college's history.[39] One result was that Oden uncovered a piece of Carleton lore from early in the last century about a predecessor, David Cowling, that he believes is highly instrumental in Carleton's saga.

A parcel of land adjacent to the college was for sale and Cowling had the vision that it would be smart for the college to purchase it. Cowling's problem was that the college was in very poor financial shape and his plan to invest major funds in this land deal was sharply questioned by colleagues and critics. Oden picks up the story: "In the late 1920s when Carleton was broke, every month there was a question of whether we could meet the payroll, and a major grant we were supposed to receive we didn't get.... And so in an era when we were broke, President Donald Cowling had the notion of buying several hundred acres of not very productive farmland adjacent to the campus, and eventually turned it into a nature preserve or an arboretum. Students voted against it, faculty voted against it. Our students said, 'we can't do it. We don't have the money.' He did it anyway." Though nearly Carleton's version of Seward's Folly, Oden reports that "right now, interview any 10 Carleton students and ask them what most matters about this campus; I guarantee 8, and I predict 10, will say, 'Oh, the arboretum.' "[40]

Even though Cowling consulted and worked with others, it can be lonely at the top, and as president he "bore the brunt of the criticism for so dedicating so much land, and there were those who thought in championing an arboretum at Carleton, the man had lost his grip." Oden adds humorously: "May we all suffer such moments of imbalance." He views the Carleton presidency as strengthened by predecessors like Cowling, who "fought and finally succeeded in persuading others that establishing a large tract of land for an arboretum was not an act of irresponsibility" in its tradition.[41] This legacy provides continuing guidance, Oden asserting that when facing major decisions, the institution's past helps him "try to figure out as I look at what's coming up whether this is in the category of spending those chips now, and I try to think of where I am in my own time."[42]

In order to lead as Carleton's president, Oden believes he must get to the "what" and "why" of the campus (as he previously did at Kenyon). He has discovered three critical components at the heart of making Carleton what it is: geography, sense of personal proportion, and intellectual courage.[43] Oden's detective work produces an understanding of the richness and meaning of Carleton's heritage.

The Carleton saga starts with the fact that from "eight miles east of here to Billings, Montana, you are in what I think of as the Great Plains or America's High Prairie, America's most characteristic landscape, the Great Plains, and what does that mean for us?" This creates in the Carleton culture an emphasis on "value and results over rhetoric," in which the important point is, "I don't know where you came from or what your credentials are. What can you do?"

This prairie spirit with its embrace of the practical leads to a second constituting element of Carleton: people who "value a sense of humor, and especially at our own expense." Oden counsels first-year students that those "who are full of themselves are rarely full of anything interesting." It is a perspective that Oden finds important and that shapes the campus ethos: "To the extent that you could see all of everybody in life as occasionally doing things that are ridiculous I think [it] helps you not to take yourself so seriously."

Finally, this environment makes the college "a very hungry-to-learn place." As evidence Oden cites an annual student-created video used in orientation. Recently screening that year's version of the video, he reports that "they ask students why they came to Carleton. Over and over again they say, 'what I really care about is what makes things tick. I'm interested in learning, and that seemed to me something that Carleton promises.'" From these testimonials and other elements of Carleton's saga, Oden concludes: "Because we don't take ourselves too seriously, because we value results over rhetoric: 'I don't care what you have: a PhD from Harvard. Can you do something at all?' That also makes us a little bit more willing to be open to learning. What matters is what you learn next, not what you did last week." And the label for this trait is "intellectual courage."[44]

From this snapshot of presidents, their institutions, and their stories, three major themes emerge. First, presidents can influence in different ways the capacity of colleges and universities to feature and to uphold openness and inquiry into the world of ideas. Cole notes the importance of her predecessor, Willa Player, ensuring King's speech would be heard by permitting it a rightful place: within the sanctuary walls of the academy. Oden emphasizes the importance of "intellectual courage" as a label for Carleton and as the seed for open inquiry and learning.

Second, there are the particular demands at religious universities in the contemporary era. Keohane and Laney show how presidents of religious campuses engage in a balancing act to preserve, while reinterpreting and shifting, the institutional saga. In confronting the challenges of today's world, these presidents must use leadership to juggle the competing positions and sensitivities of at least two groups with strong attachments to the university (and here there is some similarity to more secular colleges and universities as well). On one hand are those who believe any change in core beliefs is anathema. They want only the fundamental values, believed to have served well historically, to continue providing a consistent framework to guide the university. On the other hand are equally committed constituents, albeit with their criticisms, who view those same core beliefs as standing in the way of the progressive responses and actions demanded by contemporary challenges. Keohane and Laney manage to satisfy both of these loyal factions by developing positions on controversial issues that are rooted in founding principles on which there is reasonable and broad common agreement.

More than at secular institutions, locating wide-ranging consensus requires extra sensitivity in navigating change in the face of the diversity of today's disputes and demands. The bottom line: presidents of religious colleges and universities—but in reality maybe presidents of all types of institutions—must conceptualize and navigate the capacity for institutional change by invoking the words of the old hymn: "New occasions teach new duties."

Finally, context is not everything, but it is terribly important for presidents and has an impact on the length of their tenure. The long view of where a college or university has been is critical in determining decisions and actions in the present, as well as its hoped-for expectations for the future. Once again the balancing act for presidents is crucial. At times this means that patience and years of investment must be exerted in order for an institution to reap the dividends of presidential vision. At other times, presidents need to be able and willing to cash in chips rapidly, seizing a moment and opportunity, as with Cowling at Carleton, in order to make and leave an imprint on their institution's future. Sometimes these moments come at crisis points for a campus and at other times they are more simply part of continued growth and change. In either case, presidents have the responsibility to confront present realities and to place a significant imprint, a "long shadow," on their colleges and universities in their march into the future. In the process, presidents form and reform the saga, and bear witness in leadership to the legacies they inherit from predecessors and forbears.

NOTES

1. When Cole accepted the call to become Bennett's president, the college had been put on probation by its accrediting body for reasons of financial instability. She faced not only the task of fixing that problem, but also that of enhancing the profile of the college in terms of admissions and improving its present fund-raising to address both the sanctions concern about its fiscal situation and its longer term future by building its development prospects and capacity.

2. Johnnetta Cole, president, Bennett College, and former president, Spelman College, interview by author, June 2, 2003. Cole prefaces these remarks by saying, "There is a great tradition here."

3. Ibid. Cole mentions a commemorative tape of the King speech located in the college's archives (there is a sense that it was thought to have been lost), and gives it to me when I leave. King's talk that evening in 1958, "No Room in the Inn," provides an early glimpse of the preaching, philosophy, and rhetoric that later catapulted him to the national stage.

4. Clark, *The Distinctive College*, p. 235. As I point out in *Leaders in the Crucible*, p. 33, n. 2, Clark coined this term in this classic work.

5. In the course of my research, I have had the opportunity to study and interview three of the last four of the presidents of the University of Michigan: Harold Shapiro (1980–87), James Duderstadt (1988–97), and Mary Sue Coleman (2002 to the present), as well as studying James Angell, who served in the middle to late nineteenth century and is viewed by many as one of the "giants" of the American college presidency. In an interview in 1995, Duderstadt uses the terms "international conglomerate" and "entrepreneurial university" to describe Michigan, which at the time was a $5 billion-plus per year operation and had economic power significantly larger than that of many countries.

6. Mary Sue Coleman, president, University of Michigan, interview by author, July 23, 2003. She amplifies this point further, commenting about the plaintiffs and the situation in her Athletic Department:

> Why should they talk to us? Why should they admit anything to us? This was not in their interest....but the institution felt, and I think it was precisely the correct thing to do to get to the bottom of it. I think that what happened sometimes during these things with athletics [is] if somebody wants to really cheat, they can get behind any rule. But what you've got to always do is to be asking the question, and I have this suspicion...that in that era when all that was happening...that people didn't want to know. People in athletics who should have known didn't want to know, and so they didn't ask any questions. Now maybe they really didn't....And maybe they legitimately say, "We didn't know it was going on," but they should have seen kids driving cars that they could never have afforded. They should have been able to figure out that....Where were they getting money to rent the apartment where they lived? What was going on here? Why weren't they asking the questions? And so my stance and Bill Martin's [her current athletic director's] stance and our current coach's stance is, "You leave nothing to chance. You keep asking the questions." Now you can still be fooled if somebody really wants to....If you really want to cheat, you can still be fooled, but you shouldn't be fooled because you are not out there saying, "I want to know these things."

7. Mary Sue Coleman, "Coleman Statement, November 7, 2002, http://www.umich.edu/~newsinfo/Releases/2002/Nov02/r11070a.html, p. 1.

8. Ibid.

9. Ibid., p. 2

10. "U-M responds to NCAA decision," University of Michigan News Service, press release, May 8, 2003, http://www.umich.edu/~new/Releases/2003/May03/r050803a.html, p. 1. For a complete version of the NCAA sanctions on the University of Michigan as a result of this case, see http://www.ncaa.org/releases/infractions/2003050802in.htm.

11. For elaboration about Duderstadt's program, see Nelson, *Leaders in the Crucible*, pp. 103 and 170. Previous diversity and affirmative action initiatives at the University of Michigan were undertaken by Harold Shapiro as Duderstadt's predecessor.

12. Mary Sue Coleman, interview by author.

13. Nannerl Keohane, president, Duke University, interview by author, June 2, 2003.

14. Ibid.

15. Ibid.

16. Ibid.

17. For example, both were forced to navigate, and did so successfully though not without difficulties and acrimony, the issues of gay and lesbian partner human resources' benefits and same-sex unions in their university chapels.

18. James Laney, former president, Emory University, interview by author, April 27, 2003. Laney indicates that this language is contained in a letter of transmittal dating from the time when Emory College was moved to Atlanta around the time of World War I to be joined with Emory University.

19. Ibid.

20. For a perspective on how significantly Emory changed during Laney's tenure, see Jim Ault's documentary film, *Leading Out* (see chapter 1, n. 14). The interviews Ault features include those with faculty, administrators, trustees, and other key stakeholders at Emory throughout Laney's 16-year presidency. One of the clear conclusions is that Emory changed and changed significantly during this time.

21. James Laney, interview with author.

22. Ibid.

23. In *The Distinctive College,* Clark uses Antioch, Reed, and Swarthmore as case studies of colleges in times of crisis and significant turning points and shows how the leadership, presidents, trustees, and faculty, navigated these situations in ways that strengthened the institutions, even as they disagreed and argued over the best courses of action.

24. Frank Rhodes, former president, Cornell University, interview by author, July 22, 2003.

25. Frank Rhodes. "Interview with Harry Kreisler," Institute of International Studies, University of California, Berkeley, Conversations with History series, March 31, 1999, http://globetrotter.Berkeley.edu/people/Rhodes/Rhodes-con2.html, p. 3.

26. Ibid. Rhodes explained this same situation in the interview I conducted with him. It is also important to note that Donald Kennedy makes similar points about the situation at Stanford in the early to mid-1970s prior to his presidency, that is, the twin troubles of an institution shaken by the protest events of the preceding decade, coupled with internal budget and fiscal difficulties, compounded by a difficult national economic picture. Donald Kennedy, former president, Stanford University, interview by author, August 29, 2003.

27. For example, when James Hornig became president of Brown University in the early 1970s, Brown had been on a trajectory (for nearly a decade) of deficit budgeting, compensating for the annual fiscal gap by drawing on its discretionary endowment at levels that would have completely depleted it by the end of the decade, a span of less than eight years or so.

28. Rhodes, "Interview with Harry Kreisler," pp. 3–4.

29. Enlarging on the theme of how things have turned around, Trachtenberg asserts that "This growing reputation, this 'saga' of the George Washington University, is recognized and internalized increasingly by students who are here, [by] high school students who are applying, by faculty teaching courses, [by] administrators managing departments and by our alumni, all of whom have a greater appreciation for their association with GW than ever before." Stephen Joel Trachtenberg, president, George Washington University, interview by author, May 7, 2003.

30. Ibid.

31. Ibid.

32. Ibid.

33. Joan Marans Dim and Nancy Murphy Cricco wrote a book by the same name, *The Miracle on Washington Square: New York University* (Lanham, MD: Lexington Books, 2001), which tells the story in detail. For another account of New York University's recent history and rise to prominence, as well as a discussion of John Sexton's leadership as both Law School dean and president, see Kirp, *Shakespeare, Einstein, and the Bottom Line,* pp. 66–89.

34. John Sexton, president, New York University, interview by author, June 29, 2004.

35. Ibid.

36. Ibid.

37. Ibid.

38. Ibid.

39. Oden notes that he always makes a point of learning the history of the institution he has been chosen to lead. Later we will read his further reflections on why this is essential for a leader. In two talks during his inaugural ceremonies at Carleton, Oden focuses

at some depth on Carleton history and the college's intellectual mission and purpose. See his inaugural convocation address and his inaugural address, http://www.carleton.edu/inauguration/speeches.php3?id=2.

40. Robert Oden, president, Carleton College, interview by author, August 26, 2003. A visit to the Carleton campus confirms the beauty and sanctuary that the arboretum affords the campus community and adds to the landscape of the campus. Oden points out that the college has "returned it to a tall-grass prairie," close to what it originally was, with the exception of the bison that were likely once there.

41. Robert Oden, inaugural convocation address, October 25, 2002, http://www.carleton.edu/inauguration/speeches.php3?id=2. In his inaugural address, in thanking a number of predecessors, Oden gives thanks "to President Donald Cowling for transforming Carleton from a small, regional college into one of international standing and for, this is quite personal, for embracing Professor Harvey Stork's idea that the College devote precious resources to the Arboretum when many thought such a lavish expenditure indicated that President Cowling was losing his grip." As president, Oden used this Cowling precedent to make a purchase of additional land adjacent to Carleton, and the personal note in the preceding quotation reflects his modus operandi, previously visible in his Kenyon presidency, of making decisions to add land abutting a campus not only as a resource per se, but as a buffer and hedge against the development of property outside the college's control.

42. Robert Oden, interview with author.

43. The following material is excerpted and distilled from the Oden interview.

44. Oden is a president who loves small liberal arts colleges. He has a unique sense for these places and understands why people love them and what it takes to make them greater. But he is undoubtedly not alone. There are dozens of presidents at other, similar schools, as well as at larger colleges and even universities, and many more predecessors at all these places that have a similar passion for their places and for their unique and individual sagas. For example, Katherine Haley Will's inaugural address as the new president of Gettysburg College, "The Voices of Gettysburg," mirrors in part Oden's conception of saga by highlighting the many voices that have historically echoed through and around the Gettysburg campus, including those of two U.S. presidents, Lincoln, in his address at this place, and Eisenhower, whose farm was located there and who maintained his main office as a former president on the college campus. Katherine Haley Will, inaugural address, October 17, 2004, President's Office, Gettysburg College.

PART TWO

The Contest for the Middle: Can the Center Hold?

Arguably the major challenge facing today's college and university presidents can be boiled down to a simple question: are presidents, and if so to what degree and with what success, able to locate, to define wisely and articulate publicly, and to urge consensus toward a center—educational, philosophical, and moral in nature—for their institutions and for their campus constituents? Navigating the path toward this goal is a continuously complex and dauntingly difficult responsibility. The task might accurately be portrayed as one of inhuman proportions, or at the very least as one testing the powers of human intellect and persuasion of most mortals. Matching the magnitude of this challenge to the presidency are President Eliot's characterizations of presidents as having "no equal in the world" and labels like primus inter pares. However, even these fall short, failing fully to capture the reality of expectations or to express the true nature of the leadership demanded of today's college presidents.

By the nature of the office, presidents are at the center of the great educational, social, cultural, and political controversies of the day. However, this is really no different from the situation historically confronted by predecessor generations back to the Colonial colleges. Presidents must make smart and wise, as well as politically savvy, decisions about the use of their bully pulpits to address these issues and concerns. They cannot (nor should they) jump into every fray and controversy lest they diminish their authority and reduce their influence. But there are numerous challenges, controversies, and concerns in which presidents indeed should and must be heard in the public square inside and beyond the gates.

Thus, I am contending that the major task and primary responsibility of today's presidents is to be voices in the middle. At first glance, finding a middle path appears an easily accomplishable goal, one entailing little sacrifice or expenditure of hard-won and difficult-to-replace political capital and personal prestige. In fact, it is the opposite: the mission to articulate and define the "center" is quite difficult and demands great courage of presidents.

This is not a wishy-washy presidential quest that simply attempts to satisfy everyone with lowest common denominator solutions. Rather, and counterintuitively, shaping a center for the academy, one in which full, unrestricted conversation can take place, one that is as politically unbiased as possible, is a critical moral responsibility of presidents. To seek and articulate a moral middle of the university requires the utmost intellectual insight, persuasive powers, and educationally well-grounded thinking. It entails moral leadership, leadership with consequences no less profound than those associated with the presidential "giants" of a bygone era.

As they always have been, presidents are charged and challenged by saga, creed, and the divergent desires of constituents and colleagues to work diligently in the quest to make the center hold. This is more complicated today than in previous eras because what constitutes the middle and the common ground is much less obvious, much less clear and simple. Therefore presidents today have to work harder than their predecessors to identify a center and move constituents toward it. Convincing these multifaceted and often mutually exclusively competing constituencies that the very mission and purpose of the college and university are part of that center is a difficult, some might argue impossible, task indeed.

However, staking out the claim that this is in fact the core of the university is *the* profound presidential task and challenge. Presidents have always been responsible for leading from the middle, but in an era now long gone by when the spectrum of politics, ideologies, religious beliefs, and demographic diversity was much more narrowly defined than in the present, this task was simpler and success more easily attained. A major shift occurring both within and outside the gates of the academy in the contemporary era is the higher profile and unavoidable presence of vastly diverse cultural forces and the pressures spawned by these increasingly diverse constituencies in the life of colleges and universities. The clear result is that campuses and their leaders must both recognize this substance and candidly address these realities.

In purely demographic terms, the diversity in society has not changed substantially in recent decades, but awareness of diverse populations and their interests has become greater, and their bearing and claim on the academy have grown significantly. Programs and initiatives designed to respond to diversity often are read and received as a challenge to the deep-seated values and principles of the university, its fundamental beliefs constrained because they were shaped and designed to satisfy the predominance of more exclusively homogenized constituents and stakeholders. As the conception of diversity has expanded, more perspectives and contentious positions develop that are simply outside of what used to be considered the middle ground. In this environment, presidents are forced to redefine the "center."

This pressure of enlarged diversity forces creates greater proportional weight on today's presidents both to shape and to engage a "new" middle, to work on making the "center hold." All this while the "center" is more and more frequently torn by centripetal forces. Balancing these forces and the demand of presidential responsibility for solutions has become much more a raison d'être of the office than was the case for the predecessors of today's presidents. A closely related and intertwined trap for presidents is that as they engage this difficult process of leading into and from a center, they become easy targets of critics whose loyalties and agendas are rooted in personal and group politics, ideologies, and identities, and who are outside and threatened by that middle ground.

Given these broad constituent and political pressures on presidents, the question and matter for consideration is the nature of the content and rhetoric of the voices of contemporary presidents as they have to grapple with these issues of diversity. How do presidents deal with the subtle and not so subtle dynamics of diversity inevitably arising in episodes within and beyond the gates of their colleges and universities?

These pressures on presidents come in an array of discrete, often intersecting, issues. Conflicts among and between campus groups precipitate discussions of the free speech and the civil discourse in community to which the academy aspires. Admissions and recruitment programs designed to increase diversity in student and faculty ranks spark widely competing reactions from disparate constituents about educational philosophy, pedagogy, and content. Battles and debates have frequently raged in recent decades about the "canon."

Presidents thus grapple with two major and intertwined challenges: first the pressures inspired by diversity and second the shadows cast by political correctness and the ideological battleground. The dilemmas and constituting elements of battles over diversity and political correctness—racial matters, access, free speech and free expression, the free interchange of ideas, the political pressures on the university—combine to form the truly overarching major problem that must be addressed in today's academy and to define what presidents must engage: the obligation to locate and to make the center hold.

CHAPTER 4

The Dilemmas of Diversity

The challenge of diversity is viewed, quite correctly, as a relatively recent phenomenon in the life of colleges and universities, and therefore equally recently in the forefront of the agenda of presidents. Indeed, the major push to diversify campuses and to address the many attendant issues linked to the growth and development of more diverse populations and programs within the walls of the academy began five decades ago, in the 1960s. In that era, colleges and universities were by and large forced, at times exhibiting some willingness, to react to the political pressures brought about by the black civil rights and other social movements, especially the movement for women's equality, of the time. However, as in many contemporary "revolutions," historical context and a sense of perspective that often only time allows are routinely critical and necessary.

Neil Rudenstine is among the prominent college leaders of the last 20 years to speak in the public square about this issue, especially as it relates to questions of how to develop diversity on campus. For those who claim that he was not sufficiently vigorous or in the public view on issues of consequence while president of Harvard, his record on this as well as other issues suggests otherwise.[1] Rudenstine offers a longer range view about the roots of the relationship of diversity to the life of colleges and universities.[2]

Rudenstine begins with the influence of diversity at America's colleges and universities in the middle to late nineteenth century. While well into Harvard's long history, this is a hundred years prior to the diversity "revolutions" of the mid-twentieth century. Citing a predecessor thought to be among the "giants" in the presidency, Rudenstine claims that Charles Eliot was well aware of the difficulties of making a university community more diverse. Diversity inevitably creates "friction and turbulence" as well as sometimes making "the experience of being a student more difficult—and, at times, even alienating." In language applicable today, Rudenstine notes that despite these potential and actual rough patches, Eliot "insisted on the importance of a more open, diverse, and even disputatious university, where a 'collision of views' would promote 'thought about great themes,' teach 'candor' and 'moral courage,' and cultivate 'forbearance and mutual respect.'"[3]

As contemporary presidents and their institutions seek educational justifications for encouraging diversity, they could not find language more precise and to the point than Eliot's. His philosophy was that gathering students from a wide variety of backgrounds would "allow them to experience 'the wholesome influence that comes from observation and contact with' people different from themselves."[4] Rudenstine points out an often excluded and ignored aspect of today's debates about diversity and multiculturalism, one that goes to the heart of the necessity of locating a center that can hold. Eliot stressed the need for common ground to emerge from the encounter with difference, for the fundamental values and requirements of a democratic society and nation to prevail.

Rudenstine contends Eliot, "saw that an inclusive vision of higher education not only would benefit individual students, but was also essential in a heterogeneous society whose citizens simply had to learn to live together if the nation's democratic institutions were to function effectively, and its ideals were to be fulfilled. He insisted, in other words, on the link between diversity in education and the requirements for citizenship and leadership in a diverse nation such as ours."[5] Would that many of the arguments today about diversity had at their base the enlightened rationale and goal that Rudenstine urges.

Having anchored his views in this historical perspective, Rudenstine adds an interesting anecdote about Henry Adams. He cites Adams writing (in *The Education of Henry Adams*) about attending Harvard during the Civil War and having as roommates "a trio of Virginians" including the son of Robert E. Lee. From this experience Adams "recognized 'how thin an edge of friendship separated' him and the Virginians 'from mortal enmity' on the brink of the Civil War."[6] Whatever tensions are manifest on campuses today, it is difficult to conceive of anything as tense or difficult as relations between students from the North and South during the Civil War. Eliot's Harvard managed these tensions in the spirit of the value of diversity, and we can only conjecture about the value this attitude of diversity conveyed to Harvard students like Adams. Like an unearthed fossil relic, Harvard was home to a diversity "experiment" undertaken a century before those begun in the era of the 1960s.

Rudenstine also weighs in on the contemporary era, beginning with the immediate post–World War II period and the revolutionary changes in higher education wrought by the GI Bill and great increases in student enrollments. Among other changes were the decisions to establish more sophisticated admissions selection criteria. In light of these changes in admissions and speaking of more recent court cases such as the Bakke and Hopwood decisions (and presaging the

University of Michigan Supreme Court cases), Rudenstine contends that "we can see these legal conflicts as bringing to a head the clash between a particular 'meritocratic' idea of educational quality—defined largely in terms of statistically measurable academic achievement—and an equally strong idea of education associated with the concept of diversity, including different forms of knowledge, the variety of human qualities and talents, and the multitude of perspectives on experience that are obviously not very measurable in statistical terms, but are not less real for that."[7]

This clash between supporters of "merit"—the strength of higher education and of the nation is built on a meritocracy—and supporters of the idea that groups of people can or should be singled out for special consideration and treatment creates a major ongoing battle inside and outside the academy and for presidents today. It is certainly at the heart of the many controversies over affirmative action and other attempts to right past wrongs.

In drawing this discussion of diversity to a close, Rudenstine, with typical irony and more than a little humor (despite the seriousness of the issue, but as a way of driving home the point more firmly and emphatically), turns to a hypothetical situation. He suggests: "Let us suppose, for a moment, that Harvard were to subscribe, in a consistent way, to a statistical 'meritocratic' view. What would happen, for example, if we were to take only those students with the very highest test scores and grade point averages, going mathematically from top to bottom, until the entire entering class was filled? The results would almost certainly be very curious." It would be curious indeed, especially in terms of what Harvard and most colleges, especially the most selective among them, seek in their student bodies. "It is not at all clear, for example, how many of the students, chosen in this way, would be very talented in the arts," Rudenstine argues, "since certain creative abilities do not correlate at all strongly with SAT scores—or even with high grades in many subjects. It is not clear how many students with a capacity for leadership we would have in such a class—or individuals strongly committed to public service; or how many students who have exceptional and unusual abilities to understand other people, or to penetrate complex human and societal situations." Putting the icing on the cake in the form of leverage to address certain constituencies and as a strategy to defuse criticism of affirmative action and of other special admissions efforts, Rudenstine wryly adds, "or students who are good at ice hockey, or who are descended from our alumni."[8]

Donald Kennedy's tenure at Stanford, 1980–93, lies near the middle point of the 40 or more years of contemporary history, from the early 1960s to the middle of the first decade of the twenty-first century, of the controversies over racial issues and affirmative action. Kennedy is an insightful leader, not afraid to say something unpopular or to tackle issues others might normally (and understandably) seek to avoid. Kennedy's foray into the sensitive minefield of racial politics is a case in point.

In fall 1988, Kennedy released a statement to the university community about race, in response to several campus incidents that had occurred.[9] His concern is with a perceived backlash against programs and initiatives designed to promote diversity. This focus is an aspect of racial issues frequently overlooked except in times of crisis incidents when racial hatred or threats of violence make this focus unavoidable. Kennedy distinguishes between the "hard" and the "soft" backlash.

The aspiration to depoliticize reactions to and feelings about tense racial politics in a campus community may make Kennedy appear a Don Quixote figure. But he is serious and his intent is to alter, even if only slightly, the course of campus discourse and politicking on sensitive issues of race. Kennedy also presses toward a middle ground, trying to get the center regarding race to hold.

He views the "hard backlash" as the phenomenon that results from those who use "the racism-on-campus issue as an opportunity to advance the view that too much has already been done for minorities." By contrast, the "soft backlash" is insidiously the "disaffection of those who have believed in and have fought for equal opportunity and full minority participation" but who have concluded that they "aren't wanted and that they should expend their energies for social improvement in other ways."[10] Kennedy believes Stanford and other campuses are divided into camps regarding the extent and value of diversity initiatives. The camps are composed of otherwise "good," well-intentioned people, who make more difficult the concerted strides of others to advance progress on racial issues. On one side is a group that actively attacks what has been done as more than sufficient (or maybe feels that nothing at all should have been done). On the other is a group abandoning the playing field of support for programs and efforts designed to promote racial balance and understanding, out of a sense either that others have taken over or that they have done all they are able.

It would be easy to quibble with Kennedy's declaration that these are the two major groups of people in campus communities and society who are roadblocks to racial progress. However, his concern is more broad and deep. Connected to the types of backlash is an unnecessary, in Kennedy's view, tendency of campus groups to link their particular political agendas to racial episodes that occur. This happens with great frequency in the academy.

Kennedy judges this posturing even by individuals and groups that would otherwise be sympathetic and supportive as "too much is too much." In his community letter, Kennedy cautions students that too many of them do not understand "why racial incidents are so frequently followed by demands that bear little relation to the circumstances or the environment in which the incidents took place." The impact of this conflation of issues is highly negative, fuels the backlash phenomenon, and impedes progress on important concerns in the racial agenda on campuses. Speaking about both campus and society, Kennedy urges that "freeing our goal of racial understanding from this heavy political weight would, I think, make it easier to achieve—and also reduce the possibility of backlash."[11]

The challenges to the presidential ability to hold the center in the face of the polemics of campus diversity take many forms. James Laney provides behind-the-scenes insight about dealings with sensitive racial issues and about his tactical development of a broad context for grappling with racial problems.

During one racial episode at Emory, black students began a sit-in. Laney decided the best course was to meet directly with the students about their demands.[12] In preparation for an open public meeting, and as was his "custom," Laney wanted "to get out ahead of them. I wanted to try to grasp what it was they were after and then formulate what we should be doing and make it an offer rather than a concession." Laney regularly used this strategy to diffuse campus controversies, while still addressing the needs and expectations of students. He adds, however, that his tactic of reaching out to protesting students occasionally boomeranged. When, as in this case, the press would run headlines along the lines of Laney "meets with them and says we're going to do this," members of the Board of Trustees would occasionally become concerned that he was "caving in to their demands."[13]

Even though this trustee criticism was usually mild, it is not something Laney or any president wants to let pass. Laney's response was to focus board members' attention on major themes—turning them to a "center"—of the big picture of Emory's agenda rather than concentrating on the minutiae of the moment. He viewed the responsibilities of his office as to engage and to guide the board by centering on the purposes of Emory at its founding and as a late-twentieth-century university. Laney would draw the trustees to a philosophy of the university's contribution to education and to its increasingly diverse students: "We're working on justice. Justice means that people get treated right and fairly. They get supported, and at a university that means they have genuine support, they get encouragement and affirmation so they can do their best. And that has social and financial and academic implications."[14]

An art of the college presidency is the ability to broker agreements in ways such that the constituting ideas can withstand criticism from constituencies on and off the campus. But this art is dependent on the basic political skills required successfully to navigate and to draw together consensus. Laney did this by placing larger principles and values in the forefront of his own thinking and that of key supporters and decision makers, in this case, the Board of Trustees. The modus operandi and working definition of his leadership was to develop and frame consensus: "I think in those instances what you try to do is to reach back to some common ground and then develop it in a way that it may not be unassailable, but it has logic and coherence and you do it with an appeal to their innate sense of what's right." Realistically, "it doesn't always work—and it certainly doesn't work one hundred percent, but it works some," but Laney concludes optimistically that "with people of decent goodwill it works."[15]

Laney worked to formulate a middle ground, a broad consensus, all the while fully aware of the divergent and differing views of colleagues and constituents. Shaping such an inclusive unity in the face of diversity's divisions "was not just a solution to a campus problem. This was an attempt to come to terms with real issues that we all face. And one of the things I felt most keenly was that I used every occasion I could in public or in meeting to educate. [Not to be] didactic, but to explain why—and not just why I wanted to do it—but what was involved in all this."

Undoubtedly Laney had constituents who viewed the "center" he was crafting as flawed, maybe even morally or ethically wrong, as a basis for the university's decisions and positions. Laney knew how to get his way, but he also knew how to work with others to reach concerted goals. He also possessed the capacity to put his persona in the middle of student protests and the demands of situations characterized by divisive conflict. John DiBiaggio is another president who embodies this approach.

DiBiaggio held three presidencies, at the University of Connecticut, Michigan State University, and Tufts University, spanning nearly 25 years (1979–2002), a combined tenure that places him in the category of what today are called "career presidents."[16] Two stories of DiBiaggio's encounter with issues of diversity are instructive about the value of a president's personal touch in highly emotional and passionate situations. The first centers on gay and lesbian students at Tufts, and the second is concerned with harassment of women at the University of Connecticut.

In both of these episodes, DiBiaggio's personal touch and leadership style in student life matters is an example of the continuing active and significant role presidents play in campus communities. Active personal engagement is critical in resolving conflicts and in crafting educational moments from what otherwise are viewed only as tendentious controversies, beneath a president's dignity and involvement.

Throughout his Tufts presidency, DiBiaggio consistently reached out to gay and lesbian students. He regularly appeared and spoke at annual "coming out" and Gay Pride marches and rallies, symbolic occasions designed to call for public commitment to groups on the margin and to stress the need for civility in the university community. His straightforward message at those events was simply, "'I'm glad that we're on a campus that you feel comfortable in groups, that you feel that you can publicly display your feelings.' And I said, 'Thank goodness for that for all of us.'"[17]

One event that catalyzed a reaction from the Tufts gay and lesbian community resulted from the action of a university religious group, Campus Crusade for Christ. The organization prohibited an openly lesbian member from running for its president's post. The controversy became a tangle of interpretations of the applicability of the university's nondiscrimination clause. DiBiaggio recalls that "there were two things in conflict. One was the university's nondiscrimination policy and another was the right of assembly, the right of belief. We had two things in absolute conflict."[18]

Ironically the cause for the matter to be addressed under university policy was Campus Crusade's decision to deny the student the chance to run and to be voted for by the membership. If a vote had been allowed, DiBiaggio notes, she likely would not have been elected, because the majority of the group, "opposed to homosexuality, would not have elected her," and that would have been the end of the story. As it was, charges were brought to the student judicial board and Campus Crusade was punished by suspension of university recognition, revoking their permission to utilize campus facilities and services. Displaying concern for both sides in this battle, DiBiaggio says, "It was a harsh decision without giving [the group] enough time. And I said, 'Wait, wait. Let's just put that in abeyance for the moment and let's just ask them to take a look at their policies to make them more amenable to the university's policies.' And they did that, and the thing was resolved."[19]

Meanwhile, the gay and lesbian students conducted a sit-in to protest Campus Crusade and its actions directed at the lesbian student. In this phase of the controversy, DiBiaggio again demonstrates his trademark, "wait, wait," patience (an important leadership trait in handling confrontational situations, especially when instantaneous responses appear to be required). He held a preliminary meeting with the gay and lesbian students to learn more about their concerns. Their criticism was grounded in their perspective that the university's nondiscrimination policy did not address one important matter. DiBiaggio describes the students as contending that "'the policy doesn't speak to self-acceptance.'" Wearing his hat as an educator, DiBiaggio replied, "'Well, explain that to me. How could a policy speak to whether you accept what you are?'"

The first day's discussion ended and the sit-in continued. DiBiaggio had to leave on a brief trip and while he was away, one of the senior administrators wanted to break up the sit-in. DiBiaggio continues the story: "I said, 'No. Wait, wait.... You can't do that [arrest them] without me.... Just let them sit in for the night and I'll talk to them when I come back.'" When he returned and met again with the students, the sticking point was still their wish and demand for the policy to reflect "self-acceptance." Figuring that this matter would somehow have to be addressed, he suggested, "'Let me try to draft something and see if you could write something.'"

When the two sides came back together and the students saw DiBiaggio's draft, there was one word to which they objected. DiBiaggio asked what word they would like to be put in instead and when they told him, he said, "'Great, I'll put that word in.' We didn't do anything more than that. They all agreed, everybody left, we didn't arrest anybody."[20]

Many years before this and early in his first presidency at the University of Connecticut, DiBiaggio faced a similar moment when to his surprise, his personal presence in a crisis situation made an enormous impact. A woman university student was sexually assaulted while jogging. Female members of the community were outraged. Interestingly for a state institution, the university had a policy under which the president could declare a Day of Metanoia to contemplate a major issue. DiBiaggio used this power and a large rally was planned at which he would speak to kick off the activities of the day. He recalls: "I start to speak, and there are screams and catcalls and yells and all about every issue: racism, sexism, homophobia. And I am stunned. I'm trying to speak, and I am being open and inviting people." Needless to say, this is not a pleasant scene for any campus leader, let alone a brand-new president. The rally concluded and DiBiaggio reports that "one of the faculty members came up to me and says, 'That was wonderful.' And

I said, 'What do you mean?' She says, 'I know you're disturbed, but you realize you're the first person that's allowed these people to express themselves. You've opened up a dialogue that we've not had before. This is terrific.... They weren't attacking you. They were attacking what's been happening here.'"[21]

But this is not the end of the tale. That evening, during a candlelight march ending the day's events, DiBiaggio heard catcalls and derogatory jeers from male students in dormitories along the march route. Appalled at this behavior, he wrote a letter to the university community and subsequently spoke about his shock at this treatment of fellow members of the community. The essence of those messages was a simple testimony of what needs to be at the heart of a university, despite clashes of diversity: "I was so embarrassed for our institution and the behavior of some of our students. I hope this is only reflected [within the behavior of] a minority group, *because if it isn't, then we're not a university*" (italics mine).[22]

As at many colleges in recent times, homosexual issues at Morehouse have proved to be tense and complex for Walter Massey. Morehouse's strongly Christian institutional profile and culture and its all-male student body create an environment with a predilection for antagonism toward gays.[23] Its students (and some faculty members), overwhelmingly hail from the South, many raised in predominantly black and often fundamentalist and conservative Protestant churches. Students and parental attitudes contribute to Morehouse culture, generating a climate in which homosexuality is an enormously worrisome issue.

For Massey's administration, the precipitating episode was a physical confrontation between two students, one claiming the other made a pass at him. A fight ensued; one student, claiming to have been assaulted, pressed charges and the case ground through outside legal proceedings. Initially, with much pressure and attention from the national and local gay and lesbian communities, the case was prosecuted as a hate crime. However, the judge dismissed that charge, reducing it to assault and battery.

Meanwhile, Massey knew the college had to address the issues raised by this case. He wanted to create constructive plans to educate the campus community and to develop preventive measures for the future. In pursing that hope, he appointed a Task Force on Tolerance and Diversity that included national figures such as Peter Gomes, chaplain at Harvard University, and comedian Bill Cosby.

During the campus discussions the task force conducted, Massey steered a neutral, middle course, exhibiting empathy for both sides. He met with students from highly conservative and fundamentalist backgrounds who had trouble understanding and accepting gays, and with students who were more open and receptive, including gay Morehouse students who were "out of the closet." When the task force reported, Massey welcomed its findings, acknowledging that its "recommendations show that there are a number of things we need to do in educating our students about people of different sexual orientation, creating an overtly open community [in which] students who are gay do not have to conceal who they are."[24]

In the immediate aftermath of the episode and beyond, Massey has been very public and forthright on the impact of this tale for Morehouse and on where it leads the campus community in the future. In an opening convocation address to first-year students along with returning upperclassmen and faculty the fall after the task force submitted its recommendations, Massey comments that "although the work of the Task Force was neither exhaustive nor strictly scientific, the data it collected from surveys and focus groups strongly suggest that there is a climate at the College, particularly among students, that is not welcoming and tolerant of individuals who are gay. While I am disappointed about this finding," he continues, "I am not discouraged. I have the utmost confidence in the ability of the members of this community—especially you, our students—to address and overcome any issue that would impede our progress toward the more excellent way to which we are committed."[25]

Reflecting on the incident and its impact for his presidency and for Morehouse, Massey indicates that "I always use the whole civil rights movement as an example; do you want to change people's feelings or change their behavior? We're operating on that civil rights belief that if you are going to change behavior, first you're going to change the law. At Morehouse we're going to make it clear what the rules are."[26] Such moments are among the worst for any college leader. The best presidents can do is, as Massey attempts, to be publicly transparent (constrained by individual privacy and legal considerations) and to navigate their communities along the most constructive path possible.

Since the 1960s, colleges and universities have been forced to pay increasingly great attention to concerns about diversity and its many related issues. The panoply of concerns and demands connected to diversity has become increasingly complex, filled with tension and beyond simple or ready solutions. Programs designed to address diversity have been initiated and reassessed, albeit unevenly. There have been successes as well as many failures. In battles over diversity, religion, despite its apparent influence and power, is often perceived to be outside the major currents of debate and discussion. September 11th awakened an interest in religion, religious diversity, and multifaith as well as multicultural (itself largely an interaction of faith and belief systems) concerns. The result is that these religious forces and pressures have moved more to the forefront of symbolic and political debate within and outside the gates of the academy.

Stephen Joel Trachtenberg has wrestled with the implications that result from this "new" world of religious tension and conflict, always simmering but now more unavoidable as religious controversies inside and outside the gates of the academy have been sparked by September 11. A year after September 11, in fall 2002, Trachtenberg wades into the storm surrounding the University of North Carolina (UNC) decision to "require" a book about the Koran for the incoming first-year students. The university's intention was to open dialogue and debate on campus among people of different faiths, and to explore the Muslim faith. Opposition to their decision came primarily from fundamentalist Christian groups.

There ensued a legal fight, but despite that, Trachtenberg indicates at the very least that the "donnybrook over a book...reaffirmed the academy's justifiable faith in the power of words and ideas." He believes "we can thank our Constitution and our long traditions of academic freedom" for legally sustaining the university's right to assign the text.[27] But Trachtenberg delves a bit deeper, imagining a counterpossibility by simply flipping the players in a twist on how people would line up about the diversity at stake. He asks "what would have happened if a book on Christianity or Judaism had been assigned to the UNC freshmen.... would other groups, fundamentalist or not, have objected? I gloomily concluded that they would have."[28]

With this imaginary but not far from real prospect, Trachtenberg plumbs a crucial problem for college and university communities and for presidents in dealing with diversity and multicultural issues and the related dilemmas at the heart of the ideological battleground. The question is whether the academy can afford, at risk of eroding its fundamental values and principles, to permit those in and with power to make ideologically driven decisions about policies and programs. By using the rhetorical device of a hypothetical situation—suppose the piece of literature assigned by UNC was a book about Judaism or Christianity—Trachtenberg forces consideration about how vital, yet fragile and delicate, it is for the academy to maintain and sustain balance among these competing authorities and ideological pressures.

Trachtenberg guesses that the selection of a Christian or Jewish text would have been protested as vehemently as the Muslim one. Even though such an outcome would reveal an equally applied discrimination about diversity, he argues, "That, too, is a pity. It's easy enough these days to declare that we must promote understanding of Islam in order to heal our wounds and cure our suspicions and distrust—because we admit, we are in a state of ignorance about what Muslims believe. Yet there are many Christians who," he asserts, "know nothing about Judaism and for whom the Bible is really the Christian Testament, with maybe a little about Adam and Eve, the Flood, and the Ten Commandments thrown in for good measure. And there are Jews who know nothing about Christianity other than that its founder was a Jewish radical. Thus more ignorance and thus also another area in need of instruction and perhaps healing as well."

Trachtenberg seeks to balance and to broaden thinking about diversity, especially diversity of religious faith and belief. Lest his outlook appear gloomy, Trachtenberg concludes that these thoughts "simply underscore what seems clear enough already—that there are many forms of concrete and specific acts that we in universities can take to help heal the world."[29]

Arguably one of the most publicly visible and most discussed stories in recent years concerning race and diversity both within the walls of the academy and outside in society concerns the Supreme Court cases involving the University of Michigan. The two official cases, *Grutter v. Bollinger* and *Gratz v. Bollinger*, concerned Michigan's student admissions policies and procedures for both the Law School and undergraduate enrollments.[30] The higher education world watched these legal proceedings closely. There were and remain momentous concerns about the impact of the outcome of the decisions. The short- and long-term litmus test is to see the actual effects of the Court's decisions on the recruitment and admission of minority students, on programs and policies designed to promote and ensure diversity, and on general attitudes about race and ethnicity. These outcomes are slowly becoming apparent, but it will likely be many years before the full impact of the Michigan cases is clearly known.

The legal maneuvering on the Michigan lawsuits entered its final phases as Mary Sue Coleman entered the presidency in fall 2002; the two cases were decided in spring 2003. But because of this timing, Coleman quickly became the public "face" of the university in the months preceding, during, and following the release of the decisions. The admissions procedures at the center of the legal suits were initiated and carried out under the watch of her three immediate predecessors—Shapiro and Duderstadt in the 1980s and 1990s, and Bollinger later in the 1990s and after the turn of the century. Indeed, Duderstadt's "Michigan Mandate," launched at his inauguration in fall 1987, provided the university with its first full-blown push on affirmative action in all admissions and hiring, and on programs and efforts designed to promote and enhance diversity.[31] The impact of these policies, evolving over time, reached a zenith and tipping point that led the two litigants to bring their cases.

Without question Coleman agrees fully with the university's position and indeed has welcomed the opportunity to defend it publicly. Coleman makes this clear early in her tenure: "I am a staunch advocate of Michigan's unwavering commitment to diversity, and it is my privilege to lead this part of the fight in defense of our principles." Fleshing out this perspective, she adds: "The bottom line is that race still matters in the United States, and just wishing the issue away doesn't work." At a personal level, "It influences who we work and go to school with, who we live next door to and, all too frequently, who we have the opportunity to call 'friend.' It impacts our personal perceptions about the world and the people around us."[32] Coleman believes that "Students learn from each other as much as from their teachers, and unless they experience direct, face-to-face interactions with others unlike themselves, they cannot possibly be adequately prepared for the life that awaits them after college." In an allusion to research that the university had conducted and that would bolster its defense, she adds, "I know this is true from personal experience and observation, and we have the data to back it up. And we will strongly and enthusiastically present our arguments to the final arbiter, the Supreme Court."[33]

By pursuing these cases as far as the Supreme Court, Michigan provided a service to all of American higher education. Discussing the behind-the-scenes maneuvers and strategies that the case required, Coleman claims, "There are not many institutions that would have mounted the kind of defense and spent the kind of money [we did]. We spent more than $9 million defending ourselves, and we got a lot of work pro bono." Furthermore, "defending that case cost a lot more than $9 million dollars, but it was just this feeling that you had to do it, that you were leading the effort to stem the tide of something sweeping the nation that wasn't right." In this context, Coleman recalls that "during the time when Michigan was sued back in 1996–1997, everybody was predicting the demise of affirmative action. Nobody was giving the University of Michigan much of a chance of winning, and yet it was a brilliant legal strategy."

She makes an important point about public stands whether within or beyond the gates by presidents: "I believe that during the course of defending itself in the lawsuits that the University of Michigan changed the conversation about affirmative action in the nation in a very positive way. We track things like what are columnists saying about affirmative action in about fifty newspapers in the country. What words are used in newspaper stories?" The result was reinforcing: "We could see the shift as the cases developed."[34]

When the Court handed down its decision, Coleman released a public statement. Though the fallout from the case has been widely debated since the Court decision, Coleman publicly claims the outcome as a considerable victory for the University of Michigan and for all of higher education. She believes that "[t]he Court has provided two important signals. The first is a green light to pursue diversity in the college classroom. The second is a road map to get us there. We will modify our undergraduate system to comply with today's ruling, but make no mistake: We will find the route that continues our commitment to a richly diverse student body." The implication for the future is that "these rulings in support of affirmative action will go down in history as among the great landmark decisions of the Supreme Court. And I am proud of the voice the University of Michigan provided in this important debate. We fought for the very principle that defines our country's greatness. Year after year, our student body proves it and now the Court has affirmed it: Our diversity is our strength."[35]

Coleman characterizes the battle as a "moral issue," an "obligation of universities to create diverse student bodies because if you look over the last 50 years, we live in more segregated housing patterns now than we have ever lived in the past. Students go to mostly segregated schools de facto—by housing patterns—than ever almost in the history of this country." For the Michigan campus, Coleman guesses that "probably 90 to 95 percent of our students, when they come to University of Michigan it is the first time in any of their educational experience that most of them have sat in classrooms with somebody from a different area. And so for me, the whole issue of how we create the diversity is a moral issue."[36]

Mindful of critics of the university's position in the Court case and in the debates that followed, Coleman returns to the heart of her views of the affirmative action discussion: "There are a lot of people who disagree; they're convinced that there are some race-neutral ways to do this." However, abandoning affirmative action programs altogether makes creating diversity in any college or university population "mathematically impossible because the pool sizes.... the applicant pool sizes of the two racial groups are so disparate that we'll never get there by any other means if you can't consider race."[37] Many higher education officials, including Coleman and her Michigan colleagues, believe the "good news" was that the *Bollinger* decision did not roll back previous Court decisions, primarily in *Bakke*, that permitted the use of race as a factor in admissions. What would no longer be permissible at Michigan and elsewhere is the utilization of heavily weighted point systems, the main contention of the complainant in *Bollinger*.

Coleman believes Michigan's action on this "moral issue" affirms the value of diversity in the educational experience and the benefit that learning in a diverse environment provides to students when they leave the university to enter the workplace and life in communities. The Court cases are a "great battle fought about the educational value of diversity on the classroom." The university's rationale is not that "we're trying to redress some terrible wrong in the past. We're doing it because we absolutely believe that the nation is in a point in its history that if we don't have classrooms that mirror in part what our society is like, then we are not giving all of our students—not just minority students—the benefit of learning in a way that is going to prepare them best for the society that they're going to go into."

Continuing this line of reasoning about the positive effects of diversity in the classroom, Coleman adds: "In fact, sitting in a classroom with people who have the same kind of background that you have and the same kind of ideas that you have is not a really good educational experience at all. In fact, the best educational experience comes from people who look at the same historical information and have very different interpretations of it, and having those kinds of discussions is good." In fact, pointing to what universities can do best, she concludes that our research shows us "that the benefits last far beyond graduation, that students who learn in diverse environments are more engaged in their communities."[38]

Michigan's and Coleman's handling of these cases stands as a counterweight against critics' claims that presidents, and their colleges and universities, have out of fear and a lack of moral and political courage retreated from the public square and societal controversy. In this case Michigan pressed for a Supreme Court decision, and the institution and its presidents willingly risked their public stock and image in that battle. A much easier and less controversial path would have been to save $9 million or more, withdraw the case, and reach out-of-court settlements. Rather, they pursued the case, recognizing they were doing so in large part on behalf of colleague institutions around the country. The cost of mounting the legal battle would have been the same regardless of the size and scale of any institution deciding to enter the fray. Many, probably a large majority, of colleges and universities in the country simply could not have even begun to afford such an expense. Thus Michigan served in effect as a battering ram for its colleagues across the country.

A further outcome is that by defending its principles the university sparked and altered public discussion about affirmative action and diversity. A frequently looming question is that if not at colleges and universities, where would the research, scholarly, academic, and intellectual inquiry, and leadership on many social issues and concerns, be carried out? In this case, by forcing a national discourse about the issues at stake, Michigan performed an important and noteworthy public service. Internally the university had the good fortune of open-minded alumni and other key stakeholders who supported its stand despite disagreement with the actual implementation of affirmative action goals. Such support cannot be overlooked whenever institutions face issues as potentially divisive as those involving race and affirmative action.

But though Michigan's largesse and its willingness to expend it was crucial, it was also by no means alone in taking these cases to the Supreme Court. Presidents Cole and Oden note the briefs filed by numerous Fortune 500 corporations and by the U.S. military, supporting affirmative action and the programs the university had in place.[39] Carleton College, led by Oden, joined a group of liberal arts colleges in an amici curiae brief, and Oden outlined for his college community the contentions articulated in the brief.[40] Oden's premise is that in making admissions decisions, "among this wide range of factors is race. If it is now a century since W.E.B. DuBois wrote that race would be the issue of the twentieth century, we believe that race continues, in America and elsewhere, to effect a person's life experiences and available opportunities. Centuries of discrimination and segregation continue, and will continue, to shape the world in which we live."[41]

Oden also contends that policies governing affirmative action and diversity are grounded in another crucial value of America's colleges and universities: their rich history of autonomy. Oden rhetorically asks "why so many of the world's greatest colleges and universities are located in the United States. Among the reasons for this, I believe, is that faculty members and other educators, rather than governmental bodies, have determined policies at our colleges and universities. And among the reasons for the admired quality of American higher education is that we believe that a quality education is one which includes the experience of difference and diversity, many kinds of diversity, to be sure, but including racial diversity." Before the outcome of the case was known, Oden urged a ruling: "*We hope that the Supreme Court will continue to preserve the freedom America's colleges and universities have long possessed in allowing faculty members and administrators and other educators to define what constitutes an education of the first order*"[42] (italics mine).

Asserting that affirmative action must remain a part of the equation in college admissions, Oden notes the fact that ironically Carleton and most colleges and universities are nowhere near a quota system, given how underrepresented most minorities are in these campus communities. Regardless of perception to the contrary, Carleton and similar selective colleges do not admit "students of lesser merit" in reviewing applicant pools "because we have never defined merit mechanically or on the basis of test scores and grades alone. We rather define merit expansively, and we include an assessment of a rich variety of differing life experiences in our assessment of merit."[43]

Two threats loom behind the Court's decision and how it will play out over time. One is the capacity of colleges and universities to find constructive and legal ways to address national and institutional histories of segregation and discrimination, and to maintain the educational value of diversity on their campuses. A second, less talked about but persistent, concern centers on the degree to which colleges and universities will be able to exert autonomy in the face of potential legal constraints on their policies about race and diversity. Carleton's institutional collaboration in the amici brief symbolizes a spirit of unity if not unanimity in the higher education community on affirmative action. Whether it is getting the public attention and acclaim it deserves, the higher education community made a statement in the Michigan case. Its variety and diversity was well on display as a small liberal arts college, Carleton, tucked away in the farm country and hills of southern Minnesota, joined with other small liberal arts colleges to support the massive, almost urban university-city in the town of Ann Arbor, that is, the University of Michigan.

Rudenstine distinguishes the university from other organizations in society, characterizing the way universities address diversity. "Our experiment is a new one—hardly two or three decades old—and it is taking place in a nation that is itself deeply troubled by unresolved issues concerning race, equity, and educational opportunity," Rudenstine cautions.[44] In response to critics who argue that things are moving either too slowly or too rapidly, he takes a considered middle path: "[M]y own view is frankly evolutionary. We are unlikely to reach solutions—or, more precisely, resolutions—easily or immediately. Indeed, it is not obvious—in an untried experiment of this kind—what our realistic expectations can be. But we know there are no alternatives that are either more humane, or more in accord with the realities of our world. Our experiment in diversity," which Rudenstine assumes is here to stay, "must be pressed forward with energy and conviction, in a manner that preserves the fundamental strength and fabric of this great but also very human university." Rudenstine's thoughts about Harvard are generically applicable to the concept of the university. In language Minogue would endorse, Rudenstine assumes the university is a different institution from others: "*We are and must remain a living organism, something essentially different from a mere organization*" (italics mine).[45]

In recent decades, college and university presidents have increasingly had to play a significant role and to use political capital in guiding their institutions and society to grapple with the dilemmas of diversity. Many of these leaders and their campuses have been front and center in matters of race, equality, rights, and identity for blacks, women, gays and lesbians, and other minorities, in the passions and conflicts of religion and religious beliefs, and in the development of programs addressing diversity.

As they battle and address these difficult issues, presidents must exercise balance in guiding their institutions. The frequent absence of a reasoned consensus on campus and in society about diversity issues creates a two-pronged problem. One aspect is that the more there is a lack of consensus, the more inevitable is the likelihood that diversity issues will produce major crises and public controversy. Second, in this climate, the leadership of presidents, the images of their schools, and their handling of these crises and controversies are examined under a more critically discerning public microscope both within and outside the gates of the academy. Thus it behooves presidents to steer into the middle ground and attempt to develop broad agreement among divergent constituencies and their beliefs.

Presidents and their institutions will surely face these issues for many decades to come. Oden tellingly reminds us of DuBois's warning that race would be the issue of the twentieth century. That century left much unresolved on race matters, so race and the closely linked issues of diversity will remain a major concern in the twenty-first century as well. In addition, as Trachtenberg points out, the diversity menu now more than ever includes the multicultural pressure of religion and religious diversity, sparked largely, though not exclusively, by religious tension emanating from the events of September 11th. If the diversity docket for presidents and campuses looked full previously, that fateful day made it more so.

All these issues of pluralism, diversity, and diverse constituencies are unavoidably shot through the life of the academy. Most importantly, and given the fundamental principles of our colleges and universities, society is fortunate to have at least this one institution—the academy—as a civil, scholarly, and inquiring arena in which to wrestle with diversity. The expectation in the future, as has been the case in the past, is that presidents and the colleges and universities they lead will be the focal point for continuing the "experiment in diversity," crafting reasonable policies and programs, and doing what the academy nearly alone can do: offer the best possible education of students for life in a global and diverse world.

NOTES

1. For example, Rudenstine coauthored with fellow former president William Bowen a lengthy article, "Race-Sensitive Admissions: Back to Basics," in the *Chronicle of Higher Education*, February 7, 2003, p. 7 (and http://web.lexis-nexis.com/universe/documen, p. 2). Bowen and Rudenstine argue:

> It matters that minority applicants have access to the most selective programs, at both undergraduate and graduate levels, in both private and public institutions. The arguments that they will surely be able to "get in somewhere" rings hollow to many people. As one black woman quoted in *The Shape of the River* observed wryly to a white parent: "Are you telling me that all those white folks fighting so hard to get their kids into Duke and Stanford are just ignorant? Or are we supposed to believe that attending a top-ranked school is important for their children but not for mine?" That interchange was not just about perceptions. Various studies show that the short-term and long-term gains associated with attending the most selective institutions are, if anything, greater for minority students than for white students, and that academic and other resources are concentrated increasingly in the top-tier colleges and universities. (William Bowen and Derek Bok, *The Shape of the River: Long-term Consequences of Considering Race in College Admissions*, Princeton, NJ: Princeton University Press, 1998.)

2. Neil Rudenstine, "Diversity and Learning at Harvard: A Historical View," in *Pointing Our Thoughts*, a book of presidential speeches and writings published shortly after

he left office at Harvard. This talk, delivered to the Massachusetts Historical Society, November 6, 1996, is an interesting commentary on diversity and its relationship to learning and education. Though he is using the specific setting and example of Harvard and its history, many of Rudenstine's contentions here could easily be translated into the saga and mission of many other universities (Michigan, for example, with its notion of an "uncommon education for the common man").

3. Ibid., p. 26.

4. Ibid., p. 24.

5. Ibid., p. 26.

6. Ibid., p. 22.

7. Ibid., pp. 29–30.

8. Ibid., p. 30. The first president that I recall making this argument was John Kemeny at Dartmouth in the 1970s, when he would speak occasionally about how legacies and admissions for athletes were the original affirmative action programs.

9. Kennedy, *The Last of Your Springs,* p. 142. In this year-by-year compendium of annual issues and concerns, Kennedy has a chapter about race, presumably a major theme in his mind for that year, 1988–89. He incorporates there the full version of the statement he penned. From comments he offers, it appears to have been personally crafted. Presidents have for a fairly long time had assistants, the precursors to today's speechwriters. In assessing the rhetoric of presidents, greater significance should always be attached to what appear to be words thoroughly their own. The entirety of this chapter, "Talking about Race," is highly recommended reading.

10. Ibid., p. 142.

11. Ibid., pp. 142–43.

12. For example, included in the previously noted video documentary, *Leading Out,* produced by James Ault, is a segment on another student protest, which shows Laney meeting with his staff to discuss going before the students (in this case they were sitting in the President's Office), walking into this setting, and conversing with the students. In both my interview with Laney and in these examples, Laney's personal style of wanting to deal face to face with people wherever possible, and regardless of the degree of intensity of the encounter, is clear.

13. James Laney, former president, Emory University, interview by author, April 27, 2003.

14. Ibid. The portion of this quote noted by the ellipsis is as follows: "You know, that was hard. If they were going to take issue with us, they would have to say, 'We're for injustice.' [laughing] Well, you know that puts them in an awkward position. And I'm sure some of them didn't appreciate it." But as indicated, he underscores that the board understood his intentions.

15. Ibid.

16. The term "career president" entered the nomenclature of the college and university presidency toward the end of the twentieth century (its precise origin is unknown). It describes individuals who hold more than one (or sometimes just one very long tenure), often more than two presidencies, spanning sufficient years of professional life to constitute the bulk of the individual's career. A number of those fitting this category, in addition to DiBiaggio, have been named previously in our discussion.

17. John DiBiaggio, former president, Tufts University, interview by author, August 12, 2003.

18. Ibid.

19. Ibid. While this response by the Campus Crusade group sounds as though it happened very quickly, the process leading to the resolution about which DiBiaggio speaks took a couple of months.

20. Ibid. Unfortunately I did not learn what the one-word sticking point was in this revision of the university's policy. Another interesting side note is that while undoubtedly the university's legal affairs staff had to approve the final version, it appears that DiBiaggio undertook these negotiations directly with the students and was willing to engage in give and take, with the assumption that what was agreed to would and could pass legal muster.

21. Ibid.

22. Ibid.

23. Walter Massey, president, Morehouse College, interview by author, May 25, 2004. During the interview, President Massey supplied the descriptive material that follows.

24. Ibid.

25. Walter Massey, convocation address, "A More Excellent Way: Realizing the Academic Village at Morehouse College," September 18, 2003.

26. Walter Massey, interview by author.

27. Stephen Joel Trachtenberg, "Healing with Words and Acts on Campus," October 3, 2002, delivered to the Annual Meeting of the Jewish Social Services Agency, http://www.gwu.edu/~gwpres/speeches6.html, p. 3.

28. Ibid.

29. Ibid., p. 4.

30. The Bollinger referred to is Lee Bollinger, president of the university at the time the cases were formally filed with the Supreme Court. Bollinger went on to become president of Columbia University, from which post he continued to be actively involved and engaged in the case, testifying before the Supreme Court.

31. In her interview, Coleman states, regarding the inception of diversity initiatives at Michigan, that "the seeds for that started far before the university was sued. That started back in the late seventies and early eighties—even early seventies—when the university decided that it really needed to do something about the fact that there were so few minority students and started outreach." Mary Sue Coleman, president, University of Michigan, interview by author, July 23, 2003.

32. Mary Sue Coleman, "President's Day Talk," given at the Detroit Athletic Club, November 18, 2002, p. 12.

33. Ibid., p. 13.

34. Mary Sue Coleman, interview by author. In this portion of the interview she added the following, noted previously in her discussion of the bearing on the saga of Michigan of this part of the affirmative action case fallout:

> And so, does it mean everybody agrees with us? In fact, one of the interesting things for me in coming in at the very end of the cases when I was just sort of shepherding it through until the end, when I would go out and speak with alumni groups, there are alumni who don't agree with us, and yet there's this point of pride that the university has defended itself on principle and something that it felt was really important, even if they don't agree with us on the content.

35. Mary Sue Coleman, "Comments from University Leaders," News Service, University of Michigan, June 23, 2003, p. 1, http://www.umich.edu/news/Releases/2003/Jun03/comments.html.

36. Mary Sue Coleman, interview by author.

37. Ibid.

38. Ibid.

39. Johnnetta Cole, president, Bennett College, and former president, Spelman College, interview by author, June 2, 2003; and Robert Oden, president, Carleton College, interview by author, August 26, 2003.

40. Robert Oden, "Affirmative Action and the Michigan Cases," *The Carletonian,* February 21, 2003, p. 6. The amici curiae brief was Amherst, et al.

41. Ibid.

42. Ibid.

43. Ibid.

44. Neil Rudenstine, "Commencement Day Address: Free Expression in a Diverse Society," June 4, 1992, in *Pointing Our Thoughts,* pp. 44–45. This talk echoes Arthur Schlesinger Jr.'s book, *The Disuniting of America.*

45. Ibid., p. 45.

CHAPTER 5

Political Rightness and Ideology: The Battleground in and around the Academy's Walls

Closely connected to the push and pressures of diversity on college and university presidents and their institutions are debates engaged in and waged, especially since the late 1970s and early 1980s, about political correctness. The origin of the term itself is not precisely known. But it came into parlance in the academy at the hands of critics on the right of the political spectrum to bemoan alleged excesses in commitments to diversity, sensitivity in political discourse, and the general state of affairs in higher education.[1] In the last three decades, advocates of the political correctness critique have created and proliferated an ever-expanding number of targets in protracting and extending their claims about the wrong-headedness of the academy.

A number of focal points are among the favorite and most frequently used whipping boys: initiatives designed to promote greater diversity on campuses; anything to do with identity politics (based on race, ethnicity, gender, sexual preference); incidents precipitating questions about the content of speech and perceived censorship, and infringement on freedom of expression; and presumptions about liberal bias in faculty hiring, student admissions, and institutional posture. Political correctness critics believe numerous examples of these problems and encroachments are readily found in a wide array of combinations at all contemporary college and universities—the only exceptions being places like Jerry Falwell's Liberty Baptist College and other hard-core Christian fundamentalist schools. Foes of political correctness point to abundant evidence in a host of easily assailable programs and in the rhetoric characterizing the ethos of many campuses. The excesses of politically motivated and diversity initiatives are cited as red flags, anathema and antithetical in the academy, and destructive of its very foundations.

A great irony of the political rightness debate is the inherent embedded hypocrisy in the thinking and urgings of political correctness critics. Those assailing the academy for falling prey to the political pressures of constituents—students, faculty, administrators, trustees—who want things "correct" at the same time press their own politically correct agenda, that is, there is a right and a wrong way for the academy to be political. Equally connected to this debate is the circular problem of the Right and the Left accusing each other of capitulation to a political agenda, resulting only in rounds of polemical discourse character-ized mostly by heat and little by light and meaning. When the two sides square off with ad hominem attacks and intentionally manufactured polarized posi-tions, their behavior is not at all fitting of the intellectual discourse and dialogue expected in the academy.

A number of college presidents have spoken in the public square about political correctness during the last four decades. Their perspectives are honed in cru-cibles formed by the pressures of the political correctness debate and the ways these forces play out on campuses. The rhetoric and argument and the decisions and actions of these leaders about political correctness battles inevitably produce confrontation with the intertwined role of ideology in the academy.

One of the major constraints presidents face is the fact that the problems of political correctness, especially when connected to free speech, free expression, and academic freedom, no matter how handled, frequently become nothing other than fertile spawning grounds for more contentiousness and merely further con-firm the relentless press of political correctness itself. Without question, woven through the difficulties and dilemmas that arise and challenge presidential lead-ership and decisions is an encounter with the persistent reality of the ideological battleground in today's academy.

As one of the speakers at the inauguration of Dennis O'Brien as president of the University of Rochester in fall 1984, Donald Kennedy weighs in on the "Political Correctness" (his capitalization) environment and debate of that time. His comments, though tailored to that audience, are equally applicable today.

Steering an intentional middle-of-the-road course from which to critique both the right and left of the political spectrum, Kennedy asserts that "the idea that only one kind of subject matter, or one kind of thinking, is correct is absolutely corrosive to our kind of institution, no matter what the political vector along which it arrives." He offers scholarly and intellectual examples: "[T]he notion that history cannot be usefully interpreted from a perspective that lends more emphasis to the role of women is every bit as objectionable as the notion that some anthropologists can be ignored because they are 'biological determinists.'" Then aiming at colleagues near and far (and as the great canon debate over the Western Civilization requirement was just beginning at his home, Stanford), Kennedy sardonically concludes: "I never cease to be amazed at the vulnerability of otherwise creative and thoughtful parts of the academy to capture by doctrine.

Whether it is the development of a policy center with subtle ideological tests for appointment or the establishment of rules that would regulate certain kinds of research on the basis of their prospective end-use, it is a perversion of the purposes of the university."[2]

Kennedy hedges against criticism from both sides of the intellectual divide by using point-counterpoint examples with his feminist studies and women-oriented curricular revisionists on one side and the "biological determinists," read, for example, *The Bell Curve* advocates, on the other.[3] Though the context is different, this latter example is close to that which 20 years later got Larry Summers, then president of Harvard, into trouble over his conjecture (and a review of the actual transcript of his remarks confirms that conjecture was all it was) about the reasons for the lack of significant numbers of women in the sciences and scientific fields. In pedestrian language Kennedy says to both sides, "Cut it out. Both your houses corrode what the academy stands for." Kennedy sets a standard for college and university presidents in defending the walls of the academy from those on both sides of the political spectrum and of the political correctness divide who pervert "the purposes of the university."

Stephen Joel Trachtenberg's tenure at George Washington University (GWU) began around the midpoint of Kennedy's at Stanford and has continued well beyond. His two presidencies (the University of Hartford prior to GWU, as well as other prior administrative posts), served during the ascendancy of political correctness controversies, provide a vantage point from experience of the trends and content of the debates. Trachtenberg uses the polemics embedded in arguments about political "rightness" as a launching pad, amplifying the bearing of these contentions and issues on the academy and on presidential leadership.

Presidents, including Trachtenberg, can readily be drowned out in the contemporary culture of the "sound bite," rendering them apparently "silent," especially on critical issues. Trachtenberg's ideas are striking, thoughts from an insider's framework created to understand and address political correctness.

In the late 1980s, with the political correctness movement about a decade old, Trachtenberg presciently cautioned that "presidents need to keep their eyes and the eyes of their audiences fixed on the dangerous potential of a movement of this land some of whose caricatures are not altogether different from the scapegoating of the 1920s and '30s." Bearing in on what had been transpiring on campuses and was increasing in fervor and following, Trachtenberg argues: "[I]n short, today's president must be prepared to deal with a new ideological edge that has entered American discourse and may well intensify in the 1990s." With the likes of Alan Bloom, Bill Bennett, and a host of others in mind, Trachtenberg concludes that "In its beneficent guise, it is often called a 'search for values.' In its more ambivalent guise, it seems also to be a longing for authority and discipline."[4]

As Trachtenberg warned, critics of political correctness, yearning for authority and discipline, are convinced that rigid and conventional cultural standards are signal markers of previous eras to which they desperately desire to return. Events in the 1990s and especially in the early years of the twenty-first century produced more readily observable indicators of this pressure for greater authority and discipline. These include the responses of many American citizens and political leaders, including the White House, to September 11th, the agenda of the Religious Right, and the backlash against the cultural changes of the last four decades or so.

In the minds of many cultural and political critics, the academy is *the* hothouse incubating and promoting the worst problems of society. Thus campuses deserve to be targets of criticism, their policies and programs providing convincing evidence of the social disintegration they propagate and the political pandering they make commonplace.

Probing the dilemmas of political correctness, Trachtenberg reminds us of the post–World War II changes in the intersection of the university and society: "In the last half-century, we have become a nation of special interests. Everybody who's an advocate for almost anything tries to use everything they can to prevail. Larger advocacy groups are divided into multiple smaller groups, each with needs, wants, and wishes. I see it in the university, but frankly, the campus mirrors the nation as a whole." He believes the charges of political correctness extend beyond the usual special interest suspects of race and religion and—a reminder that these issues are by no means exclusively aimed at race, ethnicity, and multicultural and religious groups—academic specialties and other divisions in the academy. His list is a long one: "The faculty senate as a whole, the faculty of any one specific college or department; the student association as a whole, or the Black, Latino, Jewish, Arab or Native American students; those representing the physically challenged or hearing impaired; folks studying gender or race issues, life sciences or public health matters, whatever, will try to bend the will of the institution towards some agenda of their own."[5]

Trachtenberg's philosophy to deal with these complex and oppositional dynamics relies on a major theme, that of the university as a marketplace for ideas. "My individual agenda for the university has always been to try and keep it an open marketplace for all these various ideas, for formal and informal study," Trachtenberg argues. This means that "we have extended hospitality, as universities probably should, to all sorts of people—to those in front of the classroom and to those on the lecture circuit—to those with mainstream ideas and to those with fringe perspective—to people with long-standing reputations and to ones fighting to gain a foothold in legitimacy. Frankly, we hear from crackpots and geniuses, as each has their important moment of importance and/or notoriety." Although acknowledging personal politics that are probably slightly to the left of center, Trachtenberg believes that as leader "you cannot be the administrator of a large enterprise and be responsible for other people, while maintaining any sort of inflexible, didactic point of view—be it staunchly to the left or dramatically to the right."

Trachtenberg has seen it all from the leadership positions he has held: "In the '70s, I watched campuses erupt with antiwar fervor, civil rights concerns and the continuation of the Women's Movement. In the '80s, the national debt was out of control and financial aid worries colored admissions. Throughout the '90s, the focus was on the crisis in health care management and medical school, and today I fret over campus security, student housing, and international visas." However, through all the ebb and flow of different issues and emphases, his authoritative advice is that "regardless of whatever big-picture political and social issues are headlining the news, I cannot lose sight of keeping the school on an even keel. Management requires maintaining a steady course, with careful navigation even in troubled waters."

Finally, on the front of politics Trachtenberg knows well that college presidents face the problem that "if you allow some strong political statement to be uttered on the campus, you are going to have critics. Now some of these critics will be on the left—those wishing the university could, in a microcosm, take a stand and solve society's ills—and some critics are going to be from the right—those wishing the university to stay out of the fray, and *not* [his emphasis] take a stand on society's travails." Thus, as a president, "you will have to argue in defense of the First Amendment or academic freedom, even as you acknowledge that you disagree completely with the speaker and have strong opposing personal views on the issue of the day."

Keeping things on an "even keel," in "equilibrium," what Trachtenberg calls the "balance wheel" for an institution, is the primary responsibility of a president. He believes this historically important role takes on crucial contemporary meaning and value in any set of requirements of the presidential office and pulpit. This role must be played out in ways founded on respect for the passions that constitute the foundation of the free marketplace of ideas on a campus.

Trachtenberg's major argument and advice is in favor of the value of being able to lead from the middle of the road: "I have now spent 26 years as a university president constantly searching for equilibrium, and to some extent perceive myself as a *balance wheel* [italics mine] in an institution which has strong passions, made up of individuals who wish to steer it in any one of various worthwhile and even noble directions. And *my* [Trachtenberg's italics] passion," maybe the most important way for presidents to conceive the office, "is to allow all those passions to play out in the name of the healthier academic community, but also a healthier society in general."

The burden on presidents to navigate political correctness is great because their success (or lack thereof) is so public and dictates much about the shape of the academy and its culture. Is academia able to pursue its highest ideals? Will the university be able to remain a "marketplace of ideas"? Part of the current problem for both the Left and the Right is learning to put up with, tolerating, enduring if necessary the very passions about which Trachtenberg speaks. Couched at the very least in academic, intellectual, and scholarly garb, these passions are crucial to the vitality and fundamental being of the academy. Whatever the case, presidents simply have a lot of juggling to do in the face of ideologies and political correctness demands.

As president of the University of Pennsylvania, Judith Rodin faced a number of the polemical battles of the 1990s that Trachtenberg discusses. When she assumed office in fall 1993, the university was still battling against negative national press coverage of an incident during the preceding academic year that came to be known as the "Water Buffalo" episode.[6] The incident—a mix of interracial confrontation and controversy about whether the interaction involved free speech—fit the perfect criteria in the eyes of the media to be of major public interest, so they covered the story like a blanket. Media commentators, joined by a simultaneous deluge of attention from critics of political correctness, parodied Penn and Rodin's predecessor, Shelton Hackney. Fairly or not, Hackney had been tied to the establishment of Penn's speech code and its application in the case, both of which happened on his watch. Some accused Hackney of hiding behind the speech code rather than confronting the strong differences of opinion and campus divisiveness sparked by the episode.

On her way in the door, Rodin, displeased and disheartened that Penn was being publicly and in her mind unnecessarily pilloried, knew she needed to act quickly. She decided to alter the dynamic by addressing the question of the speech code. There was a great need to "restore a sense of community and a sense of dignity to the community, something that was quite fractured," and Rodin viewed the enduring aftermath of the "Water Buffalo" incident as a "teachable moment" for the community. "So I cancelled the speech code my first week as president and I said," summarizing her approach and outlining the new parameters for campus debate and conduct, "the best way to fight hated speech is more speech, so we are not going to suppress speech on this campus. We're going to try to define the boundaries of civic engagement. And so we're going to have to figure out how to become a community by engaging each other, by speaking honestly and freely, hopefully not hurtfully, but sometimes unintentionally wounding, and by bringing one another to the table so that we really can have robust discourse."[7]

In the context of the early 1990s, Rodin's position is emblematic of the turn away from reliance on speech codes as a solution to racial, ethnic, gender, and other conflicts born out of "difference." Her strategy, shared by many colleagues on other campuses, was wisely to argue for "more speech" as the antidote to hate or harmful speech. Rodin, like others, had serious concerns about these codes (the fact that they were implemented at all is both curious and an indication and reminder of how pressed by warring factions the leaders in the academy were during the 1980s and early 1990s). Questions about speech codes focused on their value, their practical application in disciplinary structures, and most importantly the many ways the codes were antithetical to the fundamental principles of the university.

Whether Rodin was a forerunner, she was certainly at the forefront with other presidents of shifting the debate and discussion away from speech codes by dismantling them.[8] The elimination or significant modification of the codes to fit within the broader framework of principles of the university created a revisionist position based on the practical realities encountered in applying those codes.

Rather than relying on codes and their inevitably unfair and arbitrary enforcement, these presidents who ushered in this revisionist position stressed that the academy had to put its faith where it belonged: in open debate and dialogue, as civilly conducted as possible.

Shortly after this incident, Penn experienced another multicultural controversy. A conservative magazine on the Penn campus made derogatory comments about the nation of Haiti and the Haitian people. Predictably, Haitian students at Penn demanded Rodin close down the magazine. She refused, asserting that free speech would not be stifled. Rather she challenged the students and the Penn community to answer what was written (which apparently likened Haitians to "witch doctors" and contained other less than kind comments) "with real knowledge and information and power. That's what universities are for. This is our distinct advantage, that we can always bring new knowledge and new information and new ideas and the power of ideas to the debate."[9] Rodin offered President's Office funds for a campus conference on Haiti. "Let's get experts from the State Department. Let's get people from the Haitian democratic movement on campus," she suggested, provoking a way of doing this right.

Also in response to this episode, Rodin created a program called "Penn Talks," a "program that seeks to keep the university community talking about even its toughest issues." It became a permanent fixture of her presidency and to this day a vehicle for the Penn community to handle controversies. Rodin used "Penn Talks" as a platform of her "bully pulpit" to keep topics and concerns in front of the Penn community and to provide her the platform to address "what the issues are and why we need to engage each other in this way."[10]

Capturing the way she faced the forces of political correctness, diversity, and ideology, Rodin rhetorically asks: "What are the civic tasks in which university communities must engage if they are to be real communities?"[11] Her answer to bridging the ideological divide is to "form communities of serious conversation around the most compelling issues of the day—issues like affirmative action, immigration, and health care. Where is the discussion of hot button, compelling social issues more likely to bear fruits than on our campuses? In doing so, we will offer our students valid experiences of active, engaged public discourse and civic involvement that may serve as life-long prototypes."

The goal in Rodin's mind is very clear. She believes campus communities must enfold a wide range of viewpoints in order to have civic discussion and engagement. When this happens, university communities are closer to generally affirmed principles of the academy—argument that considers a full span of ideas and perspectives in open inquiry, debate, and dialogue. As a result, exposure in and out of the classroom to these values at the core of the academy will more likely produce students who will be better citizens of society as a result of truly engaging others and defending their points of view, rather than being "unnaturally" protected by codes and behavioral norms artificially imposed by a politically correct climate.

Rodin defends her stand on speech codes by evoking the struggles of the civil rights movement about changing human attitudes and behavior through discourse versus legislation. By promoting civil public dialogue and exchange, "when discussions grow hot and ill-tempered, we will show that heat and anger can be handled." In the process, "we may also show we cannot legislate away bad behavior and incivility with codes, policies, and regulations....Campus speech codes and similar regulations were not able to reduce the level of intolerance or incivility," Rodin admits, "as we found so painfully at Penn, and they certainly will not moderate the ideological polarizations of our politics." The decision to abolish the speech code at Penn was made "because I believe that such measures fundamentally send the wrong message, a message that reinforces the sense of powerless individuals and of monolithic institutions, of cultural orthodoxy and paternalistic authority, and of ideological conformity and political correctness."[12]

The connection between and among the forces—cultural orthodoxy, ideologies, and political correctness—that presidents routinely face and must address could not be more plain and clear. Speech codes were a knee-jerk reaction of presidents and other administrative leaders to capitulate to pressure from those claiming to be victims of attacks and pronouncements from the Right. The problem, as Rodin points out, is that the codes were tied up in the political correctness dilemma. The codes contributed to an already "perfect storm" in which campus leaders were assailed as lacking the compass necessary to avoid caving in to special interests. Critics repeatedly used speech codes as evidence to judge college and university leaders as weak-kneed. Leaders associated with codes were vulnerable to charges that they employed a desperate solution, wittingly or unwittingly, and were guilty of sacrificing core values of the academy in order to quell "negative," unwanted speech and points of view.

Rodin's position signaled the opposite, that the president's and the "University administration's job...is to support such dialogue and debate, not to cut it off; to create an environment in which we can educate each other, not one in which doctrine or orthodoxy are legislated from on high." In her view, "[M]ust I provide 'moral leadership' to the Penn community? Absolutely. But moral leadership requires suasion not censorship, conscience not coercion. Most of all, it requires insisting that we—all of us—talk about what troubles us. Words are the life-blood of a university. For all their limitations," departing from the orthodoxy of speech codes, "even if they sometimes drive us apart, words are what bind us together in the academy."[13]

One "front" in these campus battles over free speech and freedom of expression has been the emergence of student publications, in most cases newspapers led by conservative students. The *Dartmouth Review* at Dartmouth College is a major example of this phenomenon (often bankrolled, as was the case at Dartmouth, by significant outside funding and other support). At Tufts, John DiBiaggio faced a similar conservative student newspaper, *Primary Source*, which was likewise regularly, and often to garner publicity, embroiled in recurrent controversies in the campus community as a result of its provocation of liberal students.

DiBiaggio attempted to be even-handed, at times actually defending the paper against critics. He believes a significant portion of the political correctness gulf and arguments on campus is a student-to-student issue, though he does not ignore the role and involvement of many other constituencies both on and off campus in these controversies. Despite his judgment that while the *Primary Source* students were at times "equally uncivil" in comparison to the behavior of their *Dartmouth Review* counterparts, DiBiaggio "would not intrude upon their prerogatives to express a very conservative view," choosing only to intervene "when I thought they had become so outrageous and personally vindictive towards, in particular, another student because students were somewhat defenseless."[14]

One occasion is instructive of the lengths to which students are capable of going in pursuing their agenda. Tufts learned that a student applicant to whom they had offered admission had been exposed by the press as having killed her mother, though she was not convicted of a crime because of a history of abuse she had suffered.[15] A couple of other prestigious colleges and universities had also accepted her. However, when her story became public, these schools, including Harvard, withdrew the acceptances. Before falling into a similar decision, DiBiaggio wanted Tufts to learn more. When he and his colleagues found her references and track record were unimpeachable, DiBiaggio declared that there is "a system of justice, and she has met the requirements" and therefore the acceptance should remain. The *Primary Source* editors reacted with dismay at the university's stand.

Like many colleges and universities, Tufts holds a public matriculation ceremony for incoming students. The student at the center of the controversy was, as a legitimate member of the freshmen class, to be in attendance. The staff of the newspaper "put posters all over the campus with a picture of me [DiBiaggio] and a picture of the admissions director that said 'Killers admitted.'" DiBiaggio continues: "The campus police called me and they said, 'What do we do?' I said, 'Wherever these are posted and we don't allow posting of anything, you may remove them. Everywhere else they must stay in place because this is a freedom of speech issue.'"[16] DiBiaggio clarified with his staff that while he certainly disagreed with the behavior of the newspaper staff, the posters, where posted legally, were not to be removed.

Believing that Tufts and DiBiaggio were being too politically correct (for which read too liberal, too lenient toward this entering student), the *Primary Source* wanted to use the public matriculation exercise to create an incident. Their critique was that the president should be a better guardian of the gates of the academy than to admit a student with such a blemished record. Likely they thought the *Primary Source* would receive a public relations boost even if this was accompanied by additional negative notoriety from the community, that is, they would be viewed as the true defenders of the academy, and if the university halted their public stirrings, they would become martyrs for free speech.

DiBiaggio reports that the "reaction, of course, was exactly the opposite of what the *Primary Source* wished. The students were livid with them. People went to this student's door and stuck notes saying, 'Welcome to Tufts. I'm ashamed of the behavior of some of our classmates.'" Self-effacingly DiBiaggio concludes: "I don't think I did anything extraordinary. I just did what I thought was right. But the other side of it is allowing for the expression of a view which I found terrible."[17] While his actions may not have been extraordinary, DiBiaggio avoided handing the student leaders of the *Primary Source* the bigger issue—infringement of their free speech and free expression, and certain martyrdom in some quarters—that they were certainly seeking and would have welcomed with open arms.

John Sexton of New York University takes up the political correctness debates and the ideological divide controversies in a major address, "The University as Sanctuary." The draft paper that formed the basis for this speech was eventually distributed to the NYU community as one of Sexton's periodic (he aims for twice a year) "think pieces" about the university, that is, NYU and universities generally, and other contemporary educational issues and concerns bearing on the academy.[18]

Invoking Judaeo-Christian and medieval notions about the physical and psychological "space" that defines the temple or the church (or any "holy" or sacred space, for that matter), he offers the provocative imagery of the university as a sanctuary. In Sexton's view, "increasingly, our great universities are modern sanctuaries, the sacred spaces sustaining and enhancing scholarship, creativity and learning." Sexton uses "the word sanctuary here not to signal detachment from the world, for our universities increasingly are in and of their surroundings; rather I use the term to signal both the specialness of what our great universities do, and the fragility of the environment in which it is done. What makes these sanctuaries special is the core commitment to free, unbridled and ideologically unconstrained discourse in which claims of knowledge are examined, confirmed, deepened or replaced." Sexton understands the burden that falls on presidents and other leaders—faculty and trustees along with others who guide these institutions—to protect the academy. "I emphasize the importance of acting aggressively and with every means at our disposal," describing his responsibility "to secure and protect every element essential to the general enterprise of free inquiry, the centrality of standards and the reciprocal commitments attendant to citizenship within the sanctuary.[19]

Painting the university as a "last best hope" of inspiring and rebuilding civic discourse for a civil society, Sexton knows the situation inside the gates of the academy is strongly affected by the society outside those gates (and certainly vice versa). The gravity of the situation is that "there is powerful evidence that the quality of dialogue in much of our society increasingly is impoverished— that, just when there is a need for more nuanced reflection and discussion, civil discourse seems ever less able to deliver it." "This environment imposes," Sexton contends, "an even greater responsibility on universities—always the best, and perhaps now the last best, venue for the full expression and development of ideas. We must live zealously the ideal as intellectual sanctuaries and sacred spaces where claims are tested, not only by objective measures but by informed and open debate."[20]

Sexton describes the challenge of maintaining the university as he believes it should be: "[I]t is ironic that at the time when sustaining the university as sanctuary is so important to society at large, society itself has unleashed forces which threaten the vitality if not the existence of that sacred space. Simply put, the polarization and oversimplification of civic discourse have been accompanied by a simultaneous attempt to capture the space inside the university for the external battle." Sexton judges both Left and Right: "This trend does not arise from one political side or another, but from a tendency to enlist the university not for its wisdom but for its symbolic value as a vehicle to ratify a received vision."[21]

The damage caused by politicization of the university, whether by the Left or the Right, is one of the major dilemmas facing American higher education. The underlying threats of this dilemma have to be taken seriously. While a long list of institutional needs are often practically connected to survival, Sexton views survival in different terms. He has a profound sense of what is happening as a result of political correctness and its impact on the heart of the academy. He believes the challenges presented by the political battles over the university and pushed into the "ivory tower" from without, and the battles fought within the university, are about nothing less than survival.

Conflicting sides in the ideological battleground have tried to push their particular cause célèbre into the center of the university, hoping to use the university to advance and promote their agendas. It is difficult, if not impossible, to know or make even an educated guess as to when and how the university evolved into an institution on the public auction block—"enlist[ing] the university not for its wisdom but for its symbolic value as a vehicle to ratify a received vision." Did this trend begin with the 1960s protests, with the 1970s and 1980s reaction and political correctness critiques, or with the contemporary, continuing iterations of these and other ideological battles? Or was this ideological backdrop present even in bygone eras characterized by more homogenous forces, for which read white Western and Christian males, who faced no oposition unimpeded in pursuing their agendas?

Regardless of the answers to the question of how long all this has been going on, concerned presidents, other college and university leaders, faculty, and other stakeholders today would arguably agree that the university has been pushed perilously close to, and in many cases has collapsed into, an institution that exists to "ratify a received vision." As with Trachtenberg's concern about an "ideological edge," whether in its "beneficent" or "ambivalent" guise, Sexton alerts us to the risks of allowing the vision of the university and its primary agenda to be shaped solely by external intellectuals, public figures (whether intellectual or not), and community pressure.

There are those on the left and the right in the academy and around it who view the university as a tool for a political, social, and cultural agenda. Sexton reacts with an echo of Minogue's dire warning: the university must be allowed to be the university, and if the university becomes just one other social institution, it is, by definition, no longer the university. In order to secure the future of the university—Sexton's urgent call—today's college and university leaders, presidents and their administrative, faculty, and trustee colleagues, must address this challenge.

Presidents also have self-interest in the outcome for it bears on the future of the office of president. They need to be primary architects in the reestablishment of a critical autonomy and independence, what Sexton labels "specialness," in the university. Presidents must work to protect the university from those bringing battles begun and better fought outside the university into its midst in an effort to gain an imprimatur for their positions.

This does not mean detachment from society. Pockets of the life of the university are of necessity removed and isolated from the commonweal. But most, probably the majority, of the university's purposes reflect society's needs and make contributions to it. Sexton acknowledges that "of course, the contest of ideas inside the university is not limited to issues of obvious public importance. Nonetheless, even if judged solely by its contribution to the progress of the commonweal, the traditional work of the university is a powerful generator of new responses to social concerns.... And at a time when the civil discourse is collapsing, it is necessary to assert for universities an additional and potentially pivotal role within civil society both as a powerful reproach to the culture of caricatured thought and as a model of nuanced conversation."

Adding thoughts about the university as sanctuary, Sexton suggests: "In this way, protecting the sacred space opens the university and its generation of ideas to an ever wider audience." Contrasting the difference between the ways the ideological divide and battleground is created and fought outside versus inside the gates of the academy, Sexton notes that "instead of the occasional invitation to an academic to have seven minutes on 'Crossfire,' the university can invite the public into a very different process for testing and shaping ideas."[22]

Turning from threats to the "sanctuary" of the university from outside the gates to those from inside, Sexton suggests that "there is a kernel of important truth captured in the popular political correctness debate—one that transcends political categories like left and right. Those who enjoy, in the civil sphere, certitude of viewpoint that is not open to change by reasoned argument are incapable of contributing or even participating in meaningful dialogue." Sexton maneuvers into the broad center, equally assailing ideologically hardened individuals (and groups) regardless of where they are on the political spectrum. "They cannot contribute because they treat their conclusions as matters of dogma and, therefore, expound their positions in declaratory form; they live in an Alice in Wonderland world—first the conclusion, then the conversation. They can incite discussion; they can even create an intellectual adrenaline rush; but they cannot produce insight," Sexton remarks. Connecting the political correctness problem to the ideological divide, he concludes: "[S]o also they cannot participate meaningfully in the dialogue, because they will not engage it; the exercise is a serial monologue in which they state and restate but never revisit or rethink their positions. *Thus, the kernel of truth in the political correctness debate: ideological conversation is of little or no value*" (italics mine).[23]

Whether from the Left or the Right, Sexton believes no true dialogue or dis-cussion—presumably hallmarks of the university—can take place when rigidly constructed and unchangeable positions are struck unyieldingly. Sexton is con-vinced that frequently both ends of the political spectrum are equally guilty of failure to present ideas in the forum of open debate demanded in the university.

This intractability toward addressing diversity and related politically charged issues in the academy creates major difficulties. One result is that "too many Americans—and in all honesty, too many experts and many academics—simply have not cultivated the talent of listening. One example is obvious: despite its extraordinary ethnic diversity, America is still largely an ethnocentric society; as a people we tend instinctively to devalue the wisdom, learning and possible contributions of 'the other.' The danger in academe is the development of a par-allel tendency not to listen with a generous ear to methodological, political or religious 'others,' just to name a few."[24]

Sexton's desire to grapple with the use of the presidential voice and the bully pulpit in today's ideological battleground on campus raises numerous questions. What are presidents to do in this polemical, often rigidly divided and divisive, positioning of people and their opinions? Should presidents weigh in on one side or another, and if so, when is it appropriate to do so? What type of courage (or is it merely foolhardiness?) is required when presidents publicly address issues in a politically correct minefield? If presidents remain on the sidelines, is this a sign that they are simply allowing campus discourse to sink to the lowest level? Is the smart course merely trusting that however things may play out, it is preferable (and politically astute and necessary) to enter the fray?

Sexton's response to this dilemma reflects a central point in our problematic: presidents today exert maximum courage and moral leadership first by being Trachtenberg's "balance wheel" for their colleges and universities. Comparing contemporary presidents to "giants," such as Eliot, of previous eras, Sexton admits that "to be sure, university leaders now tend to be more cautious in making pub-lic pronouncements—and perhaps not always for the best reasons. Our caution certainly does not arise," he humorously adds, "from lack of encouragement: for example, in just two years as the NYU's President, I have been urged to take public stances on everything from third world debt to whether the Knicks should have fired Don Chaney."[25]

Speaking of his bully pulpit, Sexton has "chosen a path quite different from Eliot's, and I have done so as a matter of deep and sometimes difficult principle—a principle that arises from my belief that the paramount and superceding duty of the president is to safeguard the fragile sanctuary for dialogue within the uni-versity." In order to perform this task "it is essential for the university's leader to refrain generally from expressing views publicly on any issue that is not centrally related to the core mission of the institution; to do otherwise would compromise the moral authority of the presidency in the forum and undermine the credibility of the leader's commitment to the role as guardian of that dialogic space."[26] The university president, in Sexton's view, guards the academy as a sanctuary and this allows the academy to be the place it is created and designed to be. That is a place permitting, even encouraging, broad intellectual, academic, and scholarly exploration of a limitless set of ideas by an equally limitless number of individuals. To protect the sanctuary of the university, presidents must exert the force of a balance wheel.

Rob Oden at Carleton College embodies the Trachtenberg-Sexton spectrum of advice to avoid taking sides when and if at all possible, and thus to provide balance and equilibrium. Commenting about maintaining the essential core of the college and heeding Minogue's warning about the fortunes of the university or college if they simply cave in to political and ideological pressures, Oden cites his presidential actions concerning the 2003 Iraq War. This was a "hot," divisive issue and he put a personal stamp on a way for the academy to handle the war issue educationally.

In the winter of the run-up to the war, Oden wrote an editorial in the campus newspaper about why the college should not take a position on Iraq. His argument was that if the college did so, the result would be to reduce its stature as an academic institution and violate the integrity of campus discourse. Second, Oden suggests, a president may choose to serve as *agent provocateur*. He comments that "one of my roles I have seen as a president is, whenever I see too many right-wing or left-wing speakers, or too much opinion only on one side of the position, whether I believe in it or not, to take the other." In this case, Oden continues, "I gave several dormitory talks last winter on the reasons *for* going into Iraq. I didn't think people were hearing enough of those [other views], and whether one agrees or not, it is not irrational madness. There were some intelligent and sensitive [commentators], think of Tom Friedman [of the *New York Times*].... I didn't think there were enough speakers either on or off campus saying to people there are some good reasons for contemplating this, so I saw it as my own role [especially] knowing something about the Middle East."[27] Rather than taking sides on behalf of Carleton, Oden provides balance in the interest of furthering dialogue and debate.

Oden's label for providing balance, equilibrium, and a keel for campuses is to lead from "the messy middle." He recalls a faculty member's comment at Kenyon College that "the reason you've been able to navigate the ideological boundaries or waters or storms at Kenyon is that you are yourself not an ideologue." Adding characteristics to this capacity, Oden argues that presidents should possess "a reasonable, tolerant, broad-minded, ecumenical makeup.... That is, I have spent enough time seeing the strengths and the weaknesses of ideological positions that I don't quite go there myself. I'm probably talking about fundamentalisms." Characterizing the barriers to dialogue in the university and college, Oden concludes that those driven by these "fundamentalisms" "by definition absent themselves from compromise, they absent themselves from subtlety, they absent themselves from complexity."[28]

Reflecting on the difficulties of being moderate, operating in the center of ideas and discourse, Oden adds: "The problem with mainstream liberalism, which is where I am politically, is that it's harder to defend at either end because it's so full of compromise and subtlety, and the richness and messiness of everyday life. You stand up and defend hard-core conservatism or the far left wing," speaking about the far ends of the political spectrum, "and you've got sort of certainty and clarity on your side." The creative, yet difficult course Oden suggests is "to defend the *messy middle* [italics mine]; that's a little harder. But the messy middle is, in fact where most of life happens and should happen. So, I'm in many ways in the messy middle in my own convictions."[29]

While it is important for presidents to maintain impartiality, they also must, as Sexton points out, have a nuanced view of the "whether and when to speak." Impartiality, steering in the middle, and being less outspoken than the Charles Eliot "giants" are romantically thought to have been does not mean that "university leaders must be silent on all issues. There are times where they have the right—indeed the duty—to speak."

Outlining the specifics of the president's responsibility to speak, Sexton asserts that "the clearest instances involve such issues as the role of universities in liberal democracies, access to education, the impact of government decisions on higher education, and the contours of financial aide and admissions policies. On such issues," Sexton argues, presidents should "advance a view of what is best for the university, and should be willing to defend that view openly and promote it vigorously in the public arena." Concerning the presidential pulpit and the burden of insuring that the university is allowed to be the university, Sexton concludes that "university presidents are, after all, the leaders of a certain kind of institution with a specific and important role within our culture, and they constantly should be articulating their thoughts on the role and viability of their institutions and subjecting their views to scrutiny and the standards of evidence that are themselves the ground of the university's being."[30]

Philosophically, Oden and Sexton define important presidential territory for the use of the bully pulpit. But can these ideals hold up in the real and practical world of the presidential office?

Like most presidents, Mary Sue Coleman faces the tugs and pressures created by constituencies, and she advocates pushing the university to take public positions on political, frequently politically loaded issues of the day. She begins with the assumption that presidents must affirm that the university has "moral authority." This clout, still respected, despite ebbs and flows in public perception about the position of the university in society, is ironically what makes the academy an attractive vehicle for delivering politically weighted arguments and positions.

To Coleman the starting point for university decision making on major issues is the assumption that the "university is going to change things. That carries enormous weight in this society, so it's very, very important for the university to figure out what these core principles are and not get themselves supporting one cause over another."[31] As an example, Coleman cites petitions presented by Palestinian students and their supporters pressing Michigan to divest from Israel and companies investing in Israel. The precedent the students used was the South Africa divestment position taken by Michigan and many other colleges and universities in the 1980s and 1990s.

When she met with the students, Coleman's stance was that "we decided at one point in our history to divest in South Africa. We did it." But the way Michigan got there is Coleman's key idea: "We went through a process where we had extended and comprehensive discussions on the plans over and over and over again, and," adding a defining element, "we had overwhelming support that it was morally [the] right thing to do because of the oppression of apartheid in South Africa."[32]

The South African divestment decision, enormously difficult and for many colleges and universities quite divisive, was made at Michigan according to Coleman on the basis of a final consensus that this stand was a "moral right." "That meant a core principle," for the university to identify and about which to reach a consensus that, though "it took a long time, in the end, we had worked toward building."

For Coleman, this current demand to divest from Israel does not meet the same criteria as those established by the university's South Africa divestment decision. The precedent established by the regents and the university provides a substantive rationale for responding to advocates and proposals for institutional divestment stands. Coleman as president and Michigan as an institution have a standard to guide decisions about always sensitive demands to use corporate divestment as a lever to make political statements. For her pulpit, Coleman believes a position grounded in some principle-based criteria provides some protection from "people who want to drag us one direction and drag us another direction."[33]

Nan Keohane weighs in on this approach that the university needs an institutionally agreed upon, preferably in advance, set of principles to provide wisdom and criteria for the discussion of divestment controversies. She proposed that the Duke University trustees adopt a "social responsibility policy."[34] Keohane's prediction is that if the university is not prepared, then requests for divestment and related financial pressure born out of social action and conscience "are going to become more and more common in the years ahead of us, that we're entering a new era of social activism, and the university needs to have a procedure to deal with it."

The dilemma and reality for presidents, as she sees it, is that when groups passionately advocate that the institution take a stand using its financial leverage, the response is "'that the president doesn't think it's a good idea' isn't going to be the right answer for them." In the absence of an institutional policy at Duke, Keohane employed this approach, able to say to these groups—three or four in the preceding year alone—that "I don't think the issue that they're talking about rises to the level where divestment is appropriate, because I think it's a very unusual situation where that becomes relevant," alluding to the fact that this threshold had been reached in the South African divestment controversies. Even though the groups getting this response "may not like that answer, they can accept it." However, Keohane has been around the presidential leadership barn long enough to know that "I don't think that's the right answer forever." The better course is to have the ethical grounding required in such decisions based on more deliberative thought about grander principles and moral agency than simply the "president thinks it is this way."[35]

These tense, often volatile, campus situations sharply focus the scrutiny of presidential leadership concerning the preservation of free speech and expression and of the core values of the academy when facing the tangled pressures of political correctness and battles among competing ideologies. Two major features emerge, though others are certainly intertwined.

One is reliance on the rationality of campus community members to thrash out differences. Students can behave badly and, as we saw earlier in the Tufts example, act well beyond the bounds of civility in pursuing their aims. But they are also capable of responding in civil and humane ways, as DiBiaggio notes was the case when Tufts students reached out to their peer who had been assailed by the *Primary Source* newspaper staff. Likewise, Oden's actions rely on the fundamental rationality of a campus community able to wend its way through issues and controversies. Without a presumption of rational discourse, it would be difficult for Oden or any president to provoke discussion and to present sides of an issue that otherwise would be ignored.

A second asset presidents and other campus leaders have is to enlist and to utilize faculty leadership in navigating these politically loaded and "correct" situations. In these controversies, as we will see more fully in a moment, faculty are able to do what they do best, especially in the face of hot-button and passionate topics whether sparked on or off campus: provide academically and scholarly grounded information and content, and stimulate rational, insightful, and civil discourse.

To some this would appear to be an obvious direction in which to turn. However, professors are often missing in action on the front of political, social, and cultural controversies. Faculty members are busy and they wisely view these problems as lose-lose propositions, ones that intelligent and rational people normally wish to avoid. In addition, faculty reticence is ironically due in part to the silencing effect of political correctness. This pressure is especially influential on junior untenured faculty, and on adjuncts and lecturers who enjoy none of the security of their tenured colleagues. Despite these roadblocks and disincentives, presidents can and ought to press faculty members to assume more central roles in these politically correct and ideologically driven controversies.

With these glimpses and snapshots, we turn to two more in-depth case examples of presidential leadership in today's politically correct university environment.

Late in Derek Bok's presidency at Harvard, an incident over politically charged symbols erupted, testing the institution's ideas of free speech and free expression, and its policies and disciplinary codes governing behavior.[36] The episode began when a student hung a large Confederate flag from a Harvard House residence window. Not surprisingly, and as could be expected, a group of black students immediately went to the dean (at the time the late Archie Epps) and argued that the "administration" should order the student to remove the flag. The administration response, it appears directed by Bok, was that they would not order or even request the flag be taken down (apparently no specific policy existed governing this one way or another). Rather the administration urged the complaining students to attempt civil discussion with those who were displaying the Confederate flag and to argue their case for its removal.

Instead the black students elected to fly a Nazi swastika from another dorm window. Equally unsurprisingly and as the act was designed to provoke, a group of Jewish students went to the administration and demanded that the black students be ordered to remove their swastika. Again, the administration refused to take action and as previously, suggested the Jewish students engage their black peers about their flag and its offensiveness and get them to remove it.

Interestingly this was the end of the story. In about three days, both flags were taken down and not another word about the incident was spoken. Rather than taking major institutional and likely disciplinary action, Bok and the Harvard administration chose to let this potentially incendiary incident be worked out with less fanfare and media frenzy by forcing a resort to dialogue among students and other members of the Harvard community. DiBiaggio treated the *Primary Source* students at Tufts respectfully as long as they were reasonably responsible, and thus avoided the potential traps in his response to their leafleting campaign, and Bok likewise acted in a manner that avoided making the flag episode into the larger cause célèbre it could easily have become.

As Bok's successor, Rudenstine wholeheartedly supports and agrees with the actions in the Harvard flag episode. He believes it was handled "just right in the way I would do it." Rudenstine claims these moments challenge presidents and other academic leaders "to be able to stand strongly for the capacity on a university campus for people to express their views as long as they don't directly threaten other individuals or [they] really do threaten in a fairly demonstrable way the security or order of the institution." This means enduring possible "hate" speech, distasteful demonstrations like those involving the Confederate and Nazi symbols, and providing students and others on campus "a lot of latitude to express whatever views they want to express."[37]

Rudenstine adds the qualifier that members of a community left primarily to their own devices are best able to resolve conflict, especially when they understand that a voice of authority will not prematurely intervene to solve the problem. Rudenstine also notes the important and easily overlooked point that in any community confrontation, there are bystanders who are equally affected and who can be part of the "solution." Universities are the "kind of community where symbols mean something and there are other people, not only minorities, but nonminority people who see that as more than just a flag hanging out the window but as a directly and determinably, deliberately disrespectful, and to some extent, intimidating thing." Thus the smart institutional response concerning the flag is that "you can keep it up, but let's have some discussion inside the House about what the values really are. Let's talk this out so people understand as well as they can the other viewpoints and see if we can't come to some sort of understanding." However, while this is the responsible approach, "it would be equally irresponsible not to say that in a university community that is deliberately diverse this is going to be and is known to be offensive in a fairly strong way to some people who are part of the community. And that's not good for a community over time."[38]

Thus Rudenstine would not make something like flying the flag "impermissible," but questions "whether it's doing anybody any good" and is concerned about the effect of the action on the ways "you can get along together civilly or not." As president, Rudenstine concludes that "you're going to defend the student who got the flag up, but you're going to see whether you can use it as an event that can be educative in the institution." He also recognizes the critical matter of the development of college students and their educational and growth process, a reality from which presidents easily detach themselves, "remembering always that these are kids who are only 19, 18, 20, 21 years old and are still figuring things out."[39]

Rudenstine's administration addressed two other major free speech controversies, each significant given the issues, the players, and their public visibility. These controversies exemplify the strategic utilization of faculty as a resource in addressing tense confrontations.

In 1997 Jiang Zemin, then president of the People's Republic of China, agreed to speak publicly at Harvard while on a trip to the United States.[40] Rudenstine reports that complications began with a "quite a complex set of negotiations because we were told by the Chinese ambassador to the United States that the president would not take questions." The problem was that "it's absolutely a firm tradition at Harvard that if someone is going to be allowed the podium to say what he or she wants to say," and in the spirit of the academy, "then they're going to stand for questions afterward." In response to the constraints Zemin's staff attempted to put in place, Rudenstine and Harvard countered that "we can understand that. But I think he has to understand that we have a strong tradition and that unless he would be interested in answering questions and helping to educate our students, we're not sure it's really the right thing for him to come and talk."

Harvard was able to take such a stand largely because of its power and influence. However, Rudenstine believes that more than that, it was Harvard's principles and traditions that enabled him to lay out a clear university position. "We didn't want to say he can't talk, but we wanted to give him a chance to sort of figure it out. And the message came back that yes, he would answer questions." However, this is only the beginning of the tale.

With Zemin finally agreeing to appear at Harvard, and as the required logistics were being delicately worked out, students began mapping protests against the visit on grounds of what they believed Zemin stood for, especially China's perceived repressive policies concerning dissenters and relations with Tibet. As negotiations settled the format issues for Zemin's appearance, the question for Rudenstine and his administration became "whether we could do it peacefully and securely and whether there would be or would not be disruption."[41] According to his account, there were potentially thousands of students on both sides: "Yes," Zemin should come and we want to hear him, and "No," we don't want Zemin to appear and if he does we are going to protest in ways he will be aware of.

Complications multiplied over the twin needs to ensure that the speech would be logistically handled safely and securely and to maintain Harvard's tradition of open discourse with speakers. This is where the Harvard faculty came to the rescue. Rudenstine reports that "for about three weeks before the speech the East Asian faculty plus many, many other faculty began a series of lectures, evening discussions, and teach-ins to say why this should happen and how people should think about this event and how important it was and what things were wrong with China as far as we could tell, but what things were important to try to culti-vate and advance." This use of faculty scholarship and intellectual inquiry, joined with the respect faculty enjoy among students, in preparation for Zemin's visit to campus "made a huge difference."[42]

As a result of this activity, Rudenstine believes many students and faculty shifted or modified previously embedded, strongly held positions. This set the stage for Harvard to be able to organize "free speech 'protests' on both sides in such a way that they would be visible, they would be loud." The Chinese ambassador handling Zemin's arrangements was concerned about visible and loud protests, dutifully looking to protect Zemin from seeing or hearing them. Though the loca-tion of the speech was soundproofed as far as possible, Rudenstine indicates, with a bit of Harvard chutzpah, that the ambassador was told, "We're awfully sorry, but there are going to be visible protests, but they won't intrude in any way on the evening in terms of breaking it up."

The speech came off well, not quite an anticlimax. But Rudenstine underscores the larger message that it was a "successful event in terms of what the university stood for, which was, 'Here's someone who a lot of people don't like for very good reasons. And other people felt, here's somebody who's very important from a great country with a great civilization who should be heard. And he can learn from us and vice versa.'" The bottom line and rhetorical question is simple: "How do you educate the community to get to the point where they see that the value to pre-serve is that one and that it can be preserved without obliterating other people's determination to [protest] as long as they did it within certain bounds."[43]

A second incident at Harvard while Rudenstine was at the helm concerned the tensions between student supporters of Israel and of the Palestinian cause when one of many cycles of violence in the Middle East erupted. Because of its international profile and drawing power, Harvard has both an enormous number of Arab students (Americans, new immigrants, and those on student visas) and an equally large number of Jewish students, including those from Israel, who are the most highly supportive of Israel.

The two opposing sides began organizing protest rallies to be held simulta-neously in Harvard Yard. Rudenstine, knowing that sparks might fly between them, had administrative staff begin calling "faculty members who were really responsible, thoughtful, and admired, respected faculty members," who were from

Egypt, Jordan, Israel, and other parts of the Middle East. The idea was to get them "into the Yard" where the University Security Force had placed "the two rallies on different sides of Harvard Yard and made it possible for them all to say what they wanted to say."[44] Rudenstine deployed the faculty members to the Yard, where they shuttled "back and forth between the two groups telling them to understand the fact the other people have a [different] point of view." After the day of the rallies, Rudenstine and his administrative and faculty leadership stimulated discussions in the Harvard Houses, sending these leaders and other professors to participate in further conversations with students.

While Rudenstine acknowledges that tensions remained, at least no violence or major threats occurred, an outcome that prior to the rallies was not at all certain. Reflecting on such situations, he concludes that "you can maintain speech and you don't have to choose sides between the Palestinians and the Israelis. Some people wish you would choose sides, but you better remember that's not what your job is as a president. And that also gets into another...more complicated and subtle thing: what sorts of things should the president speak out on and why and when?"[45] This central question remains and it is one presidents have to resolve in using their bully pulpits. Their take on it inevitably says much about them as leaders and about the authority of their office.

At Michigan, Coleman faced nearly identical passions and tensions, embedded in the Israeli-Palestinian conflict that was played out globally and on nearly all campuses. Upon arriving in Ann Arbor in summer 2002, Coleman immediately had to get up to speed and begin to make critical decisions about a planned annual intercollegiate conference on the Palestinian question, more properly according to her a "Palestinian solidarity conference," to be hosted by Michigan that fall.

The previous year's conference had been hosted at Berkeley only weeks after September 11th, so tensions between these groups and the conference participants were even higher and more pronounced than usual. During these meetings, near-physical confrontations occurred and some Jewish delegates registered for the entire conference were refused access to some of the sessions. The very real fear at Michigan and among Coleman's staff and in the community was that the animus of the previous year would carry over to the event on their campus.

Coleman and the leaders at Michigan heard rumors that conference organizers might again undertake to restrict access and participation or might be pressured by delegates to use similar tactics during the Michigan meetings. Because of the planning that was necessary and the public visibility of the conference on the university's events calendar, the buildup in the preceding months "caused enormous consternation both inside and outside the university."

Growing outside pressure was urging Michigan to back out of hosting the conference, a step that would likely lead to the conference being cancelled altogether. The university's high public profile and its connections with constituencies with stakes pro and con made for an extraordinarily complex situation. Coleman and Michigan faced a microcosm of today's complicated and geopolitical world with its characteristic instantaneous communications. "We had a very large Jewish population on campus. We had a large Jewish alumni group. We have the largest Arab American population here in Dearborn than almost anywhere in the United States, and we have many Arab American students on campus. And so we had this clash of forces in the way that I think most other places wouldn't have had," Coleman almost casually remarks.[46]

A standard response to this pressure normally would be that "'we have to say we have the principle of free speech no matter what.' But this was an unusual circumstance because of the notion of terrorism and how you manage that?"[47] Thus the question of principle Coleman faced was, "How do you try to keep a space within the university for people to talk about ideas, even if they're very unpopular ideas. How do you provide that?" While from a safety standpoint the institution had to avoid creating an "environment where violence can take place," Coleman had to ensure the event could proceed, but in a way that upheld, or at least did not dramatically violate, core principles of the university.

As Coleman and colleagues planned for the event, they made clear that any banning of people from all or parts of the conference as had happened at Berkeley would not be permitted at Michigan.[48] Aware of the tensions on campus in anticipation of the event, Coleman "kept the lines of communication open." "I met with the Arab community, I met with the Jewish community, and I met with everybody I could possibly meet with to give them a chance to vent to me," the intent being "that everybody understood they were being heard through this process." Even with this intense preparation "it was very difficult because we clearly were worried about the possibility that someone would get out of hand."

As happened at Harvard, faculty members came forward to join the administrative preparations in the months and weeks prior to the conference. The faculty group sought to offer ways in which they might educate students about the issues, thereby injecting more content into the debate. The modest goal was to get Michigan students at least to grasp some of the greater complexities and to engage in the style of dialogue that would be critical during the conference itself. Though not easy or simple, the basic goal was to try "to find ways, and our faculty were trying to find ways to talk about religious strife, cultural strife in a way that wouldn't focus it on the Middle East, that would not focus on the Israeli-Palestine question because the notion of the faculty—and it's correct, I think—is that the camps are so invested in their own suffering that they cannot listen. They don't even listen to each other."

Elaborating on the educational thinking she and her faculty colleagues engaged in—a most important deliberation in the academy at a time such as this—Coleman adds that "we tried to figure out ways to take it out of that context, to talk about it in other settings, other countries, other points of history, other eras, so that we could bring students to engage these issues without having to confront something that is uncomfortable for them right now in that point of history." Coleman's sense about the Michigan faculty's investment is simple and direct: "I thought that [the] care and concern on the part of the faculty was quite interesting to me and quite unique in my experience."[49]

While all this was going on both behind the scenes and in public discourse, Coleman made clear her and the university's position in a letter to the campus community. She contends that especially during times "[w]hen matters of intense emotional impact are presented on campus, it is vital that we uphold two cherished values upon which our academic community depends." Addressing the matter of how presidencies and their pulpits are best grounded in "first" principles of the academy, Coleman claims that "one is the right to explore and debate the widest possible range of ideas, even if those ideas are offensive or repugnant to some members of the community. Candid expression and open debate are intrinsic to academic freedom. We afford that freedom both to those who organize and participate in this conference, and to those who disagree with the views thus presented." The other "cherished value," Coleman cites "is the respect we owe to each other as human beings and as fellow members of this academic community. We constantly strive to build a community that is welcoming to all and that does not foster hatred and discrimination. It is especially important during difficult times and when dealing with divisive topics that we extend to one another the highest levels of tolerance and mutual respect."[50]

Coleman at Michigan and Rudenstine at Harvard draw a crucially important though at times fine and fragile line in steering the course of decisions and actions in these episodes. President Keohane of Duke captures the essence of the lived-out mission of the academy evident in these examples and provides additional thoughts about the foundation for the public stands of universities.

Though society may not always agree with the academy's positions, there are points of a general mutual self-interest. Nannerl Keohane declares that society cannot become so shortsighted as to fail in maintaining an essential understanding of the academy's indispensable role. Providing a broad framework within which higher education institutions should function, she contends that "both public and private universities, if their boards and faculties and administrative leaders have the courage of their convictions, can serve the public by allowing truth to be pursued wherever it may lead, even though it sometimes leads in directions that are, at least initially, unpopular and even unsavory," including ideas and interests that citizens might rather not acknowledge. "Those of us in the university world are convinced, on very good historical evidence, that providing a safe haven for the pursuit of truth is an extremely important public purpose, even if few members of the public may see how they stand to benefit," Keohane concludes, acknowledging the necessity of connecting in the public mind the university's value and benefit.[51]

Finally, with a touch of irony but espousing one truth of the American "experiment" in higher education—the way the nation, its citizens, and its governing structures and bodies relate to colleges and universities—Keohane identifies the covenant between society and the academy to permit freedom of inquiry. Citing Louis Menand's *The Metaphysical Club*, Keohane argues that "the remarkable thing is that American society basically bought this deal and has lived by it, even with some grumbling or incomprehension along the way. We may devoutly hope that this will continue to be true, despite some warning signs on the horizon," making clear the necessity that "we should all be vigilant in protecting this important covenant between society and academia."[52]

In contrast to previous eras in which there were tangible and pressing tensions between and among students and other members of campus communities, today's campuses witness an ever-greater proliferation of numerous large communities and subgroups (and as Trachtenberg highlights, subgroups of subgroups) that reflect an expanding range of diversity. The perceived "middle" is an increasingly smaller proportion of the whole, thus making it all the more difficult for presidents to locate an agreed-upon center. The task of convincing different ideological camps that there is some common ground, some joint, shared, universal, and historically important values with which diverse groups and individuals may be able to identify, is an enormous challenge.

President Keohane captures this reality, comparing the generations of college presidents: "I do think there are some things that are different [now]. It seems to me that we are more likely to consider ourselves having some responsibility to the diverse constituencies that comprise our institution. Since universities were less diverse in the past, people might have felt less compulsion about speaking as though they were able to reflect everyone's sentiments when they were speaking from a fairly homogeneous range." Keohane explains that "it would be odd for a thoughtful president these days not to recognize the wide diversity of opinions and views and moral commitments on the part of people in the university, and to speak as if you could just ignore all of those." Does it complicate things? Certainly "it complicates things, but it also is a richer field in which to think. It allows you to be more mindful of complexities instead of assuming that the world is relatively simple, which it isn't."[53]

In the last two chapters we have examined the broad philosophical grounding and cases of presidents and their leadership of campuses regarding three complex and complicated issues. The first concerns the varieties of diversity and related cultural, racial, ethnic, and religious passions and tensions on campus. The second concerns the characteristics of the ensuing political correctness assaults on the academy, both the deserved critiques of foolish policies and stands antithetical to the principles of the academy, and those concocted and fabricated as ploys for public consumption and play. Finally, we have seen the very closely connected ideological framework and battleground of the contemporary life of colleges and universities and its large and enlarging demand on presidents. Against this background we turn to the challenge confronting presidents to find the center, to see if Yeats's "center" can hold, to be Trachtenberg's "balance wheel," and to work in Oden's "messy middle."

NOTES

1. Among the institutions at which the battles began and the term "political correctness" was used early on was Dartmouth College, with the founding of an independent, off-campus student newspaper, the *Dartmouth Review*. For definitions and further discussion

of the label and its origins, see Bill Lind, "The Origins of Political Correctness," speech given at the Accuracy in Academia Conference, 2000, http://www.academia.org/lectures/lind1.html. For a conservative view and definition, see *Wikipedia: The Free Encyclopedia*, http://en.wikipedia.org/wiki/Politically_correct.

2. Kennedy, *The Last of Your Springs*, pp. 78–79.

3. Richard J. Herrnstein and Charles Murray, *The Bell Curve: Intelligence and Class Structure in American Life*, New York: Free Press Paperbacks, 1994.

4. Stephen Joel Trachtenberg, "Presidents Can Establish a Moral Tone on Campus," *Educational Record* 70, no. 2 (Spring 1989): p. 9.

5. Stephen Joel Trachtenberg, president, George Washington University, interview by author, May 7, 2003. The material that follows is excerpted from this interview.

6. In this episode a male student yelled to two students who, he felt, were being too loud outside his residence hall something to the effect of "Shut up, you Water Buffaloes." The two students were minority students and took the comment as a racial epithet. Penn's existing speech code was enforced as a policy to discipline the student who uttered the phrase.

7. Judith Rodin, former president, University of Pennsylvania, interview by author, August 16, 2004.

8. For example, George Rupp in his inaugural address at Columbia University, October 4, 2003, dedicated a significant portion of his speech to a series of fundamental principles for the university community, focusing on free expression and free speech concerns. This was about the same time that Rodin was taking over the helm at Penn and taking these steps regarding the Penn speech code; thus conjecture might conclude that the two were aware of each other's positions and may actually have been in contact. For a detailed description of Rupp's address and approach, see Nelson, *Leaders in the Crucible*, pp. 92–94. Ironically, also in fall 1993, as Diana Chapman Walsh was in the first months of her presidency at Wellesley College she had to confront the furor over a book published by a college professor, Tony Martin, lashing back at what he believed to be racist comments made to him over a connection he had drawn in a course, through lectures and course readings, between Jews and the slave trade. This also became a question as to whether Martin should be able to exercise free speech or whether he should be sanctioned in some manner. Walsh navigated this crisis in a manner similar to Rupp's and Rodin's approach: she censured Martin for ad hominem attacks on his attackers, but refused to censor him, on the basis that however poorly he did it, he had a right to free speech. For a detailed account of the "Martin Affair," see also Nelson, *Leaders in the Crucible*, pp. 97–100.

9. Judith Rodin, interview by author.

10. Ibid.

11. Judith Rodin, "The University and Civil Society," October 12, 1999, http://www.upenn.edu/president/rodin/civil_society.html, p. 7.

12. Ibid.

13. Ibid.

14. John DiBiaggio, former president, Tufts University, interview by author, August 12, 2003.

15. The young woman had moved from her original home to the Massachusetts area, and when a magazine featured her and the contributions she had made to the community as a high school student, someone recognized her as the individual who had killed her mother and went to the press with the information, which subsequently became public.

Technically she received a punishment from the judge, which she fulfilled, but it was not a conviction for a crime, given the extenuating circumstances.

16. John DiBiaggio, interview by author. He further indicates that the posters were put on the seats at the matriculation ceremony.

17. Ibid.

18. John Sexton, "The University as Sanctuary," draft of paper provided by the President's Office, New York University. Also delivered in part as a speech, "The University as Sanctuary," February 17, 2004, at Fordham University. The notes that follow are taken variously from each version and will be cited accordingly.

19. Sexton, "The University as Sanctuary," draft of paper provided by the President's Office, New York University, pp. 3–4.

20. Sexton, "The University as Sanctuary," February 17, 2004, delivered at Fordham University, p. 5.

21. Ibid.

22. Sexton, "The University as Sanctuary," draft of paper provided by the President's Office, New York University, pp. 6–7.

23. Ibid., pp. 14–15.

24. Ibid., pp. 15–16.

25. Ibid., p. 17. It is also worth pointing out that Sexton has a PhD in comparative religion and did his doctoral dissertation on the Harvard president, Charles Eliot.

26. Ibid. A former president of Amherst College, Thomas Gerety, makes an almost identical point that presidents' "personal views need to take second place to those views which should be associated with approval and with general support across the constituencies as the views of the institution," and that presidential utterances "ought in principle to be compatible with the widest possible range of opinions and views on the campus." Quoted in Nelson, *Leaders in the Crucible*, p. 20 and p. 33, n. 4.

27. Robert Oden, president, Carleton College, interview by author, August 26, 2003.

28. Ibid.

29. Ibid.

30. Sexton, "The University as Sanctuary," draft of paper provided by the President's Office, New York University, p. 20.

31. Mary Sue Coleman, president, University of Michigan, interview by author, July 23, 2003.

32. Ibid.

33. Ibid.

34. Nannerl Keohane, president, Duke University, interview by author, June 2, 2003. At the time she had not yet succeeded in getting her board to adopt such a policy.

35. Ibid. Keohane elaborates on the criteria issue: "I've shown the differences between the Sudan, Israel, military weapons, and the South Africa case in terms of the amount of data that was collected, the amount of evidence that divestment might matter through something like the Sullivan Principles, the long period we went through before we finally reached the divestment issue by trying other means. And I've said none of that has happened in this situation, so divestment is, at best, premature."

36. The material that follows is from the author's memory of the events, confirmed by insights added by Neil Rudenstine, successor to Bok as president of Harvard. Rudenstine, former president of Harvard University, interview by author, April 10, 2003. It also bears noting that in the interview, in his broad treatment of matters of political correctness

and ideology, Rudenstine indicated his preference and style as being proactive, especially with alumni and other groups close to the university, about his views, by implication thus indicating how he was guiding and leading the institution. His approach "on so-called political correctness, hate speech, diversity, tuition increases, a whole variety of those issues," was to raise these issues, indicating, "Well, I know a lot of you have this on your minds. Let's talk about fees at the university and why is it so expensive and is there some way to make it different or not and what is our rationale, et cetera. Or let's talk about race in admissions or are we all terribly relativists or not and what are the values that actually do bind us in a university." In addition to digging for the core values of Harvard and of the university on which they could find agreement, his feeling is that on balance "people were sort of relieved that I would bring it up rather than leaving it to them to actually bring up and, second," in a marvelous preemptive strategy, as ever in Rudenstine's style of reliance on rational discussion, "you could then actually count—because you had brought it up—on more thoughtful conversation than if it had been brought up antagonistically."

37. Ibid.
38. Ibid.
39. Ibid.
40. Ibid. The story that follows is taken from Rudenstine's account.
41. Ibid.
42. Ibid.
43. Ibid.
44. Ibid.
45. Ibid.
46. Mary Sue Coleman, interview with author. She comments that there were "thousands, thousands, thousands of responses and concern....and then we had some very anti-Semitic e-mails that were sent to people on the campus that really made the environment [more tense]."
47. Ibid.
48. Coleman amplifies on this in the following: "We had learned from talking with people at Berkeley that at some point during the conference, the big sticking point is the vision of the suicide bomber....as you might imagine, that's very much a hot button issue. So we said to the group [of conference attendees]—because we knew at Berkeley that they had closed their meeting and thrown out people who they didn't want to stay—'Sorry, in this environment, the people registered for the meeting. They get to come to all the meetings. You can't throw them out. That's not what this is about.' And we reinforced that throughout, and so I think the fact that we told them what the rules were, and we forced our rules, we weren't surprised about anything...because we had done so much preparation before it and we didn't let ourselves get surprised."
49. Ibid. In the interview I probed what in the nature or ethos of the university may have caused this response and willingness by her faculty. With a bit of hesitancy, I sense only because the question was not one she had previously considered, Coleman replied, "It's just that Michigan has so much been a place where there's the real intellectual ferment that the faculty had to think about it." In addition, although the faculty started this process, Coleman adds, "As soon as I saw that was the approach that people were taking, I encouraged it because it's very important."
50. Mary Sue Coleman, "Letter to the Campus Community," October 1, 2002, http://www.umich.edu/~urecord/0102/Sep30_02/coleman-ltr.html, p. 1.

51. Nannerl Keohane, "The Public Role of the University," address to the Duke University faculty, October 24, 2002, p. 3. http://www.dukenews.duke.edu/news/opinion.asp?id=834&catid=2,45&cpg=opinion.aslp, p. 3. Of interest in this passage is Keohane's inclusion of boards and administrative leaders in the listing of parties not only concerned about but possibly even cloaked in academic freedom, something normally associated solely with faculty and presented as solely a faculty privilege (as well as a responsibility, certainly).

52. Ibid., p. 4.

53. Nannerl Keohane, interview with author.

CHAPTER

The Courage to Hold the Center: Balancing Convictions and Passionate Intensity

In our journey we have accompanied presidents as they confront the complex issues of diversity, political correctness, and ideological battle lines in the academy. The picture that emerges is of centripetal forces created and energized by competing and often divisive constituents inside and outside the gates of the university. The challenges presented by these forces return us to a central question in deliberations about the presidency: in the contemporary era the crucial question presidents must address is whether the center of the academy can hold, and if so, how? This critically important and demanding responsibility bears on the future of the presidency itself, and certainly on the future of the university. If we grant the premise that what is at stake is whether the center of the academy will hold and if so how, then the question is what leadership is and will be required of presidents? In short, what are they able to do to address this challenge?

Though there are variations on these themes, presidents confront two clear choices. On one hand, they can allow these ideological forces, episodically waxing and waning, to play out, occasionally opposing one another and institutional leadership, and occasionally shifting to compromises, however tentative and fleeting.

There are obvious and significant dangers inherent in this passive course. While it can be successful in practice, including keeping presidents out of the firing line, a reality about these ideological constituent agendas must be confronted. By nature these ideologically advocated pressures and changes are frequently created and framed with little, if any, desire or commitment to place the core values of the university first. In fact the fundamental values of the academy are often viewed as roadblocks to more "progressive" policies and decisions.

Arguably, the university has existed in nearly its present form for centuries, and is often claimed to be one of only two or three social institutions with such longevity. Thus one might allege that the center has held sufficiently over that time, and undoubtedly will in the future. However, this approach assumes that the level of diversity and politicization in the academy will never reach a point where its impact is substantively different than in previous eras. This assumption may be true, and thus benign neglect could work as a strategy for presidents facing these challenges. However, even if this tactic worked, the risk of standing on the sidelines could have severe consequences in perceptions about presidential leadership and about the core soundness of the traditional principles of the academy.

On the other hand, presidents can lead in a fashion that seeks to define a broad-based center on which these ideological and diverse constituencies can find common ground. To do so, presidents have to engage the debate and dialogue essential to the framework of a working consensus for the life of the university. Developing a lasting consensus would require upholding the fundamental principles and values of the university in order to sustain them for the future.

The choice of these two courses of presidential action (or inaction) is framed by Harold Shapiro's analysis and warning about the inescapable gravity of the situation. "Unfortunately, the last decade [the mid-1970s to the mid-1980s] has witnessed a decline in the power and influence of many of our society's major integrative institutions. In their place, we have witnessed the development," speaking about the impact in society and on campuses, "of a kind of social hegemony of special interest groups. As one result, we are less confident as a society to make moral distinctions."[1]

In a revealing and "politically incorrect" (for both two decades ago and today) comment that dovetails with the concerns raised by Trachtenberg, Sexton, and other presidents, Shapiro continues: "[R]adical ideologies, unable to compromise on any issue, are fundamentally hostile to a social order such as ours and to the role of integrative institutions. Such groups do not include in their agendas that critical toleration of others—the hallmark of Western civilizations—that creates the foundation for social and political reconciliation and compromise. The key characteristic of our integrative institutions," here with the university foremost in mind, and distinguishing it from faith and belief systems, "is that while they do not proclaim any ultimate truths, they nonetheless provide the 'working hypotheses' which broadly govern our social behavior at any point in time."[2]

Presidents must use all reasonable power and the authority of their office to pursue the mission Shapiro urges. It is a mission essential to the health and well-being of the university. It is a mission that must be shaped and conveyed in concert with the mission and purposes of the university and college. For the sake of the university's future, the diligent and hard work of reaching consensus must be engaged. Colleges and universities must rely on their presidents to take this lead, to frame and advocate for "working hypotheses." This requires locating and articulating a center that holds together the diverse and disparate individuals, groups, communities, and cultures constituting today's campuses. It demands being able to be in and to lead from the middle. It means negotiating among and between the various factions and streams of the twenty-first century university.

Finally, presidents who set this course of locating a "center" must summon the personal courage and moral compass required to lead in this fashion. This is truer than in the exercise of other responsibilities of their office, because presidents must have personal grounding in order effectively to exert a vision that embodies the fundamental principles and values of the university. The reality is that presidents lead in the face of the intense and passionate demands of factions and individuals who perceive the fundamental beliefs at the foundation of the university as roadblocks to pursuing their cultural, political, and social ends.

Donald Kennedy cites verses from Yeats's poem, "The Second Coming," in his commencement talk to the class of 1988 at Stanford.[3] The context of his remarks is the reality of the world the graduates were about to confront on their departure from the university. In connection with Shapiro's thoughts about "radical ideologies, unable to compromise on any issue" and the need to develop "working hypotheses," Yeats's worldview places in stark relief the presidential responsibility to work in the "messy middle" of Oden in attempting to make the center of the college and university hold. Yeats's imagery anticipates the forces of political correctness and ideological thinking in today's academy, forces that tear at the center of the academy.

In the 1980s Bartlett Giamatti, former president of Yale University (later fulfilling a lifelong, though tragically short-lived, dream of serving as commissioner of major league baseball) anticipated the battles over political correctness before it even had that name. Presciently he commented about the academy's handling of diversity concerns (and, in particular, "solutions" like speech codes and affirmative action) and of the ideologies peppering campuses in the preceding decades, then beginning to become more firmly entrenched in the life of the academy. We have the advantage of a couple of decades' hindsight since Giamatti claimed colleges were falling prey to reliance on the dangerous game of codification as a way to reach "compromises" designed to quell political and ideological controversies. Giamatti spotted the resort to codes and codification as it grew and developed. He believed that the hasty use of codes to meet contentious problems caused the rejection of a traditional and tested value in the academy: trusting dialogue to develop broad-minded and broad-based consensus.

Giamatti's argument goes to the heart of the challenge of making the center hold. He contends that codification reduces values to codes and that this, in turn, displaces the historic reliance on the traditional pathway to ensure that center would hold (and by inference keep "radical ideologies" in check): simple consensus. Giamatti describes an "impulse that I can only call the codification of the academy," the result of which "is the once gradual, now visible and ever accelerating effort to encapsulate all values in codes. It is the effort to capture what at its best was a consensus—that universities were collegial institutions designed to foster within, and promote without, access, equity and intellectual excellence—and to put that consensus into a code."4 One result is the close connection between action, on one hand, based on the impulse to codify "solutions" to seemingly intractable problems, driven by the pressure for diversity, and the increasing presence of ideological and politically correct thinking on campus on the other hand.

Codification can also be utilized, as many institutions have done, to simplify and, as advocates would argue, to streamline (as well as toughen) tasks like budgeting and financial management that get easily bogged down by consensus decision making. David Kirp cites the University of Michigan's experiment with Resource Centered Management (or Responsibility Centered Management) as a budgeting tool. A dean confronted the provost, arguing that the problem with this approach was "the rationale that RCM would take the hard decisions out of resource allocation—and that the formula would drive everything, all the way down to the professor level."5 The key issue is that a formula, whether mandated from the top down by administration, as was the case in this instance, or agreed to after some consensus-seeking discussion, would eliminate the "hard decisions" regarding resources and budgeting. The dean makes Giamatti's case: however messy or time-consuming, it is better to argue a consensus than to allow a code, a systematized way of conveying values, to dictate decisions and their underlying values to the constituencies of the academy.

Giamatti confesses the extent to which he is conflicted about how and why the reliance on codification has happened. Critical of how the academy handles battles over values, he notes that "the values universities say they cherish and foster and promote have not always been fostered, cherished and promoted within them; when one considers that the society has been urged by universities to encourage access and attend to equity and excellence, but that when the broadest forms of these values, documented in codes and reduced but still energized by regulation, come back to the academy in a shape the academy does not recognize, only then do problems arise."6 This is a quandary of a "collision of values, or worlds of shared assumptions," those we elect to codify on one hand, and those borne out of consensus on the other. Giamatti's resolution of this collision of competing principles is the "hope that the codification to which I refer is a transitory phenomenon; that...we do not depend upon law for all our ideals; that we do not believe codes are more than ghostly sketches of consensus; that we do not as citizens go easily to the proposition that until everything is written down, it does not exist; and that we resist the desire to wish for a past world where absolutes looked neater, easier, more agreeable precisely because they were known only to a few, even if preached to the many."7

Shaping consensus is not easy, particularly in academic communities where inquiry, questioning, and critical analysis reign. In addition, any decision or agreement can be understood as merely provisional, because the assumptions on which it is based must be subjected to further and continual reexamination. Defining consensus, Giamatti turns to its Latin root, "to connote a feeling with, or a mutuality of, shared sentiment." Still, the lure of codification, "the act of documentation," preempting the slower process required to gain mutual agreement, "may be the best way to note the demise of consensus."[8] This threat to consensus, Giamatti was convinced, is irrevocably tied to the potential undoing of the foundations of the academy. That Giamatti had sufficient vision, along with a few other colleague presidents from his era, to see the development of political correctness and ideological problems coming to the fore is nearly uncanny. As he was departing the presidency, Giamatti warned his generation and future generations of college and university leaders that they would have to deal with these issues, intercepting them where possible and, at the least, ameliorating their negative and damaging effects on the academy.

Giamatti bears witness to the significance and merit of his ideas. He concludes that "this University [Yale] is carefully engaging in the process of dismantling a set of shared assumptions by the very act of fashioning public expressions of what were once only private privileges. This process is one that calls neither for strident applause nor for plangent lament but rather for a reasoned recognition that Nothing comes from Nothing. In such matters we do best when we remember institutions change so they may endure, endure with a sense of their purpose and dignity, which sense is what differentiates endurance from mere survival."[9] He urges presidents to be certain to ground the university in shared values and beliefs. These qualities are best, maybe only, created and shaped by the considered ideas, thoughts, feelings, and judgments of the community as represented by its constituents. In effect, presidents forget at their and their institution's peril the admonition that "Nothing comes from Nothing."

If Giamatti is correct, providing a proposition that deserves serious consideration, then a number of questions follow. How might consensus reemerge as the primary mode of discourse and decision making in the academy? How are we to move away from turning to the law, from relying on the codification of positions borne out of controversy, and from the short-cut fixes, like financial formulas, in order to reach institutional decisions? Giamatti argues that college presidents must provide the leadership for a return to consensus, regenerating an emphasis on mutuality and shared sentiment in the academy. However, this expectation pivots on the capacity of presidents successfully to steer this course. What guidance do presidents who have been there have on the ways to face and to navigate this minefield?

During his presidency at Emory, James Laney transformed the university from a decent regional institution in the mid-1970s to a noted national and international university of much greater renown at the end of his tenure in the early 1990s. He created many of the changes Emory underwent, and though social and cultural influences pressured others, even in these cases Laney capitalized on the effect of these forces to transform the university as well. Laney stressed two consistent themes throughout these evolutionary changes. One is the belief that a goal of a college or university education is the "education of the heart." The closely related second theme is commitment to education as a transformational process.[10] These assumptions underpin the framework that Laney used to define the "center" of the university.

Laney acknowledges that the values and beliefs of an older, bygone era at Emory, steeped in Christian heritage, cannot be forced on the culture of the academy in a more pluralistic time. However, he refuses to believe that just because the old homogeneity no longer holds, leaders including faculty, who are responsible for scholarly and academic content and for the curriculum (much fought over during the "cultural wars"), are reduced to "do nothing except present, in a sense, an *eviscerated kind of knowledge* abstracted from any personal qualities. Students really want to know what the faculty thinks. They want to make up their own mind, they don't want to be told" (italics mine).[11] To counter advocates for "objective," post-Enlightenment deconstructivism, what he views as "eviscerated knowledge," Laney instead argues for "human excellence," a goal around which he led key constituents at Emory—especially faculty and trustees—to rally.

Despite differences among constituents in intellectual views, scholarly assumptions, and individual agendas, Laney believes the pursuit of excellence is a core and binding concept for the university. Laney guided Emory so that "we would not have a homogeneous community" but rather a diversity embodied by having "people of human excellence."[12] Human excellence, in Laney's thinking, extends beyond the mere intellectual and is composed of a range of capabilities and characteristics that students, faculty, and other members contribute to the shape of the university community. Laney's concept of human excellence incorporates and embraces a diversity of individuals and points of view. The result was to fashion Emory as an institution that could be elastic and change but without compromising basic principles and values.

Laney's core and "center" unfolds from the establishment of this goal of human excellence. This pursuit of human excellence symbiotically stimulated "building a community, and not just being." Laney shaped Emory to be more intentional about what it would be as a university, "not just an open field where people are hired to teach the students and they just kind of gather in different parts of the field and learn." By talking about "education as formation," Laney affirmed "those habits, structures, traditions that imbue the community with things that people care about or can care about."[13]

Presidents frequently address the close relationship between the academy and society. At some points, the two are on the same page, or nearly so. At others, the university functions, in Shapiro's terms, as "servant and critic" of society. At still others the academy and society tussle for institutional authority and influence. The competing voices and interests of a pluralistic era inside and outside the gates result in an uneasy, at times unstable, relationship between the academy and society. Laney claims the university fulfills its "responsibility to society not just to give, to train a meritocracy but to train human excellence." Though Laney has a definitive philosophical approach, he admits presidents "have to find those commonalities to which you can appeal, work on. And there is no formula that I know of, but I'm convinced that it can be done." His injunction is that the university must engage this mission, "or else the idea of a common society is very, very much in doubt." Laney views the quest for the "center" as a search to embrace the "whole circumference."[14] He envisions a wide circle that can be drawn around the common life and experience of the multiple constituencies in today's academy. But his circumference still incorporates and remains true to the fundamental core values and principles of the university. If the center is conceived as this broad circumference, Laney believes it is able to hold.

Rhetoric and the judicious use of language are tools and important qualities in presidential leadership. They are even more crucial when presidents articulate a "center" and the values around which diverse constituent groups can identify and agree. Throughout his presidencies at Michigan and Princeton, Harold Shapiro probed and examined concepts of tradition and change.[15] His thoughts about the polemic of these twin elements are critical to a consideration of what constitutes the "center" of the university.

Shapiro's dilemma, obtaining today as much if not more so than when initially articulated in the mid-1980s, demands the utmost serious consideration. The university *is* based on ideas and particularly in an ideological age (even if there arguably has never been an age that has not been in some way ideological), sorting ideas from ideologies is a crucial task. When this challenge is addressed reasonably and fairly, the university is enriched. When it is done poorly, when everything simply collapses into an ideological playground and battleground, the university is harmed, if not destroyed.

Highlighting the challenge for the university and for presidents in locating the center, Shapiro begins with the last century as a time when "American colleges and universities have been transformed from quiet centers of cultural orthodoxy—largely removed from the dynamic forces propelling our society forward—to institutions fully participating in the adaptive changes that have gained us a position of world leadership." Given the impact on fundamental foundations of this historical shift, the university must be prepared to adapt and change in ways that "preserve its own sustaining traditions and values."[16] However, dangers lurk, as indicated by Shapiro's invocation of the specter of the "fervent but suspect ideologies [that] change inspires" as a threat to universities as they attempt to maintain a "center" founded on tested values and beliefs. The challenge is "to *select* from the innumerable novelties that are sure to confront us those few that will effectively transform our lives and institutions." As leading institutions in society, it is essential that colleges and universities be anchored in the substantial and fundamental traditions that have guided them in the past, so that "at their best, they might, as Alfred North Whitehead recommended, help us 'to preserve order amid change and to preserve change amid order.' "[17]

But Shapiro also turns back to the Book of Proverbs in the Hebrew Scriptures, noting its injunctions about core educational principles and objectives: "for education in wisdom and moral discipline, for the understanding of thoughtful speech, for training in the discernment of what is right and proper and ethical, to sharpen the wit of the ignorant, [and] to give knowledge and foresight."[18] Much later, medieval and Enlightenment thought contributed additional fundamental values to the academy: reason, autonomy, individual and academic freedom and independence, and contributions to society through vocations and knowledge.

Shapiro suggests that these are the "principles" at the heart of the university and they form a center that can hold. "The principles governing the special privileges and responsibilities of the university are intellectual autonomy, broad political and philosophical neutrality, and academic freedom," Shapiro declares. "Critical to this role is the capacity for independence, reflection, and ongoing appraisal of society's efforts, constrained only by the use of reason," an absolutely core value for Shapiro. Thus, "the modern university is not an instrument for solving society's problems, but a repository of the tools, the language, and some of the alternative visions needed to explore new solutions."

With this as a basis, Shapiro proposes that in navigating the political correctness and ideological battles, the university can serve as a resource for change, but in doing so, it cannot "sponsor particular movements without undermining its defining characteristic as an independent source of ideas."[19] Aligned with Minogue's contention about the uniqueness and social value of the university, Shapiro goes a step even beyond "political and philosophical neutrality" to underscore the independence and autonomy of the academy—clear American traits and qualities fundamentally grounding our college and university "system."

Shapiro links academic freedom and institutional stands on controversial political and public issues to understandings of the center. He understands the "center" of the academy as rooted in discrete concepts derived from what are considered the "in" versus "out," the internal and external, purposes of colleges and universities. "The work of the academic community is undeniably related to and supported by a particular set of values," defining the "center" of the university to include "the value of knowledge, the benefit of fair and open inquiry, respect for other points of view, and the possibility of human progress." After noting that "most universities are now on record as taking a stand on some moral issues such as affirmative action and research on human subjects," Shapiro cautions "about adding to this list. Without developing a means of distinguishing ideas from ideologies we risk the possibility of undermining the environment that supports our principal commitments and responsibilities."

Wrestling further with what should and should not be on an emerging contemporary list of core values and principles in the university, particularly in the battleground of diversity versus homogeneity, Shapiro warns that "[R]eturning to an earlier model of moral, political, and scientific orthodoxy would, however, undercut academic freedom and open discourse, transforming the character of contemporary higher education and undermining the university's capacity to make positive contributions to society."[20] The bottom line for Shapiro is that the "center" and foundation of the academy stems from a short list of qualities and characteristics. He argues that even if they are few, some "old-style" values and beliefs of earlier eras need to be maintained, for example, the "value of knowledge, the benefit of fair and open inquiry, respect for other points of view, and the possibility of human progress."

Shapiro adds to this "traditional list" of values contemporary ideas such as affirmative action (though he seems to argue that there well may be a future time limit on these policies) and protocols for research on human subjects. But he warns that expansion beyond an agreed-upon narrow list of these more contemporary values to include those promoted by competing ideological agendas would do damage to the university equal to that of a return to no longer applicable "old" values and beliefs. At the same time, Shapiro is also fully aware that in a pluralistic age, a return to a simpler, more homogenized set of values and beliefs is as impractical (if not impossible) as it is undesirable.

In addressing the problems that tear at the values defining the center of a university, Shapiro raises the bottom-line question: "How does a society committed to pluralism ever survive?" Characterizing the American national struggle for survival as "an experiment," he adds that "here is an experiment which may or may not last forever where a society based on a notion that people [who] actually disagree on fundamental issues nevertheless can find a way to get along and gradually make itself a better place." However, if American society can "get it right," Shapiro suggests that possibly "the same thing is true in the university."[21]

Shapiro, a Canadian, takes heart in the fact that "if a country can find a way to get along, we [in the university] can find a way, but only under certain circumstances." That is, it can find a way "only if we can continually remind ourselves about the values that really matter to us. Just like in this country, we could not get along if we didn't remind ourselves often of what it is that our liberal democracy is built on." Almost off-handedly, Shapiro indicates that whenever he urged constituents toward a "center," the central theme was always "We don't have to sign up for a lot of things that we all agree on, but we have to sign up for something." The crucial question about whether this can work, whether the "center" can be sustained, is that there is "a limit for the amount of difference even a liberal society can tolerate. No one can tolerate everything on common difference—that's just anarchy."[22] The distinctive characteristic of the university is its commitment "to the very liberal notion, the autonomy in the individualist self and worth of individual and their ideas," so it is "bound to be a place where people will have disagreements on issues that matter," Shapiro declares.

The way forward is that presidents joined by university community members willing to be part of this process "have to search for a framework within which thoughtful intellectual discourse can take place amongst people with differences." Shapiro concludes that this is "just what a university is if it's anything." Thus, if presidents and others concerned about the academy have the belief and courage to permit the university to be the university, then the academy may be able to embody this difficult, but by no means impossible, balancing act among disparate forces, an act that itself largely defines the "center."

Though the diversity among individuals and institutions in society is amplified in universities, there are still common points of reference and identity even among the most diverse constituents. Shapiro's prescription for locating what binds a university together consists of two things. First, "people at universities—university faculty and students—find it really quite uplifting to be reminded" about what the core values are and about "what it is that is really distinctive about what we're doing." Second, and building on the first, he indicates that "one of the ways I've expressed this from time to time is the very special role that both individuals in liberal society and the university as an institution have." This means that "an individual has many identities and many jobs. It's wrong to think of an individual as having a single identity or a single job. Their identity, values, and roles change depending which role they're fulfilling. The same thing for a university. We have different identities, we have different responsibilities, we have a mixture of things."[23]

Shapiro concludes with an interesting aside, critical for presidents and their institutions. He advises that presidents "have to take the time and effort to talk about these relatively abstract, almost philosophical" ideas, principles and ideas that are truly motivating if leaders only take the time to communicate them. Though fully cognizant of the benefits of competition, Shapiro decries the "almost pathological competition that now universities are involved in," viewing this as a pressure that can force leaders, faculty, trustees, and others to "lose sight of the values that inform what we do."[24] His major point is that presidents must avoid the latest fads that vie to be included in the "center." Pushing the fads toward the margins, where they largely belong, presidents then must focus on the core values and beliefs that form the university.

In any discussion about the "center" of the university, a central, nagging question lurks: Has the university become such a mixture of disconnected people and parts that an institutionally identifiable core and "center" no longer exists? This overarching question is prompted by Shapiro's analysis of the delicate balance between change and tradition. Lingering in this debate is the voice of Clark Kerr, the late dean of higher education and former president of Berkeley who placed his now classic label on the university in America, calling it a "multiversity."

The term "multiversity" implies an ever-expanding and growing institution, concerned little, if at all, with its roots and any prospect of being defined by a narrow core. Rather, the multiversity is chameleon-like, not only ready but by design destined to change and adapt, even if haphazardly, with the times. In Kerr's words, "the multiversity is not one thing but many things along a continuum."[25] Though focused on large research universities, the implications and reach of this label have penetrated the culture of most universities, small and large, public and private, as well as even the liberal arts college.

Kerr's "multiversity" contrasts with the more single, unified in purpose, and coherent university that preceded it. This successor version is described as "pluralistic," "having several purposes," centers of power, and clienteles. It is not unified, not least importantly in terms of community, and it is marked by "many visions...and by many roads to achieve those visions...."[26] Thus there are few unifying elements in Kerr's university. It is decentralized by nature and design, and while maybe not totally anarchistic in line with Shapiro's notion of "common difference" as nothing more than anarchy, the multiversity is highly centripetal in profile and cultural milieu.

Kerr's classic work, *The Uses of the University*, went through reprintings and new editions, as he constantly engaged his case about the university in continuing scholarly debate and argument. As he reflected on the "multiversity" as a concept, Kerr turned it ever so slightly to make even this "conglomerate," pluralistic university without "a single soul" an institution still capable of having a "center." The major iterations of Kerr's tampering with his ideas began less than a decade after the 1963 lectures on which the book was based, in his "Postscript—1972," later titled "Reconsiderations after the Revolts of the 1960s."

Kerr arrives at this new place acknowledging that he coined the term "multiversity" before learning of William James's notion of the "multiverse."[27] James's multiverse is a pluralistic state that Kerr believes fits a mainstream, even if evolutionary, understanding of the traditional principles and beliefs at the foundations of the academy. He describes a state characterized by more continual conflict, more flux, and more "free will for the individual," even if also greater "dysfunction within and between organizations." As noted, not only is there nothing threatening about conflict and about individuals using free will to act and to debate in the academy, but these values and principles are in actuality at the heart of the university.

Kerr's use of James, while complex and almost arcane, provides an intellectual grounding for identifying a "center" for the university. In the grappling that goes on to locate a center for the university that is able to hold in a diverse and pluralistic age, the image that Kerr develops is unique and important. Institutions in a pluralistic multiverse, remarkably like today's academy, feature parts of the whole that "'may be externally related' rather than only internally related...a situation where 'each part hangs together with its very next neighbors,' and where 'every part' is 'in some possible or mediated connection with every other part.'" Thus the unity of an institution or organization is of a "strung-along type" or "a contiguity."[28] This image of the "center" of the academy likens it to beads on a necklace, each independent, but related to each other by a common thread.

With this foundation, Kerr concludes that the multiversity has "a condition of cohesion at best or coexistence at next best or contiguity at least (under internal pressures in recent years, some campuses have moved from a state of cohesion to one of coexistence, or from coexistence to mere contiguity of constituent elements)."[29] Kerr came to believe that the choice of the label "multiversity" might not have been the best and most accurate description of university. Certainly the connotations that arose were not what he fully wished to convey. The new picture of the university that emerges is of an institution that is still extremely complex, in some ways disjointed, and characterized by internal competition and conflicts. However, the important change from Kerr's original ideas is that rather than abandoning its historical roots and fundamental heritage, this reconceptualized "multiversity" is able to contain many basic, integral, and traditional tenets of the academy.

So, we return to our central question: Can the center hold? Will it hold, and if so how? The answer indeed will vary among the various and diverse higher education institutions on the American landscape and as a function of their equally diverse leaders. Prospects about whether the center can hold are also, of necessity, provisional. Much of the outcome is born of the individual sagas and the discrete missions and purposes of these institutions. In addition, as presidents grapple to shape and articulate the "center" of their universities and colleges, other critical factors emerge.

The values, beliefs, and traditions of colleges and universities must be able to be uttered, conveyed, and understood within and outside the gates. Presidents must lead in ways that convince and enable constituents to seek and to sustain common agreement about fundamental institutional principles and purposes. Purpose and meaning must transcend and consist of more than simple market niche formulations and "brand." Marketing and promotion under an organizing theme and concept may be important, particularly for schools struggling for identity, for those having lost ground in the competitive admissions game, and for those needing to project a more coherent institutional profile strategically based on marketing tactics.[30] However, a true binding "center" must have constituting elements that provide a more firm and enduring foundation than possible from mere slogans, banners, and state-of-the-art packaging.

The foundations of colleges and universities must be undergirded in the tenets and principles that have traditionally served and shaped the academy. Missions and purposes must be truly defensible educationally. The delicate balance is to establish an enduring "center" that is as comprehensive as possible, without sacrificing focus and core values. Presidents and other leaders—faculty, trustees, alumni, and other influential stakeholders—must bear in mind Giamatti's basic warning: "Nothing comes from Nothing."

Certainly, defining a center and reaching sufficient community consensus in support of it is not an easy or simple task. However, in the absence of such a center, campuses face grave dangers. The allure of fads has always been a particular danger. The Yale Report of 1828 reaffirmed the university's curriculum in the face of reforms believed to be diluting the education at its competitor institutions. In the contemporary era, the forces of political correctness and Shapiro's lurking radical ideologies are among the challenges and dangers that both stand in the wings. Unchecked, these pressures will readily fill the vacuum created when institutions lose focus, are unable to articulate discrete purposes, and fail to engage debate, dialogue, and decisions essential to shape and sustain a center. Ensuring that the center will hold relies in large measure—and hence their crucial role—on the vision and power of persuasion of presidents to compel constituents, even with their diverse convictions and passions, into joining the prospect of life in the center of the academy.

NOTES

1. Shapiro, "Ethics in America—Who Is Responsible?" Elsewhere in his writings Shapiro draws a contrast between the forces of pluralism and what he labels the "cultural utopia" of various forms of fundamentalism. This fundamentalist thought framework "proclaims the superiority of one culture" over others. Many of the campus battles over political correctness and ideological differences are reducible to the cultural, whose view is superior, differences. See Nelson, *Leaders in the Crucible*, pp. 136–38, and p. 144, nn. 15 and 16.

2. Shapiro.

3. Kennedy, *The Last of Your Springs*, p. 130.

4. A. Bartlett Giamatti, *The University and the Public Interest* (New York: Atheneum, 1981), p. 181.

5. Kirp, *Shakespeare, Einstein, and the Bottom Line*, p. 126.

6. Giamatti, *The University and the Public Interest*, p. 183.

7. Ibid., pp. 183–84.

8. Ibid., p. 181.

9. Ibid., p. 184. The "Nothing from Nothing" reference comes from Shakespeare's *King Lear*.

10. James Laney, former president, Emory University, interview with author, April 27, 2003. Laney spoke about these concepts during the interview, but also wrote extensively about them, especially in *The Education of the Heart: Selected Speeches of James T. Laney* (Atlanta, GA: Emory University Press, 1994).

11. James Laney, interview with author.

12. Ibid.

13. Ibid.

14. Ibid.

15. Harold Shapiro, "Tradition, Continuity, Discovery, and Change: A Conversation with Princeton's Past." Inaugural address, President's Office, Princeton University, January 8, 1988, pp. 1–12.

16. Shapiro, *Tradition and Change*, p. 118.

17. Ibid. p. 119.

18. Ibid., p. 120.

19. Ibid. p. 128.

20. Harold Shapiro, "Is Taking Sides a Good Idea for Universities?" SCIENCE (American Association for the Advancement of Science) 225, no. 4657 (July 1984): p. 19.

21. Harold Shapiro, former president, University of Michigan and Princeton University, interview by author, July 8, 2003.

22. Ibid.

23. Ibid.

24. Ibid.

25. Kerr, *The Uses of the University*, p. 106.

26. Ibid., p. 103.

27. Ibid., p. 104. Kerr cites James's book, *A Pluralistic Universe*, as the source of this notion and of what follows.

28. Ibid.

29. Ibid., p. 105. His footnote next to the word "cohesion" in this quotation leads the reader to Kerr's citation of James Perkins (in *The University in Transition*, Princeton, NJ: Princeton University Press, 1966, p. 49) as setting "a higher goal of 'coherence' where 'all the university's activities advance its capabilities to pursue each of its missions.'" Kerr then adds: "A still higher goal might be congruence in the sense of harmony and unity," p. 240, n. 8.

30. For elaboration and numerous examples, such as the name change of Beaver College to Arcadia University and the rebuilding of Dickinson College, see Kirp, *Shakespeare, Einstein, and the Bottom Line*.

CHAPTER 7

Presidential Imprints: Securing the Academic Core from Threats Within and Without

We have been contending that the office of the college and university presidency throughout American history and into the present day has played a dramatic role in the shaping of the university. Without question, though, presidents alone do not dictate the course and future of the college and university. This is never more the case than in the imprint of presidents on the academic core of their institutions. Many other players, critics and colleagues, have a guiding and significant impact in shaping the academy and its academic life. However, the footprint of presidents is still a major factor in the creation of the university's academic traditions and values.

Given their position, presidents possess unique perspectives on the critical issues that face and frame the academic core of the college and university. The ways in which answers to the central problems in the academic life of the academy are fashioned have a direct bearing on the future shape of the university. The relationship among the critical issues of curriculum, teaching and research, and the approaches presidents use to develop and lead faculty member in addressing the academic core is highly suggestive of the academy's future.

The Reverend Theodore Hesburgh is a truly remarkable figure in American higher education in twentieth-century history. He served as president of the University of Notre Dame from 1952 to 1987, and had a vast impact both on his campus and on the nation and world. Hesburgh's service ranged from the Civil Rights and the Nuclear Regulatory Commissions to global weapons control discussions.

I met Hesburgh at his office on the 13th floor in the appropriately named, given his stamp on it, Hesburgh Library on the Notre Dame campus. An enormous depiction of Jesus in mosaic tile, known fondly as "Touchdown Jesus" because of its plain visibility from the Notre Dame football stadium, adorns the entirety of one exterior wall of this massive building.

The scale of the library is almost out of place given the architecture of the campus, but it is very much a centerpiece. Hesburgh's office windows overlook the campus in two directions and Hesburgh insisted on showing me the view of the sand dunes on the eastern shore of Lake Michigan more than 30 miles away to the northwest. A thick rug in the university colors—deep blue and gold—and featuring the Notre Dame seal is centered in the room with couches and chairs around it. The office walls and tables display mementoes and awards from Hesburgh's distinguished career. The former president's desk is very much a "working" one—reflecting his active emeritus role—complete with computer, reading lamp, large magnifying glass to compensate for some failing vision, in and out boxes, and his daily schedule on top. Hesburgh is a distinguished, almost patrician figure. An aura around him seems to radiate his priestly stature, yet he is quite down-to-earth, welcoming, not at all off-putting, and robustly friendly.

Though maintaining a slightly less rigorous schedule than once was the case (during his presidency the joke went: "What is the difference between God and Father Hesburgh? God is everywhere. Father Hesburgh is everywhere but Notre Dame!"), he is still notorious for working well into the evening, even on days when he returns from the now much less frequent travel than his schedule and prominence once demanded. Hesburgh estimates that he still lectures a couple of dozen times a year in classes taught by other professors.

A major issue Hesburgh faced early in his presidency was the need to build up the profile, the reputation, and especially the academic standing of the university. Citing it as a critical step in building up Notre Dame to the major university it is today, Hesburgh tells the tale of the vision for the library, completed in 1962, at a time when the university owned 250,000 books. Colleagues wondered whether the university even needed a new library and questioned Hesburgh: " 'Do you want to double the capacity for books?' And I said, 'No.' 'Do you want to quadruple it to one million books?' And," with his typical confidence and forward thinking, "I said, 'No, I want a three-million book capacity.' And they said, 'You're crazy. We've been around all of these years and we've got 250,000. Now you want to build a library for three million?' And I said, 'That's right, and I'll tell you something else. I hope it will be filled in my lifetime.' And today it's full."[1]

Admittedly Hesburgh is much more insulated than his secular colleagues from the consequences of touching a "third rail" of contemporary discussion about the university and college: advocacy that the academy must transcend the artificial barrier of "objective" and value-free or value-neutral knowledge. While other educational leaders no doubt believe this, it is increasingly more difficult, if not dangerous, to speak this language. This is even more true in a politically correct climate where such rhetoric can easily be decried as yielding to some conspiracy of the Right (or maybe even the Left, depending on the ax to be ground). At first it appears unsurprising that Hesburgh stakes out this territory, given his particular perspective as a priest heading a major Roman Catholic university imbued with its traditions and values. But is Hesburgh really so alone in his concept of the university?

Hesburgh's philosophy of the university and its academic center is certainly framed in the crucible of his perspective as a religious, Roman Catholic educator and leader. His counsel about the university is classically in the tradition of Cardinal Newman. Like his predecessor, Hesburgh has a broad understanding of the university that transcends parochialism, without pushing it altogether out of the picture. His analysis of what makes a great university is directly and understandably tilted toward the transcendent, toward the highest human values he believes are inculcated in the foundation of all universities and in higher education broadly conceived. But as we will see, Hesburgh's concept of the university also mirrors that of contemporary presidents—all of whom he speaks of as friends, personally and fondly—presidents such as Kennedy at Stanford, Rhodes at Cornell, and Shapiro at both Michigan and Princeton, universities that are more secular and are clearly more mainstream. Minus his religious trappings, these presidents still share Hesburgh's concern that a relentless pursuit of objectivity, of science in the absence of human constraints and values, and of an education designed for nothing other than practical applications, is a severe problem and threat that educational leaders must address.

Speaking at a meeting of the then Council of Graduate Schools, Hesburgh carefully uses broadly inclusive language designed to bridge the secular-religious divide (though language that is dated by exclusive gender references), contending that the university is "by nature at the service of the good as well as the true. Universities are first and foremost essentially dedicated to discovering and transmitting truth—but too long we have harbored a false dichotomy between the true and the good. What is humanly, or divinely true for man is also good for man. I do not believe we can be effective champions of the truth without some commitment to the good."

Treading, close to crossing, the fine line between Shapiro's characteristic of "political neutrality" toward a more partisan position, Hesburgh fears that "there seems to be a real moral vacuum in many of our universities today. We might ponder what this meant in Nazi Germany when great universities allowed themselves to be prostituted to inhumanity in the name of moral neutrality." However, his conclusion rests in the mainstream contention that change in the academy cannot be permitted to override and erase tried and true traditions, especially those embedded in the foundation of the university. "If universities are to face the changes of our times effectively, and not be swallowed up in the change, each one of us university people must," delineating the value of the bully pulpit, "be men of courage, of commitment, dedicated to justice, to the great human values of Western Culture unafraid to speak out whether it is popular or not, knowing where we stand and why, unashamed of our moral, as well as our intellectual, commitment."[2] With this assertion, Hesburgh places himself in the mainstream of his presidential colleagues: they are responsible to be guardians of the gates of the academy and must speak forcefully for the "good," for "justice," and for the broad human values vital to the university and to a higher education.

Later in his presidency, Hesburgh revisits this theme, critiquing the claims of objectivity at the base of the scientific method. The danger is that though appropriate for science and technological fields, the scientific method "has also given us the specter of a value-free world that is on the brink of destroying itself....It has placed great power in the hands of those who have few priorities beyond their own political, social, or economic aggrandizement." Hesburgh connects the problem of objectivity versus subjectivity to the curricular arguments in the contemporary struggles of colleges and universities to identify what courses and content should be taught by faculty and required of students. His response to these debates about the canon is "a call for faith on the religious level, and humanistic studies as central to all education. There is...a need to reassess our total concept of higher education, adrift today, to re-establish the centrality of such subjects as philosophy and theology, literature and history, art and music, and the inevitable value content of political science, economics, anthropology and sociology."[3]

University curricula have been debated almost from time immemorial. Many leaders of the academy—we are reminded of Laney's warning that the university cannot be reduced to offering "eviscerated knowledge" devoid of human issues and concerns—support this call for an emphasis on the humanities and for the assertion that even the social sciences incorporate and reflect "values," that is, they should not be purely construed as objective subjects, neutral toward values.

Near the end of his presidency, Hesburgh focuses the dilemma confronting educational leaders concerning the moral aspects of a university and college education. He argues that what needs to happen is "not too popular in modern universities and colleges: defining what we are really trying to do, what we most fundamentally believe higher education to be, what we deeply believe these future leaders should learn from us." But this suggestion is simple compared to what Hesburgh next proposes: "Doing this will require something even more unpopular in modern universities and colleges, spending a few moments to consider transcendentals like the true, the good, the beautiful, and the moral imperatives that flow from them, if indeed they are very relevant to what we are educating young persons to be, what will really qualify them to lead us out of the present wilderness to a better future."

Arguably Hesburgh could be ignored as merely indulging in a jeremiad. However, his counsel is still relevant today, even if the danger that the university would lose its moral bearings has evolved more slowly than he might have predicted. His advice is still applicable and relevant: "I need not insist here that if we, the faculty, do not see the road ahead fairly clearly, it is unlikely that we will surmount this moral dilemma in time to help our present students become effective leaders in a world of considerable moral confusion."[4]

Hesburgh calls for the university to incorporate and address a moral agenda, particularly through its curricula and the way these shape the students' education. Stripped to its most basic level, Hesburgh is "only" arguing that the academy needs to know more clearly what it is doing and why. He believes that as these questions are sorted out, leaders—presidents and faculty members in particular— inevitably cannot avoid considering the moral components integral to education and to student learning.

There are great similarities between the territory Hesburgh maps out and that of other contemporary presidents, such as Shapiro. Shapiro does not use Hesburgh's precise religious language (though Hesburgh is also a master at finessing his religious emphasis, drawing listeners to broader, more inclusive and generic assertions), but Shapiro makes use of many of the same assumptions and reaches remarkably similar conclusions. By refusing to fear stepping into consideration of the moral and spiritual foundations in the university and in higher education, Shapiro shows that this perceived "third rail" in discussions of the academy is not so untouchable after all.

In his inaugural address as president of the University of Michigan, Shapiro outlines the idea and the essential role of the university as both "critic and servant." He plumbs the heritage of this notion, claiming that "over time, society's support for this dual concept of the university as an institution both serving and criticizing society has been ultimately sustained by faith in rationalism, faith in knowledge and science, and faith in the resulting notion of human progress. Perhaps one of the most distinctive ideas of Western civilization is the idea that nature, by itself, cannot achieve full potential. Rather, what is needed is a mutually beneficial interaction between nature, science, and mankind."

So far this assertion about rational thinking and the good of human kind is nothing very different from mainstream, Enlightenment and modern, understandings of the basis of the university. But this boilerplate claim is followed by a shift in emphasis that injects moral and spiritual considerations essential to Shapiro's concept of human progress. "The university plays an increasingly central role in this process. In the end, we all live under the sway of ideas, and the idea of progress in both our material and our moral or spiritual condition has been an increasingly dominating idea of Western thought," Shapiro asserts. A coda hammers home his point: "[T]he university now plays a critical role in strengthening the positive correlation between progress in science and the development of new knowledge, and progress in a moral and spiritual sense."[5]

It is no surprise that enormous struggles ensue at major research universities in response to any attempt at incorporating ideas related to "progress in a moral and spiritual sense" into the mission and curricula. But Shapiro believes this is part of the quest for what the university does and therefore is part of what the university is. In his mind, there is an undeniable connection between moral and spiritual progress and the prospect of the university: "[T]hus, we have responsibility for providing an education that not only develops an individual's technical expertise, but relates an individual's experience to the broad human landscape of which we are a part, and moves them to a purpose and capacity beyond themselves."[6] This aspiration becomes less theoretical and indirect when, for example, issues like affirmative action and recruitment of minority students are discussed and policies are adopted or changed.

At the same time, arguments about public sector funding and financial support are connected to debates over what the academy should be, and these arguments are unavoidably injected into the life of universities and the leadership of presidents. Pressures related to public support create different, but no less serious, threats both to the fundamental foundations and to society's conceptions of the university than do battles and disagreements over whether the academy can or should be value free. Federal and state funding of public as well as private institutions has become much less dependable and substantial during the last few decades of the twentieth century and the early years of the twenty-first century. These financial pressures affect presidents and the ways they deploy their leadership resources, especially in the face of trends—tax policies and revenue, public perception and support, and red flags raised by citizens about what goes on inside the gates of the academy—that are often outside their immediate control. Thus, presidents must be prepared to adapt and accommodate to changes in the flow of public money to their campuses.

Federal and other public sector funding has become a mounting problem for colleges and universities, that has grown as their dependency on these sources has increased since World War II. The post–World War II era marked the beginning of significant public student aid through the GI Bill, and of vastly increased and for decades increasing (as a result of the Vannevar Bush report) amounts of federal research support pouring into universities as well as to colleges. Kerr's idea of the "multiversity" was the first major attempt to conceptualize and describe fully these dramatic changes and their impact, especially as a result of major injections of public funding, already underway between the late 1940s and the early 1960s. This revolution continued for at least another couple of decades before federal investment and other public funding streams began to level off and decline.[7]

The reality of the dramatic change in public support over the last four decades can be seen at Michigan, where state support fell from 70 percent of the annual general fund in 1960 to 36 percent in 2000. This led James Duderstadt to remark acerbically that Michigan "used to be state-*supported*...then state-assisted, and now we are state-located."[8] His successor, Mary Sue Coleman, recognizes that government funding reductions force presidents of public institutions, like the University of Michigan, to function more like presidents of private universities. She and her public-institution colleagues have no choice but to dedicate the time and resources of their offices and their universities to raise increasingly larger proportions of money from private donors and other nongovernmental funding sources.

Donald Kennedy is a high-profile voice of the academy addressing the impact of enlarged support for science and related research in the university. He reflects on Vannevar Bush's *Science: The Endless Frontier*, viewing it as "a metaphor

[that] represents a momentous decision that decanted the mechanism and the resources for supporting science into the institutions responsible for training the next generation of scientists." Evaluating the level and quality of university research from nearly every imaginable angle, Kennedy concludes, "There is no question that the decision was good for science." But he quickly interjects the question: "[W]as it also good for the universities? That is a harder question."[9]

Grappling with this "harder" question, Kennedy's concern is about the institutional dependency that resulted from increasingly heavy reliance on federal funding. "The growth of dependence on federal funds among state-supported as well as private research institutions has blurred the distinction between public and private. The University of Michigan and Stanford might both be described as quite similar federal universities. This blurring has been accompanied," Kennedy unsurprisingly notes, "by a subtle but steady increase in government ambitions for control, which are justified under the all-purpose principle of accountability."[10]

The specter of the "federal" (or federalization of the) university is unsettling and is a grave issue of gravity for presidents. The issue boils down, among other concerns, to the threat financial control and leverage pose to the autonomy of colleges and universities. This freedom and independence is a critical and long-standing tradition, highly prized and at the heart of the uniqueness of higher education in America. One aspect of securing this independence, and another critical challenge for presidents, is the need for presidents and institutions to collaborate in pursuing the highest quality of higher education for the nation and society, and in defining the research agenda of individual faculty members and institutions in ways that preserve and protect academic values. If the American university is to maintain its historic independence, presidents must collaborate with faculty and draw leadership from the professorate that will secure academic values of autonomy, freedom of inquiry, and the expansion of knowledge within and beyond the gates.

Kennedy views the pressure of government oversight and its potential to erode core principles and values of the academy as relentless. The extent of this impact can easily be overlooked even among those who follow such things closely and may be affected most profoundly. The general public and even closer constituents of the university such as alumni or even faculty may in many cases have very little sense of the overall effect of governmental intrusions within the walls of the academy. "In the past ten years, government agencies have made determined efforts to regulate access by particular groups to unclassified university research; restrict access of foreign nationals; place restrictions over academic researchers publishing their own data; and pursue newly claimed regulatory authority over something vaguely defined as academic misconduct," Kennedy declares.

Perforce in the post–"Endless Frontier" era, universities are involved with government funding and government work. But the dangerous prospect is that "when institutions serve utilitarian purposes, they invite political intervention. Absent the growth in federal control we have seen, I suspect that state university governing boards might not have become as ambitious as they have, and might have stayed in their traditional oversight roles." The impact of this creeping oversight intrusion can be observed, Kennedy contends, in the reality that "three great public university systems—Michigan, California, and Minnesota—are in desperate disarray over efforts by political regents to assert control over traditional academic functions. It is a very serious situation, so far without significant opposition or public outcry."[11]

This combination of funding pressure and governmental intrusion presents challenges to presidents and to the shape and definition of the university. In response, presidents need to solicit and ally with faculty in the preservation of values undergirding the academic core of the university. This central role of faculty in the life of colleges and universities can be easily overlooked. In the present climate and gazing into the future, the major issues presidents must address concerning faculty members fall into two broad, though inevitably linked, categories. The first concerns the degree to which faculty members identify their home campus as a place of primary loyalty and affiliation. The second centers on the amount of contact professors have or are willing to have with students, especially undergraduates at major research universities.

The troublesome threat of funding pressures on academic values in the university is evident in considerations of the external sources of faculty support. Faculty work is highly dependent on federal and other research funding sources, and these sources can distract faculty from on-campus responsibilities and even compromise governance duties. When professors are drawn away from their duty to the curriculum, course content and requirements, and student advising, presidents have little power other than to cajole faculty to remain engaged.

Presidential concern centers in an area of vulnerability regarding faculty involvement with undergraduate teaching and course offerings within the curriculum. This is particularly sensitive given its relationship to questions of the cost of education. The public is fully aware of rising undergraduate tuition costs, and that courses have large enrollments, are often heavily overenrolled, are not consistently offered, and are taught in many cases by graduate assistants. These problems fuel public perceptions that presidents and faculties are inattentive to the shape and care of undergraduate education. This concern about expense is a soft underbelly at both elite, costly private colleges and universities, as well as at their public counterparts. The "bargain" of subsidized public education means little if parents and citizenry believe that students' education is being shortchanged.

Though, as a scientist, Kennedy focuses on science faculty in the following comments, they are applicable to all faculty members regardless of discipline. He believes that faculty members in today's campus environment are "more peripatetic. Their membership in the invisible international academies of their disciplines is far weightier in their lives than their attachment to their own university and their students. It is this disengagement," citing a prominent higher education colleague (and someone who came very close to being a college president himself), "that caused Henry Rosovsky . . . to speak of the secular decline in the civic consciousness of his distinguished professors."[12]

Additionally, Kennedy is concerned about the importance of faculty relationships to students.[13] He links faculty-student interaction to the overall way the university should be shaped; stated simply, "we need to return students to the center of our institutional concern." Injecting the word "moral" into the calculation, Kennedy adds that "[t]he argument for this is not a kind of moral abstraction, it is intensely practical." In the face of arguments to the contrary, Kennedy contends it is difficult "to think of an academic scientist, even among the most distinguished colleagues I have had, who has not contributed more through the students he or she has produced than through his or her own work."[14]

Another issue for presidents in sustaining the academic core of the academy directly concerns their relationship with faculty. Presidents need to develop the professorate that they would like to have and one that will work in the best long- and short-term interests of their institutions. First as dean of the Law School and now as president of New York University, John Sexton has developed novel strategies to recruit outstanding faculty, at times getting into the controversial game of stealing "stars" from other institutions. His goal, beyond the obvious raising of the profile of the university, consists of two strategies that reflect Sexton's stewardship of academic values at the heart of NYU.

The first strategy is recruitment of faculty willing to commit to long stays at NYU. Sexton's rationale for this tactic is to build continuity in the composition of the faculty. Obtaining long-term commitments by attractive professors, noted in their fields, has also enabled Sexton to use their willingness to join the NYU faculty as leverage to attract others of equal (or even greater) reputation and quality. The second strategy is to encourage synergy between and among faculty members, and in their relationships with students. Sexton confirms the notion that the best faculty work is not exclusively faculty members' own research and writing, but rather the work done in the course of educating students, and in faculty members' intellectual and scholarly interactions with colleagues.

Sexton seeks to locate a "center" of the academy that links to an understanding of the "ratio studiorum," an ideal similar to Cardinal Newman's idea of "first principles." In his inaugural address he develops this center by linking a definition of the university and its core concepts to the role of faculty, listing features of the university—speaking both about NYU and broadly and generically—that he believes are essential for its health in the future. The first "is that we will place a new demand on ourselves, one that insists that we be able at any given time to articulate our institutional mission—what might be called our ratio studiorum. And we must ask how each move we make advances our overarching goal."[15] In a similar vein, Frank Rhodes underscores the need for a "clearly articulated and broadly acceptable statement of mission, goals, and programmes" as an essential step in any "meaningful discussion of the effectiveness of individual institutions."[16]

Attacking assertions that the ivory tower is disconnected from reality, Sexton claims that "universities of the future, in a far more reflective and deliberative way, must connect the strengths they possess to the changing world in which they operate."[17] Building on this assumption and addressing faculty and their responsibilities in the academy, Sexton reveals a bias against the growing contemporary characterization of faculty members as "independent contractors." He argues that "we must recast our notion of what it means to accept the title of 'professor,' moving away from a concept of the tenured professor as an ultimate independent contractor toward," revealing the core need that the academy be coherent, his "view that each person who accepts the title 'professor' simultaneously accepts a fiduciary duty to the entire enterprise of learning, scholarship and teaching."[18]

In Sexton's world, professors must be more than just individuals passing through institutions with little or no sense of accountability or investment in the essential tasks of teaching and learning at the heart of the campus. The faculty role and responsibility for the "center" could not be more transparent and vital. Arguably, this is not a novel idea. However, the way faculty practice their craft, even at elite liberal arts and other colleges and universities that emphasize teaching, raises the question of whether the investment of professors in the classroom and teaching is waning. Sexton wants faculty members more fully engaged in the life of universities and colleges, a step he believes to be essential to their vigor and quality.

For decades, intense debates have been waged inside and outside the gates of the academy about the balkanization produced by partitions between and among the many academic disciplines. At major research universities like NYU, the necessary major academic and professional divisions and schools create further walls and barriers among them and with the institution itself. Aware of this problem, Sexton argues that "the university of the future must transcend the limits too often imposed by traditional boundaries—captured in words like 'department,' 'school' or even the word 'university' itself. Clearly each of these words has utility, but we cannot permit borders to become barriers. We can be distinct without being isolated."[19]

Over half a century ago, Robert Hutchins at Chicago was among the first to point out this balkanization as an example of what ails the university. He also argued, as continues to be true practically and pragmatically, that universities could be less profligate in their use of resources if they did not have to cater to the inevitable duplications and unnecessary overhead costs that result from divisions and divides in the academic culture. While not quite as radical as Hutchins, Sexton questions the needless separations that turn boundaries from borders to barriers. He believes these divisions negatively affect the life of the university. As an alternative, Sexton also suggests a higher calling about the idea of the university as a more truly and intentionally collegial institution. Sexton extends this critique of barriers to relationships among colleges and universities, wondering if through a superior shared sense of commonality and less rigid definitions of type, category, and status, they might collaborate more strategically and systematically.

Many in and out of higher education view with concern the trends, which some believe to be rapidly accelerating, in recent decades and years of faculty members associating and affiliating their work and loyalty with colleagues nationally and globally. The obvious question is: what effect do these professional identities and points of identification have on their attachment to their "home" institution, and to the students and colleagues with whom they should focus their intellectual and scholarly energies? Sexton recognizes there are no simple solutions to these pressing and perplexing questions. The professorate possesses and prizes the autonomy and control that exists over professors' own "work." At the same time, most people in and out of the academy, including many faculty members, believe professors owe an engagement with students and colleagues at their "home" campus in return for the financial and other security of their appointments.

Sexton believes simply that the university must not permit "the unhealthy separation...of the research enterprise from the teaching enterprise."[20] Incentives and indicators that create an impression to the contrary must be avoided. Sexton knows this is a challenge of walking the fine line "not to discourage faculty loyalty to disciplines or even to stifle their taste for celebrity," rather producing an "appreciation that one of the best tools for inquiry and insight is examining intellectual formulations not just with colleagues in the same discipline, wherever they are located, but with colleagues in the same discipline and in other disciplines within a scholar's own university." He assumes that the "home" institution makes a difference: "[T]here is a richness at home, sometimes discovered quite serendipitously and without the affirmative act of seeking conversation, that can be invaluable to the scholar. And, concomitantly, we must engender in our faculty an understanding that time spent with students (in and out of the classroom) is both rewarding in itself," appealing to their self-interest, "and enabling of the general enterprise which supports them."[21]

David Kirp argues that while many senior, tenured faculty bemoan and sometimes condemn the trend of using part time lecturers and adjunct faculty, they have done nothing to voice their concerns or to use their considerable power to address the compensation, security, and professional courtesy inequities that already exist and are getting worse for these marginal part-timers.[22] Estimates vary, but there is general agreement that nationwide adjunct faculty members and other part time lecturers teach well over half the courses offered at colleges and universities (not counting those taught by graduate assistants).

Sexton tackles the self-interest of faculty in the professorial pecking order, especially those who are senior, tenured professors, as it relates to concern about the use of full time faculty versus the growing use of part time faculty. Wading into this minefield, Sexton argues that "faculty of the common enterprise university will reverse conventional assumptions about seniority. They will understand that, with regard to institutional direction, senior faculty, even as they exercise authority, must view themselves as standing not just at a shaping point but at a listening point." Despite their enormous numbers, Sexton contends that "the generation in power," looking to the future of the professorate and the university, "must accept that one of their most crucial roles is to hear and heed the voices of the next generation of leaders."

Acknowledging that "this strategy for institutional continuity and organic, consensual evolution may not win ready acceptance from some who have climbed to the pinnacle," Sexton clings to a vision that the changing and future environment "in which our universities and their faculties now function often will mean that research and learning on the issues of the day will be shaped more easily by scholars who are younger in years or experience. So the common enterprise university must resist a hierarchy that restrains younger faculty and makes them wait their turn. Instead, we must foster an iterative and progressive process—one empowering inter-generational relationship across its faculty."[23]

In the face of this problem about the future direction of the professorate, Sexton proposes a solution based on "three broad categories of faculty, by and large outside the tenure system." Sexton views the adoption of this model as instrumental to the changes occurring and forecast within the academy and as critical to the ways faculty members invest in their work and professional identity. His three categories and proposed titles for faculty members are "Master Teachers," "Global Professors," and "Adjunct Faculty," the last-mentioned not to be confused with current applications of the term.

Sexton's Master Teacher would "be chosen through a rigorous academic review process to join the faculty because he or she has been adjudged to be capable of conveying the most advanced stage of a discipline and of appreciating the creative side of the venture, while possessing a particular ability in the classroom and a special dedication to the enterprise of teaching." Though these individuals would have research agendas, they would tilt "the personal mix of research and teaching more dramatically in the direction of teaching than would be appropriate for one seeking tenure."[24]

Duke University and other elite universities have similar faculty cadres to those Sexton advocates in the form of "clinical" or practitioner professors who know their fields well but who do not emphasize research in their work. The major difference is that Sexton's idea of the Master Teacher also leans more in the direction of an intellectual or public scholar. This type of faculty member fits his concept of the university because of the expectation that these professors will be dedicated to undergraduate teaching and to involvement with students outside the classroom in terms of advising and guidance. This is the paramount and critical standard Sexton is urging.

Sexton's second category is the Global Professor, comprising international faculty members who would commit to both permanent and visiting arrangements with the university. Their presence as teaching faculty and scholars serves Sexton's idea that the university of the future must be truly global in scope. The final group of professors in this scheme is that of the Adjunct Faculty, who would truly be practitioners, bringing an appropriate and important blend of "how theory works in practice."[25]

Sexton believes, almost as a creed, in a forward-thinking picture of the transformation of the university. He wants faculty to commit to the "common enterprise" and thereby play a crucial role in developing the evolution of the idea of the university. If the university professorate represented primarily by its senior faculty could be convinced to accept this philosophy, indeed no small feat, the ensuing new faculty blood would do two things. First, their presence would prod new thinking and change in the often rigid and traditional perspectives of current faculty. Second, these new faculty would serve as bellwethers of the very changes Sexton believes are inevitable.

For Sexton the emphasis on community is also rooted in a classical and distinctively American sense of social compact. "The faculty of the university I envision will display excellence in scholarship and teaching," he argues, "but they also will manifest a dedication to common enterprise." Certainly not naïve about the uphill climb toward this goal, Sexton acknowledges that "some potential faculty may be allergic to this ideal; but for many, the very demand will appeal to their higher and more aspirational conception of themselves, will raise the standard of their ambitions and will affect every aspect of what they do." "For them the mutual obligations of the social compact," invoking his baseline assumption and its ideal, "will be a positive and even irresistibly powerful magnet."[26]

Though merely snapshots, these stories tell of the battle for the academic center of the university as crucial to the concept of the university. In this arena of decisions in the academy, we must heed the warning Kirp offers in response to his portrayal of Duderstadt's philosophy while president at Michigan. Kirp quotes Duderstadt after leaving the presidency as contending that his successor's administration, despite its intention to retreat from his more corporate and market-driven approach, "won't be able to resist management by markets." Kirp quickly adds that this "criticism misses the mark. 'Leave it to the market' is itself a political statement, a default of institutional leadership and an abandonment of the idea of the university's mission."[27]

Presidential leadership and philosophy can and must leave imprints on the "idea of the university." In terms of the faculty's role in this crucial task, presidents certainly cannot "order" professors to do anything. However, presidents possess enormous powers of influence that should not be overlooked. These include incentives that can be incorporated to create movement of the faculty in certain directions. Presidents also have the power of persuasion that comes with the bully pulpit. We turn our attention next to this time-honored platform that presidents have historically and traditionally used to make utterances, to exert influence, and to establish legacies in the public square.

NOTES

1. The Reverend Theodore Hesburgh, former president, University of Notre Dame, interview by author, June 26, 2003.

2. Theodore Hesburgh, "The University in the World of Change," delivered at the Fourth Annual Meeting of the Council of Graduate Schools, December 10, 1964, University of Notre Dame Archives, Theodore Hesburgh Speeches, 1947–1967, Box 141/21, pp. 22–23. To be more politically correct, might Hesburgh today substitute "world" or "the best of human culture"?

3. Theodore Hesburgh, "The Future of Liberal Education," February 9, 1980, University of Notre Dame Archives, Box 142/15, pp. 13–14.

4. Theodore Hesburgh, "The Moral Dimensions of Higher Education," delivered at the first joint meeting of the Association of Universities and Colleges of Canada and the American Council on Education, October 13, 1983, University of Notre Dame Archives, Box 142/20, pp. 6–7.

5. Harold Shapiro, inauguration address, April 4, 1980, Harold T. Shapiro Collection, Ann Arbor Commencements, Michigan Historical Collections, Bentley Historical Library, University of Michigan, Box 178, pp. 8–9. Also in Shapiro, *Tradition and Change*, pp. 112–13.

6. Ibid., p. 11.

7. Kerr, *The Uses of the University*, p. 142. The rapid decline in state appropriations in the early 1990s and the beginning of a slight mid-1990s rebound are shown on p. 174, fig. 2.

8. Kirp, *Shakespeare, Einstein, and the Bottom Line*, pp. 124–25.

9. Donald Kennedy, "Universities: Costs and Benefits on the Academic Frontier," personal paper provided by Office of President Emeritus, Stanford University, p. 1. See also Kennedy's fine, aptly titled book, *Academic Duty*, which outlines and discusses the responsibilities of leaders and faculty members for the academic life of universities. Also see his essay, "The Lost Art of Teaching," *Stanford Magazine*, January/February 1998, pp. 1–6.

10. Kennedy, "Universities: Costs and Benefits on the Academic Frontier," p. 4.

11. Ibid., pp. 4–5.

12. Ibid., p. 5.

13. We have noted previously Frank Rhodes's comments, based on Cardinal Newman, that the university's purpose is reified, "One-by-one, person-by-person, student by student: that is the basis for educational success. It is also the basis of a free society, and the secret of a great university. Universities will remain great only to the extent they are great student universities, as well as great centers for individual learning, discovery and outreach." From "Thoughts on the American University at the Dawn of the Third Millennium," p. 38.

14. Kennedy, "Universities: Costs and Benefits on the Academic Frontier," p. 6.

15. John Sexton, "Inaugural Address," September 26, 2002, provided by President's Office, New York University, p. 5.

16. Frank Rhodes, "Reinventing the University," in *Reinventing the Research University*, ed. Luc E. Weber and James J. Duderstadt (London: Economica, 2004), p. 9.

17. Sexton, "Inaugural Address," p. 6.

18. Ibid., p. 8.

19. Ibid., p. 9.

20. John Sexton, "The Role of Faculty in the Common Enterprise University," delivered as part of Northwestern University's President's Teaching Series, provided by President's Office, New York University, May 6, 2004, p. 7.

21. Ibid., p. 8. As dean of the Law School, Sexton initiated a consortium of selected faculty, dubbed "The Enterprise" (often with the modifier "general" or "common"). This group was gathered to think about the faculty's and the institution's future. Sexton's philosophy of the university is grounded in the importance of community, and he believes faculty must embody this principle in their teaching and scholarly work.

22. Kirp, *Shakespeare, Einstein, and the Bottom Line*, pp. 85–87. For example: "Meanwhile, professors who unhesitatingly protest the working conditions of janitors in Los Angeles and picket companies like Nike for their treatment of pieceworkers in Indonesia have

generally been mute about the plight of these not-quite members of the academy" (p. 86). Sexton is in the crosshairs of Kirp's critique. However, Kirp also seems to agree, as evidence here suggests, that Sexton is concerned about this issue and attempting to do something about it.

23. Sexton, "The Role of Faculty in the Common Enterprise University," p. 10.
24. Ibid., p. 14.
25. Ibid., p. 17.
26. Ibid., p. 18.
27. Kirp, *Shakespeare, Einstein, and the Bottom Line*, p. 129.

CHAPTER 8

Life in the Bully Pulpit: Choices and Dilemmas

n May 1970, John Kemeny had been president of Dartmouth College for just over two months. He was confronted, as were presidents across the nation, by the stunning news that four students on the campus of Kent State University had been shot and killed by National Guard troops.[1] Students there along with thousands of others at hundreds of campuses had gathered to protest U.S. involvement in the Vietnam War and revelations of the previously secret bombing campaign in Cambodia.

On the evening of the Kent State slayings, Kemeny was scheduled for a regularly weekly appearance on the campus radio station. He had initiated this practice at the beginning of his presidency to signal his and his office's accessibility to students. Over the airwaves that evening in a remarkable extemporaneous address, Kemeny cancelled classes for the remainder of the spring semester. He urged students and faculty to devote the time that would have been dedicated to normal classroom education to a more important educational task: discussion about the war, about the state of national debate and politics, and about citizen responsibility. Kemeny stated that he would place this action before the faculty, but that their voice and vote could only confirm not overrule his decision. However, he acknowledged that this pronouncement, crafted in hurried consultation that afternoon with students and faculty on different sides of the war issue, would expend some of the goodwill that had accompanied the beginning of his presidency. These leadership "chips" are not unlimited and this single decision could well have cost Kemeny a great deal.

More than almost any other responsibility, presidents must know when and how to use the bully pulpit. Given the diversity of presidential styles and temperaments, and the range of issues that confront their office, it is no surprise that presidents are not unanimous in assessments and guidelines about how best to use their public platform. However, there are principles that presidents have in common.

In this instance Kemeny did what he felt he had to do. He grasped the authority of his pulpit to lead the campus through an undeniably trying and difficult time. The conditions and issues at stake—Kemeny equates this national crisis as on par with the Revolutionary War period—compelled him to action even as he recognized its potential to sacrifice the long-term future of his presidency.

Kemeny's feat bears witness to the complex intersection of factors at play in considerations about the bully pulpit. Presidents make choices and have to decide about utterances they wish or feel compelled to make. They must wisely judge the severity and urgency of the social, political, or educational issue and concern at stake. They have to decide what influence they are actually capable of having. Finally, presidents must contemplate the constituencies inside and outside the gates and their reaction to anything that might be said from the pulpit.

Kemeny used the bully pulpit on the occasion of his talk that May evening in what seems almost another era. But that era of the 1960s and early 1970s was the first major moment in the history of the college and university in America when student protests and commitments were joined with national concerns and political movements, in this case focused on civil rights and the Vietnam War. Ironically, many initiatives believed to be rooted in political correctness—minority recruitment and admissions, refashioning of curricula, concern about the relationship of the academy to corporate investment and influence, and the negative reactions to them—were spawned in this era.

The presidency of Ted Hesburgh, a contemporary of Kemeny, began a decade and a half before the late 1960s and early 1970s. Hesburgh is in many ways unique as a university president. He headed a high-profile religious university, deeply rooted in the Roman Catholic faith, that grew significantly in national reputation largely as a result of his evolving personal leadership and image. He was a prominent, resilient presidential figure, almost a throwback to an earlier era, whose persona and office commanded great authority and respect within and outside the gates of Notre Dame.[2] Those who believe that the public voice of today's college and university presidents has been reduced in comparison to what it once was might point to the Hesburgh-Kemeny era as a dividing line in the visibility and role of the bully pulpit. Prior to the 1960s, presidents were thought undeniably to possess the platform of the bully pulpit, and they regularly and with little inhibition used it.

After the early 1970s some observers think presidential voices and the use of their pulpits became restricted and diminished. I believe that this view over-romanticizes some bygone era and judges unfairly and without clear evidence the pulpits of presidents who have served in recent decades. The 1960s were a period of grand tensions and polemical politics, a climate that put many presidents on the spot. The political and ideological frame inside and outside the academy has evolved between that time and the present. Since the 1960s, one lesson presidents may well have learned is to be more cautious about public utterances. But this has not led to silence in the ivory tower.

Hesburgh reports that during the 1960s "student revolutions" he kept a small pocket-card "necrology" of the names of presidents, most whom he knew personally, who lost their jobs because of political and social pressures. With a sense of resignation in his voice, Hesburgh claims that he stopped listing them when he got to 250.[3] Perhaps this was simply a fetish of Hesburgh's, or a sign of the times, or both. Hesburgh alone may have been maintaining such a contemporaneous record of "failed," suddenly-concluded and terminated presidencies, but his accounting confirms the worst estimates about what happened to a number of presidents during those tense times.

At Notre Dame it might be said that Hesburgh was always using the bully pulpit. The following episode at Notre Dame resulted from student concerns reflecting a broad political spectrum, and from protest by some against the Vietnam War.[4] Hesburgh's actions are indicative of his leadership style and despite the passage of time still carry lessons today.

A student leader called Hesburgh late one night and asked to meet with him. He came to the office (Hesburgh was famous for being in his office late into the evening and always prepared to meet with students) and told the president about a war protest rally on the main mall of the campus scheduled for the following afternoon. The student was there on behalf of the rally organizers to invite Hesburgh to speak. Hesburgh was known to be a friend of then-President Nixon and some thought he was a hawk on the war. Whether the students had a definite idea about what he would say is not clear. No doubt their primary interest was to have him simply as president and as the featured speaker. Hesburgh agreed to come the next day.

Hesburgh was asked to speak first and recalls that "I had a sixth sense, which I think you get on these jobs some of the time," contending that his came "from the Holy Spirit." Though he had been to many similar rallies, his sixth sense told him this was different. Hesburgh knew well that as president a failure to handle moments like this well could easily prove disastrous. So uncharacteristically, though his custom was to speak extemporaneously, he decided to write down his remarks.

He wrote out "seven reasons why the war is wrong." He recalls that the gist of the message was that "'99 percent of you guys and gals out there are against the war. But I think if you were to walk through this town [South Bend]—it's an immigrant town—there are Hungarians and Poles and Irish and Italian and Belgians.' And I said, 'This is a pretty tough, down-to-earth, American citizenry.'" Mentioning his seven points he then added, "'I assume that 99 percent of you would sign this in a minute, but just think that you're not the only people in America. These people [of South Bend] built America and they're solid people and there are probably 30,000 households or more. Some of them are first and second generation.'"

Then Hesburgh turns the force and power of his bully pulpit on the students: "'I want to give you a challenge. See if you can get 80 to 90 percent of these people to sign this statement why the war is wrong.'" He added that most of these conservative, immigrant citizens would be in favor of the war and that the students would have a difficult time convincing them to endorse the statement. Hesburgh told the students the rest of what he would do: "'If you get at least 40,000 of these filled out—most of them I hope will be filled out against the war, but that's your problem—but if you get them, I'll deliver them to the White House so that you're not just doing this as an empty gesture. And it will get a little publicity.'" He concluded the talk quickly, saying, "'I guess that's all I have got to say on the subject,'" and by commenting that college students were only a small part of the people making up the country and that unfortunately their protests often merely gave them bad press because they were, after all, nothing more than college students.

After a quick detour on a campus errand, Hesburgh returned to his office where 40 or so students from the rally were already waiting for him. He took them in and they said, "'We buy your proposition and we've got to get copies of your talk.'" We were fortunate because I knew this was going to be an important thing and I had a copy and I wanted to think about it for a few hours." He then had his secretary make copies, and the students "went out and made 40,000 copies and distributed them all over the campus. And all these kids went down house by house."

The students spread out in South Bend and Hesburgh reports, "I'll be darned if they didn't come up with about 40,000. They had a heck of a time getting them," because of major pockets of support for the war and because many questioned the students in their face-to-face meetings along the lines of, "'What do you mean it's a bad war? Why aren't you over there doing something?'" But Hesburgh concludes that "it was a good experience for all of them and it was a kind of high point" in terms of the way the antiwar protests often went. As good as his word, Hesburgh delivered the petitions to the White House.[5] All in all, Hesburgh used the presidential office as a teacher with his students, seizing the occasion of this protest as an opportunity to create more of an outcome than simply a rally on the mall.

Among contemporary presidents, Nan Keohane believes there are three arenas of choice and wisdom concerning presidential use of the bully pulpit. Keohane assumes that there exists "a responsibility of those in the university sometimes to use the moral authority of the university itself by speaking out, rather than simply providing a haven for expression by faculty members speaking for themselves."[6] This underscores the position of the university and the way in which institutional stands can complement (or possibly disagree with) the voices of individual faculty. However, there is an opposing camp that disagrees with this type of stand and contends rather that the university as an institution has no business at all using its moral authority in this way.

The first threshold Keohane believes presidents must cross in making decisions about whether to use the bully pulpit centers on the major principles of the university (echoing Cardinal Newman's notion of "first principles") and the responsibility to protect these values at the foundation of the academy. Arguing, debating, exhorting in the public square for these core values is well within the province of the president. Because these values are fundamentally important, ducking this responsibility would raise questions about presidential leadership. Keohane's parameter in this case is to use the bully pulpit "where an issue has clear relevance to the other public purposes of the university. Few would deny that the president ought to make his or her voice heard when the basic goals of the university are at stake—support for research, financial aid that makes education more accessible, threats to academic freedom."[7]

This plank in the use of the bully pulpit is relatively straightforward; after all it should be expected that presidents would guard the most hallowed turf, the "first principles" of the academy. But Keohane's second arena of choice is more debatable: "where the university has an interest but the connection is less clear cut.... [These] are matters where members of a university community are likely to hold widely differing views as citizens; this means that special care should be used in deciding whether and how to speak out as president."[8] The problem is that these areas are gray because of the ready potential for disagreements about what is and is not "connected" to the university, and because of divisions among constituents about what stand, if any, might be worth taking.

For example, in the Michigan Supreme Court case, President Coleman tried to persuade to the contrary some constituents who, even while applauding the university's stand, believed that affirmative action was not directly connected to the university's core values and principles. Certainly affirmative action and minority advancement are not on Keohane's narrow list of research, accessibility to financial aid, and academic freedom. Coleman's opponents—alumni and other key supporters—felt the university's diversity initiatives were simply outside Michigan's primary mission. However, their sense of loyalty drove them, at the same time, to recognize the importance of Michigan standing up for its autonomy by fighting in court for its affirmative action policies. Keohane is not saying that presidents have no right to speak out except in cases where a university's "first principles" are clearly at stake or members of the community are reasonably united in their opinions. Rather she argues that in the cases where clarity and unity are absent or hotly debated, presidents must maneuver with greater care than where connections to university core values are more evident.

Keohane's third arena of choice for the bully pulpit concerns "issues where there is serious disagreement about whether 'the university' has any business getting into a topic at all—issues like divestment from South Africa, support for the government of Israel or the rights of Palestinians, perspectives on war in Iraq, corporate ethics, sweatshops and boycotts." She continues by arguing that it "is [in] these areas that presidents must determine their course of action very carefully, realizing that a large contingent of those who care about the university will disagree strongly with whatever presidents do—including doing nothing."[9] For example, where might issues like divestment from South Africa, or the analogous pressure for similar strategies concerning investments in Israel or the Sudan fall? Using Keohane's template, these would be judged as not directly "connected" to the basic values of the university. However, we have seen the University of

Michigan and its regents argue that in the case of South Africa a clear matter of moral right and wrong was at stake, and the university was already involved because of its investments. Even in this case, jumping to conclude that the South African divestment precedent is applicable to other instances will generate more than its share of disagreement within and outside the gates.[10]

Keohane believes that judgments about choices in the use of the bully pulpit pivot on an adage about ethics: not to decide is to decide. In this way, she stands on their heads questions about whether to use the bully pulpit, and about the moral and political consequences of refusing to use it in the face of pressure and controversy. In some cases presidents may duck a public issue or question with little or no loss of prestige or authority. In other circumstances presidents can lose more by saying nothing than by saying something. This is where things become most difficult. Presidents have latitude to use the bully pulpit, but they have to consider who will be on board? Who will not be on board? To what extent are the feelings and reactions of constituencies a major factor in the decision process?

Keohane also links the bully pulpit to debate about political correctness and ideological battles in the academy. She is concerned that leaders of the academy, be they presidents or faculty members, frequently hide behind the argument that everything is and always should be "objective," using this as an excuse to restrain public commentary. Her opinion about this minimalist position is: "I find it hard to accept the viewpoint that many of my colleagues in university presidencies would affirm—that the only place we can stand comfortably *as* presidents is on the 'objective center,' that our only role is to make sure freedom of speech is not impaired for others and that both sides are heard."

But does this place presidents on a slippery slope? Does it mean subjectivity is unleashed, making fair game of any issue and the way it might be addressed? These questions run smack into the political correctness battle for the center of the university. Concerned that those who are able to speak for the university will wall themselves out of the public square, Keohane contends: "Some of my colleagues use, as an argument for neutrality, the fact that both sides in contentious issues are attempting to capture the 'moral authority' of the university. No doubt this is true; but if that 'moral authority' is never used by those who *can* speak for the university, then in what sense is there any moral authority at all?"[11]

Though calculating and cautious, Keohane affirms that presidents have both the right and more crucially the duty to make public utterances based on the "moral authority" of the university. Whether it is the president of Harvard or the president of a community college in the Midwest, the institution, the "university," by definition has "moral authority" and carries moral weight. But institutions cannot speak; only people can. This is precisely Kemeny's point in his radio address: the decision to cancel the semester was his alone as president, not somehow the college speaking. Keohane's corollary is simple yet profound: moral authority—presidential and institutional—ceases to exist if not effectively utilized and voiced.

The oft-repeated argument is that compared to the "giants" of old, contemporary presidents are found wanting in their use of the bully pulpit and moral persuasion in the public square. Keohane tackles this perception head on: "Quite a few people these days deplore the fact that university presidents have become a bunch of wimps, concerned only to raise money and keep peace—pale shadows of the giants who walked the earth in ages past, whom an entire society revered as moral arbiters. I have no desire to be a wimp, but also no illusions," acknowledging the problem she and her colleagues confront "about becoming widely recognized as moral arbiter even if I wanted to."

But this still begs the question of what prevents today's presidents from gaining the perceived high profile of their forbears? After all a president as "recent" as Hesburgh, his tenure overlapping with the first years of Keohane's lengthy presidential career, was able to attain and possess such stature. Keohane's reply to the question of what has changed captures part of the problem. The way things worked for the "giants" is "simply not the way things work in our society of sound bites and talk shows, a society that no longer easily accords moral leadership to anybody in whatever post."[12]

Reality is that ours is a "sound bite" culture, one in which presidents and their utterances are squeezed out of the headlines and of the public view by fast-paced news cycles and by a compressed attention span. In the earlier twentieth century, presidential inaugural addresses appeared in full text in newspapers. Today, a college or university is fortunate when a president is inaugurated if a press release with a few choice quotes and some coverage of the event appears in print or televised media. The "content" of what a president says is simply not of sufficient public interest, except to the few "insiders," faculty, fellow administrators, alumni, and maybe students, to be examined closely or to engage broad public discourse.

However, there are ways for presidents to get public play, even if they cannot quite become the "moral arbiters" of old. Presidents more and more are using op-ed essays in major newspapers as a part of their platform. Some are still publicly visible enough to appear on radio and television, though unfortunately much of this attention has been limited to athletic scandals, or problems such as major alcohol-related and other student life crises.

One service that Keohane provides is to clear a path leading presidents outside the boxes that constrict the bully pulpit. Breaking out of these constraints is not simple or easy. Faculty, trustees, and alumni send messages that presidents exist exclusively "to raise money and keep peace," and they should therefore keep quiet about controversial issues. Some presidents, it must be admitted, are quite happy with these restraints because they make the public pulpit part of the job relatively safe. The tasks of raising money and keeping the peace are not terribly difficult to accomplish. What president would want to complicate these expectations, unnecessarily rocking the boat by using the bully pulpit to speak to a public issue? But Keohane counters these presumptions and the inertia they inspire. Whether inside or outside the gates of the academy, presidents still must make "right" decisions about when and how to use the resource of their pulpit. Keohane believes that "it's much tougher to find the common ground for a moral voice on issues outside the university." This is because with regard to issues outside the gates, it is "a lot harder to argue that this is something the university ought to be engaged in" when there is "clear evidence that members of the university community disagree profoundly" in the first place about engagement in external issues.[13]

Even if the "giants" are a thing of the past, there are still ways in which today's presidents can and must use their bully pulpits to address the issues and concerns of the day, whether inside or outside the gates of their campuses. While it is a balancing act, for sure, successfully using the bully pulpit is by no means impossible. Keohane declares that "moral authority may become moribund if it is never used; but it is also squandered if it is used too casually."[14]

Among the social and political issues Keohane confronted as Duke's president, one is a case study of the criteria she suggests as parameters for decisions about the bully pulpit. The issue concerned a boycott of the Mount Olive Pickle Company, a major regional pickle manufacturer near the university in eastern North Carolina. The boycott—local, regional, statewide, and beyond—began in response to employee working conditions and to the political reality that unionization was not a likely step to be taken to address employees' problems. Thus the only pressure that could be applied was by consumers.

Duke's involvement began when its Dining Services manager decided to join the boycott by ceasing university purchases of Mount Olive products. He informed Keohane of his action and she assented (though retrospectively, noting her preference for prior consultation about the decision). Subsequently a group of Duke students gathered detailed information about Mount Olive employees' working conditions, pay, and treatment. Aware of the Dining Services' stance, the students presented their evidence to Keohane, requesting she affirm the purchasing decision as an official university stand on the boycott. She agreed to do so "at least for a period of time," deciding that "the best strategy was to sustain it for a while as we began conversations with Mount Olive and use it as leverage to say, 'We want some serious opportunity for change here.'"[15] As a result of this action the university fashioned a working partnership with the owners of the company to make substantial changes for the workers.

This case falls between two of Keohane's categories about presidential stands: those in which the university has an interest in an issue but its connection to fundamental university principles or values is not clear-cut, and those in which there is broad and firm disagreement about whether the institution should be involved. In the pickle boycott, the university's connection was as a large purchaser of the company's products, capable of exercising economic sanctions that might pressure Mount Olive in its relationship with its workers. But there was also disagreement within the campus community about whether the university should in any way be involved. Some of Keohane's senior advisors questioned the decision to pursue this strategy of involvement, because they concluded that the boycott question "was far enough away from daily life here that a number of people thought I was getting pretty far off the mark." However, Keohane disagreed and exercised her belief that there was "no question that this was the right thing to do."[16]

Another situation drawing the attention of Keohane's bully pulpit was Duke's leadership in addressing the issue of foreign "sweatshops" producing athletic apparel and products that capitalize on collegiate names and logos. This was an issue of major significance nationally and even globally. Based on her experience with university stands on difficult social and political issues, Keohane is convinced that portraits of today's college and university presidents as "nobody's taking any stands" are simply unfounded.[17]

Donald Kennedy agrees with Keohane's criteria for the use of the bully pulpit. His fundamental ground rule is "that the president speaks not only for himself but for the legal entity of the university, that is, for the ownership of the Board of Trustees."[18] He points to the "germaneness criterion," that is, when a president uses the bully pulpit, the issue "ought to be something in which universities have a special interest." However, in certain circumstances, Kennedy argues, a president can act more independently and thus "leap over" the germaneness bar.

Hypothetically, he suggests that while as president you "don't go on and make a general statement about the new drug approval process, even if you're an ex-commissioner of the FDA, unless it has something to do with the university." However, because of its direct impact, "you might very well say something about a national selective service policy if it affected large numbers of your undergraduates." Kennedy also believes that the president must know "something so that he is taken seriously. . . . he ought to have some expertise." In exercising the responsibilities of his office and pulpit, Kennedy tried to restrict himself "to things in which there was a legitimate institutional interest, because it involved our student body or faculty or the campus community in some way, or because one or more significant constituencies here had a deep interest in some concern or decision that would affect how well they did their work."[19]

Mary Sue Coleman draws attention to another arena that presidents can utilize to speak on public issues. These are instances where a president's academic and scholarly background and knowledge can and should be brought to bear. For example, given her scholarship in biochemistry and health research, Coleman believes she has both a right and responsibility to speak about the problems of the growing population lacking medical attention and health care insurance. She pursues this through national involvement with the Institute of Medicine and views this as an absolutely justifiable place for her to use her pulpit.

Presidents who are academician-scholars bring to the table professional specialties and credentials that create platforms from which to exercise public commentary. James Freedman was a legal scholar in the fields of freedom of speech and the press. This expertise and knowledge bolstered his voice and complemented his personal moral outrage in criticizing the journalistic abuses of the *Dartmouth Review*. While Freedman possessed the authority of his office as president of Dartmouth, his position was even more powerful precisely *because* of his scholarly command and experience.

Coleman also believes she can use the public pulpit to address social and moral wrongs. Racial problems in society and the response of colleges and universities to racial inequities and injustice are prominent issues for her. Coleman frames this issue as the "obligation of universities to create diverse student bodies," a premise that assumes universities to be major players in rectifying long-standing racial dilemmas and inequities, and assumes that diversity programs and initiatives are potential solutions to be explored and employed. This obligation "is a hugely important issue," but one Coleman recognizes that not "everybody agrees on." The disagreement within, as well as beyond, the gates of the academy is not whether there is a major national problem—most camps at various points on the political spectrum would likely agree—but about the remedies, and specifically whether they can or should be race-neutral. Coleman believes racial problems and inequities cannot be adequately addressed in race-neutral ways, or put another way—obviously based on Michigan's court battles—in the absence of affirmative action. She assumes that "unless we solve this problem, race is going to continue in our country to be the issue that causes us just immense pain and problems." Possibly with the exception of the military, "right now, universities are really the only place in this society where . . . people of different races really get together."[20]

Still, there are legitimate arguments about whether rectifying racial problems is part of the core purposes or principles of the academy. Michigan's notion of an "uncommon education for the common man" embedded in its saga reflects a fundamental institutional value that can be interpreted to include affirmative action designed to reach "all" of the common people. But Coleman still extends her pulpit to an issue—racial diversity and justice—that has its genesis outside the university and on which there is fair disagreement inside and outside the gates about methods that could or should be used as a "solution." The good news for Coleman is that the precedent of the Supreme Court case provides some leverage and support for her position: The university has a legitimate hand in the solution to this societal problem so long as the institution's conduct and policies are within the provisions and constraints of the U.S. Constitution.

There is yet another angle to the connection of a university's moral authority to the presidential bully pulpit. Put simply, presidents need to guard against constituents questioning the judiciousness of use of the pulpit, especially if the judgments are about failure to uphold the institution's respectability and about abuse of its "moral authority." Certainly the actions of presidents will always be subject to interpretation, and presidents must be alert to the nuances of the opinions and positions of their constituencies. What constitutes a substantial or significant portion of community members on one side or the other of an issue? What happens when there are significant divisions among groups in opposition to and support of a position a president takes? Where are the trustees in the mix? In navigating these issues, presidents must recognize the goodwill they possess, if they do not squander it, and the accountability they must accept in exercising the bully pulpit.

John DiBiaggio believes there are two judgments to be made about the use of the bully pulpit. First, the matter at hand has to be something of "consequence." If the president perceives a matter to be of consequence, then it *could* be (but by no means definitively is) a reason to speak out. A second, contingent criterion must then be met. For DiBiaggio the question is: "Is this something political enough that someone has, not because of them but because of the office they hold," thinking of his role as president, "the potential to have an impact, an influence, a decision." When this is the case, leaders have "a responsibility as citizens to speak up."[21]

Presidents regularly face decisions about issues that can be, and often are, reduced to matters of "right" versus "wrong." These moral judgments are inevitably made within the political contexts of the academy, and thus constituent groups are often arrayed on an issue that a president has addressed. DiBiaggio claims the voice of faculty members can prove to be crucial in these situations. Though faculty are unlikely to support every stand a president takes, they must understand that civic engagement on issues of the day is part of the job of the president.[22]

The fine lines governing the use of the bully pulpit and the reactions of the community on and off campus to presidential positions should never be underestimated. Tom Gerety, former president of Amherst College, tells of a late 1960s predecessor who joined a protest against the Vietnam War at a local military base.[23] The protesters intended to be and were arrested (whether the president was among this group is not clear) and a few months later he stepped down from the Amherst presidency. In theory, his resignation had nothing to do with his opposition to the war and participation in the protest. But the confluence was not lost on members of the college community at the time and was clearly not lost on Gerety. In this instance, whether fairly or not, the Amherst president was judged as unwisely using the authority of his office in his war protest.

Neil Rudenstine counsels caution, and advises that presidents recognize the limits on the reach and the use of their pulpits. His concern is with the potential for presidents to overplay their clout and to make unwise decisions about their influence in ways that rebound in resistance from colleagues and constituencies. He suggests two major lines of argument about the latitude of presidents to speak out.

First, in broad agreement with many if not most colleague presidents, Rudenstine stipulates that it is impossible to divorce the individual in the office from the role of president. Given the visibility and public profile of Harvard, Rudenstine faced both the curses and the blessings of the ways in which he was viewed and treated as president by those outside the gates. But the role carries perceived supremacy from the inside, where the president "is inevitably going to be seen and recorded and felt by, if nobody else, the students and faculty at your own campus and the staff. And they are not going to be thinking of you as an individual. They have to deal with you as a president. There's just simply no way you could strip yourself of that power."

His second claim about the president's role and the bully pulpit is that without hesitation "you speak out on what the core values of the institution are and you defend them. And when a core value is [in] dispute and in contention or under attack, then you have not only every reason but an obligation to speak out, because it has to do with the very purpose of the institution you're supposed to be leading."[24] Defending this territory is a clear, incumbent responsibility of the university president.

But Rudenstine adds a counterdistinction, regarding moments when the criteria of core values and fundamental principles are not at stake but presidents are regardless drawn to use their office and pulpits. "When the value, however interesting, good, important, or worthwhile it might be," Rudenstine argues, "has to do with things that really are germane centrally to other parts of the perfectly, legitimately, parsed-out universe of the country or the world, then you better be careful."

He cautions about the negative prospect that a president's use of the pulpit to make political, social, and ideological points can result in the eliminations or reduction of freedom to think freely and to explore the limits of inquiry by those who might be intimidated. Misuse of the bully pulpit in this way can dampen the speech of members of a campus community, both students and faculty, especially untenured professors. If presidents get out on this thin ice of issues outside the central mission of the university, Rudenstine warns, "what you say on those issues has an impact on your students or faculty whether you like it or not. And that impact does exactly the opposite of what a president ought to be doing," which is the protection contained in the idea "that you can say what you want without fear of any recrimination."[25] Anytime presidents stray into major social and political issues outside the gates, they simply have to exert great care.

Rudenstine returns to settings where core principles are at stake. For example, if a governmental or other policy external to the academy "happens to be the policy on scientific research or student aid or diversity" and it touches "a core value educationally, if you happen to believe it [does], which I do and I think you can make the case for it," then a president has every right and responsibility to engage the debate. Rudenstine draws a firm line of division with regard to these issues to encourage presidents to avoid matters that do not "really touch essentially on educational core values." Whenever this line of demarcation is crossed, "then I think you really are beginning to misuse the institution and your position." Though there are no guarantees that problems will be avoided by taking this cautious approach, Rudenstine argues that it at least protects the freedom of expression of members of the community. "If a core value isn't to allow students and faculty at all levels to be able to express themselves on an issue of importance without thinking they might be penalized, especially by the president or part of the system, then I don't know what it is," Rudenstine declares.[26]

Whether one likes it or not, Harvard is an incredibly powerful institution both within and outside the world of colleges and universities, and a major player on many different fronts. Rudenstine embraces this influence, especially Harvard's potential to throw its weight around when necessary. Rudenstine's critics believed that, though the balance and fairness of the judgments are questionable, he was too reticent and cautious in the use of his and Harvard's voice during his presidency. His record paints a picture to the contrary. Ironically, his successor, Larry Summers, was vulnerable to critics on the other side of this argument, that is, that he was too outspoken, too often lacking wise restraint.

Rudenstine's key question about whether presidents should engage their or their institution's pulpits is: "Who's likely to get the best results?"[27] He believes that at times it was preferable collegially to let other schools than Harvard and their leaders be in front on certain issues. Thus in some instances, what might be viewed as Rudenstine's reticence about getting involved was in fact a calculated decision to remain out of the limelight so that others, often better positioned on specific issues, could move to center stage.

However, Rudenstine was more aggressive, feeling compelled to enter the fray "on issues where I thought I didn't see anybody playing that role, like diversity," in cases where "we had a tradition at Harvard and a real stake in it and where other institutions were more vulnerable to being chopped up if they took or played a lead role in it." In situations when Harvard could stand up, on behalf of others, to very political constituencies, Rudenstine believed "it was very important for me personally—and for Harvard—to be out and front: (a) because I didn't see anybody else, and," fully acknowledging, maybe even reveling in, Harvard's institutional muscle, "(b) I knew as an institution we could take it. Nobody was going to push us around."[28]

Comparing the presidential pulpit today to the age of the "giants," Rudenstine adds an interesting twist. If there has been some compromising of the presidential voice in recent years, the cause has been more due to institutional and cultural changes affecting presidents rather than to some dramatic change in who the presidents are and whether they have the courage to speak forcefully in the public square. Rudenstine thinks two factors are foremost.

The first is changes in the culture of colleges and universities. In some cases these changes have resulted in a reduction of the reach of presidential authority. As examples, Rudenstine notes the shift only in recent decades in trustees' involvement in tenure cases, previously the purview of presidents alone, and the righting of wrongs as a result of battles now won against prejudiced and restrictive policies of the pre–World War II era, when "Harvard had only about two Jewish faculty members."[29] While there are always some new wrongs, many of these more egregious "attitudes would be unthinkable today."[30] However, sometimes these past wrongs continue to be the springboard for presidential utterances. One example was Jim Freedman's forceful talk when he was dedicating a new Hillel Center at Dartmouth in the last months of his presidency. In his address he openly decried Dartmouth's anti-Semitic attitudes and those of Ernest Martin Hopkins, one of his esteemed predecessors, which resulted in the college's restrictive and minimal Jewish admissions quotas for years.

A second and closely related change is the fact that because of generally accepted progressive social assumptions today compared to previous eras, "other values are going to be greater and more important and more central and more endurable than the president's own views or the corporation's own views except on strictly educational matters and values." Because there may be a broad consensus on many formerly divisive issues and the idiosyncratic ideas of a president might more likely be judged outside this mainstream, "you can be outspoken today, but the price of being outspoken may be a cost on your own faculty and students, on your institution, that you don't really even know or you don't want to know." Rudenstine's warning is that if a president "goes too far," there is a likelihood that "you won't last and you shouldn't last," because you would have violated the basic principles and expectations of the institution concerning the use of the presidential pulpit.[31]

The situation Rudenstine presents creates an intriguing prospect that presidents of today have to face. Is it possible that two seemingly contradictory but possibly complementary forces are at work? One is the contention that the diversity and complexity of constituencies and viewpoints, especially those based in ideology, have created a narrower center than was the case when the spectrum of perspectives was far more homogenized. The second is Rudenstine's point that society has at the same time, literally during the same historical period, become more progressive and enlightened. That is, a general consensus has developed, leading to a refined and superseding set of core social and cultural values—commitments regarding civil and human rights, acceptance of the value of diversity through affirmative action and related initiatives, and expanded democraticization of decision making and participation—governing the lives of institutions, organizations, and individuals. In this rendering, though there are detractors who resist this "progress," in general an expanded and refined social compact has become generally accepted. Thus, as presidents locate and articulate a "center" from which to speak out and guide their colleges and universities, they are both helped and hindered by this shifting cultural environment.

Presidents can find themselves supported by the existence of a broad consensus about a moral center widely accepted and embraced by significant majorities of people, regardless of political and cultural differences. From their pulpits, presidents are able to tap into this "center" as the continuing "experiment" at the heart of the unique American democratic and liberal progressive tradition. However, this same broad consensus can restrict the latitude of presidents to speak about critical issues because, in an ironic twist, any questioning of these new modern shibboleths could cause knee-jerk criticism and debate from those who do not share the consensus on who believe it stifles free thinking and inquiry.

Any discussion of the bully pulpit of the presidency must encounter the inevitable issue of the degree to which presidents speak for themselves versus the degree to which they speak for the college or university. When Kemeny commented about the Kent State killings and his actions in canceling classes, declaring a day of mourning, and calling on his faculty to "have meetings...to bring about collective wisdom as to what we can do for the remainder of the week and beyond," he acknowledged that "while institutions as such cannot effectively take stands on controversial issues, individuals must take stands." Juggling the fine line of presidential authority and the latitude of leadership, he adds "I am painfully aware of the fact that no college president can use this prerogative too often or he loses his effectiveness. And yet events have taken place during the past week which make it impossible for me not to exercise this prerogative."[32] Given the crisis that Kemeny faced, traditional guideposts may go out the window. As Donald Kennedy points out, rules are fine, but presidents must have latitude to "make exceptions only in cases of extreme urgency, because there will always be moments" when they must decide and act.[33]

Whatever latitude presidents possess, they must develop reasonably consistent principles for engaging the bully pulpit. They must be as clear as possible with constituents about what they are doing and why. While there are inevitable crisis moments that challenge the academy and call for responses from inside the ivory tower, many of the matters presidents face are quite routine. They must create expectations for their pulpit and how they will utilize it on a day-in and day-out basis. These choices in the use of the pulpit of office involve both style and substance. Presidents are like preachers: as a function of the office they possess a pulpit and must decide the pastoral and social concerns to present to their "congregations." Rob Oden claims there are a number of inescapable issues embedded in the academy that need to be at the forefront of life of campus communities. To address these matters in the social fabric he uses his pulpit in two major, overlapping ways.

The first is the public ceremonial and ritual role of the president.[34] Oden believes these opportunities are of increased importance for college and university presidents in part because the role of ceremony and ritual has become less important in society. Presidential public occasions are "moments to talk about what matters." Paradoxically, Oden believes that finding the right language to talk publicly about ideas, such as love, friendship, and the spiritual side of life, that matter is simply difficult for most people and leaders. Because these concerns are the focus of private thoughts and conversation, leaders are vulnerable when they speak about them publicly. Despite the risk, Oden views public occasions as "freighted moments and presidents have to use them," and says that he needs to ask, "what are the hard things which need to be talked about?" He adds that especially in times of tragedy, "the president simply cannot delegate what will be said to the community and how that will be done."

Oden was president of Kenyon College on September 11, 2001, as the campus shared the national sense of confusion and shock. Classes continued without interruption, a decision Oden made and one with which most administrators and faculty agreed. But as occurred at many campuses, faculty members reacted by wanting to do what academics do best: organize panels and formal discussions. Oden resisted this faculty pressure for forums to discuss what had happened, its geopolitical and national implications, and what might happen next. He simply saw this approach as inappropriate for the moment and contended that faculty panels and forums should not be scheduled for at least for a week or so. Instinct told him that in the aftermath of such a cataclysmic shock, the campus community should rather have a few days for reflection, for grieving, and for informal discussion. However, Oden admits that if the faculty had actually voted, he would have lost. But he persisted in his view and the faculty chose not to vote, in an interesting echo of Kemeny at Dartmouth in 1970.

Oden's second principle about the use of the presidential pulpit begins with a question: "How do you lead your own life?" He believes that presidents must ask this of themselves and that in the larger scheme of things, posing this question is integral to the life of the academy. Oden raises a critical point about the personal responsibility and standards of public behavior underlying the presidential pulpit.

In a talk at Kenyon, Oden used a phrase, "time famine," that he felt certain he had read somewhere but could not remember where. Wanting to be extremely careful and to underscore the importance of avoiding plagiarism anytime, especially in a talk to the community, he publicly indicated that a search using all the latest technology and techniques had not located an author of the quote. He was only able to say, "I know it is not mine."[35]

Oden uses this example not to extol personal virtue but rather to point to valued and fundamental principles in the academy. He believes that plagiarism and the lifting of others' work by noted scholars and writers are an assault on professional and public standards of behavior. Stepping over this line threatens the ability to maintain the integrity of "the canons of the work we do and the lessons we do" in the academy.[36] At the fundamental foundation of the university, "we possess a model of inquiry which relies on subjective, but nonetheless substantive questions and answers," Oden declares. His point is simple yet profound: the academy must hold itself (and presumably be held by others) to the highest standards in order to maintain its status as a distinctive and distinguished institution in society.

One aspect of the college or university presidency today, one I would argue has ever been such, is the expected fidelity of leaders despite the relentless personal pressures of the office. Frank Rhodes's simple judgment is that presidents need to have at the heart of their leadership an integrated sense of the fundamental principles of the university. Such a core understanding and the clear communication of it will not inoculate presidents against criticism and complaint. Inevitably there is a diversity of reactions to any president and to the directions a president aspires to take with regard to an institution, and the consequences will include dissent, dislike, and resistance. To a large extent, presidents are on a scaffold constructed of regular and continual judgments by their constituents. However, a failure to hold fast to the fundamental values of the academy in the conduct of their office—decisions, philosophy, and choices about the use of the pulpit itself—will rebound negatively on presidents, even drawing criticism from those who might otherwise support them.

Noting the daily claims and nature of the office, Rhodes asserts, "I don't think the presidential pulpit is confined to great speeches on great occasions. I think everything, every single thing you do, is a pulpit." The relentless public visibility lends to an almost pastoral role, and to Rhodes the presidential pulpit "is a living sermon." He ticks off a bill of particulars: "the way you answer the phone, the way you greet a janitor, the way you talk to a student walking across a quad, the way you interact at an alumni reunion, the way you deal with the mayor of a city where you live or with the governor of the state in which you're situated. Every single thing you do—and the way you teach a class—is a statement, is a sermon, not because you have anything great to offer as an individual but just because of the office."[37] Presidents are continually "on duty," with the rare exceptions of escape for some planned, and occasionally unplanned, personal, "down" time. Acknowledging the paucity of personal time created by the demands of the office, James Duderstadt notes that during his presidency at Michigan the only time for thinking was when he was stuck in airports longer than planned.[38]

Harold Shapiro adds that on any occasion when he was to speak publicly he always wanted to say "something of substance," no matter the setting and no matter what else might be expected. For example, he notes that even when speaking about athletics to an alumni group he would "never talk about the won-loss record." Rather he "would talk about things like can intercollegiate athletics survive in this current framework? Or how does what's going on in youth sports impact what goes on at the collegiate level?" Shapiro offers an important watchword: "I never liked to talk about nothing. I never talk about something simple, I never talk about something trivial. I never talk about making people feel good because [it is] embarrass[ing] to talk that way."[39]

John Kemeny behaved similarly. As Dartmouth's president, Kemeny always had something of substance to say, certainly at prime public occasions but also in the most mundane of places such as monthly full staff meetings. A faculty joke at Dartmouth during Kemeny's tenure went along the lines that with the entire faculty (that time more than three hundred academics) arrayed against him, Kemeny could "win" the argument, would be able to carry the day. Kemeny's power to deliver in these circumstances was also due to the substance of his thinking and ideas, and his ability to communicate that wisdom from the presidential pulpit.

But even this day-to-day focus of the pulpit still connects to the ideals of the university: "And so you're on parade whether you like it or not—I won't say 24/7, but every time you're doing anything in public—attending a concert, being present at an athletic event—every single thing you do is a statement," not just an ordinary statement but engaging the force of the office "for or against the values for which the university stands." Ignoring the conventions and snares of political correctness, Rhodes asserts that "those values are essentially the values of Western Civilization in the Western World." While he "simply does not know enough to be sure" whether "maybe there are great universities that have the same values in other cultures," Rhodes contends that these values are grounded in the fact "that the universities of the Western world were invented by the Christian church." In his analysis, the ideals at the core of the university are the "heritage of a committed community—a community of integrity, a community of openness, a community of civility, a community where knowledge is seen as the pathway to understanding and a wider sense of service."[40]

Rhodes suggests that a presidential style that adheres to the creedal foundations of the academy is most critical in times of crisis, controversy, and disagreement. Concerning these "great historic values" of the university, Rhodes asserts that "without preaching every day about them" a president still "can and must exemplify those values in a way that you behave in every situation." This is especially true "when you're confronted with people with whom you profoundly disagree— things like the South African boycott question, for example." Leaving to our imagination his position about the divestment issue, Rhodes adds, "I disagreed with many of the people who were members of the campus, disagreed with many of the trustees, disagreed with most of the faculty if the votes mean anything." "But the way you handle disagreements, and the sensitivity and courtesy and the civility of handling difference on the campus," Rhodes stresses, "is one of the great lessons that you have to teach." His bottom line was "how to disagree without being disagreeable." Finally, asserting that a foundational principle of the academy is a "model of inquiry which relies on subjective but nonetheless substantive questions and answers" and pushing back in a politically correct era, Rhodes concludes, "If we so shelter our comments, if we so constrain our comments that we never disagree on anything, we've actually failed the test of truth."[41]

In exercising all their responsibilities, and especially in the use of their bully pulpits, presidents must resist being made into demigods and being put on pedestals. Because of their influence, presidents face constant pressures from different groups and constituencies to speak out on behalf of their causes. Aware of the potential to be drawn willy-nilly into all manner of causes, John Sexton confesses that "in fact it is very easy" as a president "to get demagogic." But the main reason he avoids taking sides and positions is that maintaining more than just the appearance of neutrality helps "to build up my moral capital so that I can provide the broadest possible dialogue inside the university, and, in appropriate cases, exclude people who do not accept the rules of discourse of the university."[42]

The tugs and pressures of ideologies, the demands for consensus-making, and the need to consider earnestly the voice of constituents lead many to believe that the authority and power of college and university presidents has become severely curtailed in recent decades. Rhodes disagrees, convinced that the authority and influence of the presidency remains solidly in place and as crucial as ever in defense of the core ideas of the academy. Those principles include "institutional autonomy, the academic freedom of the faculty, the rights of individuals to due process and a fair hearing. These are fundamentally important values on the campus." In upholding these values, "the president, in one sense, is the person who has to embody those values. There is no one else. The trustees are only there a few days a year, and although they're the ultimate authority of the university—the constitutional authority—it's the president who day-to-day embodies and guarantees those values."

In addition, the role and capacity of presidents to protect values inside the gates is connected to the actual as well as perceived image of the university outside the gates. Rhodes reminds us of the critical and indigenously American notion about higher education, that "because universities exist because of an unwritten social compact, they're accorded enormous freedom—institutional autonomy, academic freedom, being excused from paying taxes, being supported by the public with gifts and taxes—in exchange for what the public sees as the public good of scholarship and professional education, and with the understanding that they will be impartial and responsible in the use of their knowledge."[43]

However, this long-standing and hard-won social compact is not so uncritically or universally accepted and therefore is more fragile than in previous eras. From many quarters, questions are regularly raised about the "benefits" accorded to colleges and universities, public and private. The "old" practical arguments about the large number of employees, the taxes they return to states and municipalities, and the positive institutional economic impact including the purchasing power of students do not play as they once did. Allegations about larger than necessary tuition increases, property acquisitions in surrounding neighborhoods with no tax trade-off, and perceptions of liberal political bias lead citizens, government leaders and legislators, and the media to be highly critical of higher education.

Accompanying these concerns is a desire for tangible, short-term results that makes the citizen and other stakeholders less willing to accept the rationale of the more theoretical, longer-term benefits and value to society of the university: the pursuit of knowledge, new discoveries particularly in the sciences, technology, and medicine, and nearly universal access to educational advancement. But maintaining this social compact is critical to the foundations of the university and is the basis of its relationship to society. Presidents are crucial as a bulwark to defend the academy and to argue that the best interests of the ivory tower are synonymous with the best interests of society.

The manner in which presidents are perceived in their pulpits dictates and defines perceptions about them as decision makers, as leaders in the eyes of administrative colleagues, faculty, students, alumni, and trustees, as dependably wise figures in times of crisis, and even as fund-raisers in the inescapable gathering of resources and capital. Therefore, presidents must capitalize of this platform of their office. How do they define when and how to use these pulpits? What are the boundaries of the presidential pulpit? How do presidents make wise decisions about public utterances?

Though by no means exhaustive, the following conclusions are evident and critical. First, the presidential office carries enormous weight, and to maintain its dignity and influence, presidents must be prepared to sacrifice individual freedoms of speech and expression for the good of the commons. But they ought to be mindful of Rhodes's injunction that if "we so shelter our comments, if we so constrain our comments that we never disagree on anything, we've actually failed the test of truth."[44] Achieving the balance is not easy, but it is essential to sustain important values of the academy as well as practically crucial in sustaining presidential leadership.

Second, presidents should frame issues and concerns in light of the fundamental values and principles of the university. This requires having a working set of assumptions about what those principles are. Building on that framework, presidents need to be able to communicate views regarding matters about which they are expected, obligated, and responsible to speak to constituents.

Finally, presidents should heed the advice to speak about what matters, to talk about things of substance. The use of more symbolic, pastoral, "living sermon" speech and action is crucially part of the presidential pulpit, important to members of university communities as well as to those outside the gates.

The bully pulpit has evolved hand in hand with changes in the presidency in recent decades. It has been and is being reinvented, and will require continual reformation in the future. There is no doubt that the pulpit continues to be a critical part of the office of the college and university president, and presidents are rightly expected to speak out on issues of concern, on things that matter to those inside the gates of the academy and to the larger society and world beyond. However difficult and tendentious the choices made in its use, the bully pulpit will remain available to presidents as long as they recognize and grasp its relationship to the inherent moral authority of the university and of their office. In the future, as in the past, presidents will shape this platform, and done rightly it will remain a foremost feature of their leadership, public image, and persuasion.

NOTES

1. This story is covered in greater detail in Nelson, *Leaders in the Crucible*, pp. 18–20. I return to it here as Kemeny's leadership is emblematic and iconic, though he would likely resist the labeling of himself in this way, and captures the moral leadership of presidents and their use of the bully pulpit.

2. The Reverend Theodore Hesburgh, former president, University of Notre Dame, interview by author, June 26, 2003. By his own estimate, Hesburgh accepted 16 U.S. presidential appointments and accepted untold other appointments for service on national education organizations and bodies.

3. Ibid.

4. Ibid. The story is as told by Hesburgh, including the accompanying quotations, in the interview.

5. Ibid. Hesburgh follows this up with some of his advice to President Nixon on a previous occasion. Here we see his influence on the national stage and in ways that were in the best interests of college-age students. He says he and Nixon discussed two things. About the first Hesburgh suggested:

> "You ought to get the vote for the 18-year-old kids because if they can be picked up to go to war and maybe get killed as a lot of them do, especially the poor, they ought to be able to vote for their commander-in-chief. Do you agree with that?" And he said,

"I do indeed, and I'll work on that." And he did, and within a year, the 18-year-old vote was reality.

Regarding the second, Hesburgh advised,

"I think it's high time that we had an all-volunteer army. And my guess is that if you study this and decide to do it, you'll have just as good an army as you do today, maybe better, because they will have signed up freely. And you can cut out the guys who aren't qualified." I get a call the next day from the Secretary of the Navy, and he said, "You and your big mouth." And I said, "What's up?" And he said, "The boss called me in today and I'm now chairman of an All-volunteer Army Commission." And he said, "You're the first one who's going to be a member." So, a year later, we got it [the report] out and a year later we had an all-volunteer army.

6. Keohane, "The Public Role of the University," p. 5.

7. Ibid., p. 6.

8. Ibid.

9. Ibid., p. 7.

10. In fall 2005, Dartmouth College's Board of Trustees passed a resolution partially divesting their portfolio of holdings in companies doing business in the Sudan as a protest against the genocide in Darfur. Dartmouth was one of the first major colleges to do this, but others have followed since.

11. Keohane, "The Public Role of the University," p. 8.

12. Ibid.

13. Nannerl Keohane, president, Duke University, interview by author, June 2, 2003.

14. Ibid., p. 9.

15. Ibid.

16. Ibid. Keohane speaks passionately about this, indicating that she personally viewed the conditions in which the Mount Olive employees worked and that she believed the university could and did intervene successfully to change that situation. She appears to have been persuaded by the students' passions but more so by the fact that they had done the necessary research, gathered evidence, and were able to engage in a debate and discussion about the situation and the actions that might be taken.

17. Ibid.

18. Donald Kennedy, former president, Stanford University, interview by author, August 29, 2003.

19. Ibid.

20. Mary Sue Coleman, president, University of Michigan, interview by author, July 23, 2003.

21. John DiBiaggio, former president, Tufts University, interview by author, August 12, 2003. The array of issues on which DiBiaggio exerted leadership and influence spanned an interesting range. They include while president of the University of Connecticut battling against a linkage at the federal level between student financial aid and registration for military service; speaking out against an initiative by the CIA, then headed by William Casey, during the Reagan administration attempting to prevent colleges and universities from having foreign-born scientists study and research in America because they might steal secrets; and taking on the governor of Massachusetts publicly, including in an op-ed piece in the *Boston Globe*, for removing all the money, by an executive order, from tobacco cessation programs in the state. He concludes his reflections, noting there are times when a variety of factors and

constituencies need to be balanced, "But when it's crystal clear in your eye, when you see an absolute wrong being done, you can't tolerate that. You just simply cannot sit idly by."

22. Stephen J. Nelson, "Presidential Profiles," John DiBiaggio, March 2001, www.collegevalues.org.

23. Thomas Gerety, president, Amherst College, interview by author, July 27, 1994.

24. Neil Rudenstine, former president, Harvard University, interview by author, April 10, 2003. Enlarging on this issue of constricting or worse eliminating someone's right of expression in the face of a forceful presidential position on a hypothetical issue about which a president might have spoken out, Rudenstine adds, "And if I make the statement about whether we should or shouldn't [do something,] whatever I may strongly believe, and there's a faculty discussion and 11 assistant professors say something that's different from what the president just said, and they think [this] might possibly endanger how they're perceived and whether they might get promoted, that's bad. That's *very* bad. [Strong emphasis] Those assistant professors shouldn't be put into that position any more than the students should be."

25. Ibid.

26. Ibid.

27. Ibid.

28. Ibid.

29. Ibid.

30. Ibid.

31. Ibid.

32. Jean Kemeny, *It's Different at Dartmouth* (Brattleboro, VT: Stephen Greene Press, 1979), pp. 22–24. Kemeny's talk in its entirety is also available in A. Alexander Fanelli, *John Kemeny Speaks* (Hanover, NH: Dartmouth College, 1999).

33. Donald Kennedy, interview by author.

34. The following is taken from a phone interview with Robert Oden, March 22, 2002, while Oden was president at Kenyon College, and Oden's subsequent article, published in "Presidential Profiles," www.collegevalues.org.

35. Robert Oden, "The Time Famine of the 1990s," dinner talk, August 19, 1999, provided by President's Office, Kenyon College.

36. Ibid.

37. Frank Rhodes, former president, Cornell University, interview by author, July 22, 2003.

38. James Duderstadt, president, University of Michigan, interview by author, March 6, 1995.

39. Harold Shapiro, former president, University of Michigan and Princeton University, interview by author, July 8, 2003.

40. Frank Rhodes, interview by author.

41. Ibid.

42. John Sexton, president, New York University, interview by author, June 29, 2004.

43. Ibid.

44. Frank Rhodes, interview by author.

PART THREE

The Present and the Future: Presidential Prospects

CHAPTER

The Presidential Post:
Inside the Job

The span of duties of college presidents and the constantly changing situations they face are without question profound. For all of the on- and off-the-mark comparisons with corporate CEOs, the job of president in the academy is in another league. The college presidency is simply and vastly more complex and demanding. Presidents are regularly and relentlessly pressured by seemingly unending problems and dilemmas, diverse constituencies with competing interests, large and small debates over matters equally great and trivial, and expectations that they consult, adhere to democratic process, and commit to rational discourse.

Carleton's Rob Oden relates the story of a college presidential counterpart who hailed originally from the corporate sector commenting that the difference between the corporate world and the academy was that "we make snap decisions in business, and then mop up the agony for six months. In the academy, you have a process that seems agonizing for six months, and then the decision is reached. So, it's agony or process on one hand or the other." But, Oden rightfully concludes that, regardless, "it's a lot of process anyway," and that is itself a marked difference and a different reality for leadership.[1]

Presidents are expected and required to be able to meet and address everything thrown at them. They are to look effortless, with no public or private whining. They are to do all this with little note or recognition of the dogged behind-the-scenes work necessary to create institutional stability, to adhere to reasonable process and rational discourse in decision-making and pronouncements, and to keep campus life on an even keel. Presidential insights about these less visible aspects of the office reveal much about both the style and the substance of the office, including their role as teachers and educators, their accessibility to colleague administrators, staff, faculty, and students, their use of leadership capital, and the subtleties of their commitments and endurance as leaders.

Anyone who has thought even cursorily about the college and university presidency knows that it is both physically and emotionally demanding and draining. Acknowledging the personal wear and tear, DiBiaggio nonetheless points out that it is a pretty good job or there would not be so many people who want to do it. Frank Rhodes, arguably one of the more successful later-twentieth-century presidents, suggests that the burdens of office can be alleviated and ameliorated, despite the personal toll expected and extracted from presidents.

"First, personal exhaustion takes a terrible toll. Lack of sleep, no time for exercise, shortened vacations, and repeated involvement in crises are the warning signs on the road to personal exhaustion," Rhodes declares. Facing this reality, "only a disciplined routine, a managed calendar, appropriate delegation, a willingness to say 'no,' effective personal support staff, and the unswerving personal conviction," to Rhodes a critical part of belief in what you are doing, "of the ultimate value of the university's work can prevent personal exhaustion." In Rhodes's opinion much of the stress is self-made: "Overburdened university presidents do not suffer burnout; they create it, inflicting it upon themselves by their lack of responsible work habits." The problem is compounded because "the campus is unlikely to prosper if its leader is so worn down by the burdens of office that he or she conveys a sense of joyless routine and weary resignation."[2]

Close-up views of the expectations of and demands on presidents certainly confirm the picture Rhodes paints. However, opinion is more divided about the practicality of the suggested solutions. Rhodes's formula to prevent pressures from crushing presidents hints at throwback images from earlier eras that may be impossible to emulate today. However, despite the fact that contemporary hurdles to minimizing the pressures are quite real, Rhodes's ideas are worthy of deliberation. "The antidote?" Rhodes rhetorically asks, regarding the burdens of office: "[S]erious reading, continued teaching, participation in lectures and symposia of substance, maintenance of meaningful research interest, nurture of the inner life: These are the means of intellectual grace, the essential basis of the scholarly community." Rhodes continues: "The effective president's schedule will have a place for each of them, though not, inevitably, to the degree the president once enjoyed as a member of the faculty." This means that presidents should teach and try to maintain some scholarly activity even if only minimally keeping up with their field. However, Rhodes acknowledges, "[T]he pressures of the day will converge to squeeze out these activities." But this "must be resisted. Time must be found. Space must be made and it can be done."

Rhodes left the presidency in the early 1990s, and while the pressures may have increased somewhat since then, it is inconceivable that things have changed that much in the last decade. He says, "I used to escape to Cambridge University for three weeks every summer, to read and write on Charles Darwin. I found that time precious, not only because it gave me time for reflection and renewal, but also because it allowed me to see Cornell in perspective; to view affairs from a reasonable distance."[3] Oden follows Rhodes's advice, taking three to four weeks' vacation every summer, though not without some "work" but primarily as a respite (in his case favoring his avocational interest in fly-fishing).

Many of the "giants" would take nearly the entire summer off, albeit with a full scholarly agenda of reading and thinking, something no doubt impractical today. But Rhodes's notion that presidents could benefit from the habit of a "retreat" as part of a summer routine merits reflection.

Rhodes' image is of presidents on duty nearly 24/7, constantly on stage, performing all manner of duties and activities. Most of the impressions constituents construct about presidents are based on public occasions and perceptions that develop with time and exposure. An often-neglected part of the presidential role is as educator and teacher. Despite assumptions that, compared with their predecessors of earlier eras, today's presidents have little time to meet with students, many contemporary presidents manage to reach out and connect to students. For example, Rhodes would have "have a breakfast with students every week," with students signing up in groups of 25 each. One outcome was "how many students I meet at reunions and other places who say to me, 'You know, you said something to me during that breakfast that had a profound impact not just upon my time as a student, but on the kind of person I've become.'"[4]

Reports of other presidents about personal interaction with students counter the image that such involvement died off with the passing of the era of the giants. These episodes also reveal an imporatnt day-to-day aspect of the job of being president. With regard to these interactions with students as a quality in presidents, one can imagine the following possible interview question as part of a presidential search process: what was the most significant moment you had with students and what did it mean to you and to them?

Throughout more than 20 years in three presidencies, at the University of Connecticut, Michigan State, and Tufts University, John DiBiaggio's habit was to dedicate time to weekly open student office hours. One student visit began with a one-on-one discussion but subsequently led to a meeting of the student with the Tufts Board of Trustees and then concluded with a postgraduate coda.

A student representing a campus environmental group dropped in on DiBiaggio to discuss a hydroelectric company in Quebec, Canada.[5] The students in the group had been researching and studying this company's plans for a new dam project. If undertaken, the project would cause the flooding of lands inhabited by native, indigenous people, and in the process also impact, the students were convinced negatively, the natural ecology and habitat. The students knew that Tufts had investments, albeit modest and almost inconsequential in the context of the university's overall financial portfolio, in this company.

The student shared the group's thinking and protest with DiBiaggio and challenged the president to get the trustees to divest from this stock. The students asked that DiBiaggio should meet with the chief of the Indian tribe that was going to be displaced by the flooding of its land. DiBiaggio agreed and subsequently met the chief, but the students additionally wanted a discussion of the investments and the impact of the company with the full Board of Trustees. "I had all these students, and they were very emotional, presenting me with all kinds of material. And the leader insisted that he speak with the Board of Trustees," and so DiBiaggio reports, "I said, 'Absolutely.'"

DiBiaggio followed through and arranged for the student to attend a board meeting and make a presentation. Presidents are often viewed as too busy for day-in, day-out student concerns, and trustees, very busy people themselves, would generally and rightly expect their presidents to protect them from this sort of intrusion upon their normal executive business and decisions. DiBiaggio thought differently. He indicates that the student who had talked with him was "very passionate, and an older trustee who was an engineer and had a huge, worldwide engineering firm, said to this youngster, 'Well, let me ask you, you're worried about the ecology, so what if we don't have hydropower. What do we have then: nuclear? Would you rather have nuclear? More fossil fuels?' And it went on like this." The board meeting was a seminar of sorts, but also a clash between young and old, youthful ideals and real-world experience, and vested interest—the power of the purse—versus moral convictions about the influence of financial leverage.

After the board meeting, which DiBiaggio portrays as civil but clearly a discussion at loggerheads, he met again with the student. He told the student, "you've made your case. I'm going to go to the board divestment committee and I'm going to ask them to divest us," practically splitting the difference "of only a couple million dollars. Somebody else will acquire it. But I respect how carefully you've stated your case, and having listened to you, on the basis of what that is, I'm going to recommend this."

DiBiaggio leveled with the student, saying that "several of our board members are not going to be happy with me for this." The student was almost apologetic for causing trouble, but DiBiaggio insisted the case had been made well and the argument was convincing enough for him to make this recommendation to the board. However, he added a piece of "fatherly" advice: "As you grow older, you're going to appreciate what my definition of maturity is, and that's a tolerance for ambiguity. You're going to discover things are not going to be so black and white for you because you're going to realize there are variations of gray in this whole business because as that trustee said to you, there are other issues here that are equally compelling, and arguments can be made on both sides." DiBiaggio reveals that his guess that some trustees would not be pleased with his proposal proved accurate. However, as a testimony to his relationship as president with them, "They knew they had to support me."

There is a coda to this story. Following graduation, the student went to work for an agency involved with energy and environmental issues. The now Tufts alumnus showed up one day at the President's Office to schedule a meeting. When they met, he thanked DiBiaggio for his support in negotiating the discussions with the trustees on campus a few years earlier, but said there was something else he wanted to discuss. The student acknowledged, "You know, I've had to make some decisions in my job, and now I understand what you meant because it isn't always black and white." DiBiaggio was pleased to hear the student's reflections about the educational moment they had shared a number of years before, and views the story as emblematic of the big and small things presidents do and their opportunities to influence students.

Often, student interest in appealing to their president is directed to press proposals for the college or university to take monetary or symbolic action to indicate political and moral stands. Nan Keohane had similar experiences with groups requesting discussions with her about major national and international (as well as local, in the case of the Duke pickle boycott) issues of economic injustice and social inequity or variations on these themes.

A group of Duke students were in a course in which they studied the situation in the Sudan and the slavery, civil war, and "horrific" circumstances facing its people. The students became increasingly passionate about the issue and wrote a 35-page group paper for their professor. They submitted the paper to Keohane, who found it to be "quite well done and quite thoughtful." They also presented to her "a petition saying, on the basis of my own statements about moral leadership, they thought I should support divestment from the Sudan."[6] Keohane explained to the students that nowhere in the paper did they make the argument that divestment from the Sudan would make any difference. However, she agreed to meet with them to discuss their position in more detail and depth.

"We did meet for a couple of hours," Keohane says, pointing to a large conference table across the way in her office, "the day of the great ice storm back in the fall while everybody else was going home" for a school vacation. "We stayed and talked for a couple of hours about their paper, about their claims, so that I could argue both that I was really impressed by what they'd done to learn about the Sudan and that I admired their moral commitment and I'd much prefer students to care about something than to be apathetic and care only about their latest sorority rush or something" of less merit and importance.

However, while applauding the students for their ideas and arguments, Keohane told the group she thought "they were mistaken that this was a situation where divestment was relevant." But from her perspective, she "certainly engaged them" and they "knew they had been heard," even if their president was not persuaded and was not about to turn their plea into a petition for action by the Duke Board of Trustees.[7] Keohane adds that this incident was evidence and a reminder that Duke needs a "social responsibility policy" to deal with such student appeals and petitions. Her concern, which she took steps to address, was that such requests would, absent predetermined direction or guidelines, merely be left to the president's or the board's discretion.

Johnnetta Cole tells of a moment during her Spelman presidency when a public talk led to a probing discussion with a student. Cole spoke in the chapel, and as was her custom had begun the talk with the invocation, "Our Mother, Father, God." After the meeting she was returning to the president's house when a student caught up with her in what Cole describes as "enormous pain."

The student was very upset at the thought of God not being exclusively "Father." Cole remembers that "it took an hour of sitting and talking about it. I had simply challenged the very basic notion" of a patriarchal religious and personal view "that really oriented much of her world."[8] At some length, she explained her beliefs to the student, playing a role as educator and counselor. Cole believes this episode, early in her presidential experience, taught her about leadership responsibilities and reach, especially the need in public settings to be careful to explain herself more clearly. With regard to the presidential pulpit and the weight of words and rhetoric, Cole notes the reality that "much of what a president says is going to be taken as 'the gospel of the institution.'"[9]

In this brief encounter, Cole confronted the public exposure inherent in the presidential office. Few otherwise successful presidents in recent years have felt more severely the impact of public vulnerability than Donald Kennedy, in his case as a result of the grant audit affair at Stanford. Kennedy has been consistently forthcoming about the personal and institutional embarrassment that resulted from this contretemps and its negative fallout, and has acknowledged responsibility for this affair happening on his watch.

Kennedy's tenure was undoubtedly shortened at least a bit by this drama, his intention to step down being certainly connected in the minds of many to the events that unfolded in full public view. In his last commencement address, Kennedy speaks "personally, and from the heart, because if our tradition of teachable moments means anything, the best gift I can give you as you depart is a frank accounting of my own learning in the last few difficult months."[10]

Following a detailed replay of what had happened and the damage it had caused the university, Kennedy's personal, final comments are revealing for a public figure. "There is a deeper personal dignity that takes the hard shots with grace, doesn't look for the nearest place to dump the blame, and—above all—doesn't whine," Kennedy confesses and counsels. Offering encouragement and advice to his audience he adds, "No one can take your dignity away from you, but you can lose it. It is very much worth keeping."[11] In a farewell testament, hoping students and others might draw the "right" lesson from his personal travails, Kennedy urges they not "draw from my experience any negative conclusions about the perils of leadership. Leadership . . . entails risks. But it also brings joy and satisfaction. You should know that I would not consider trading," taking the bad with the good, "even for relief from the last several months, the extraordinary privilege I have had here for eleven years."[12]

One debate about leadership centers on whether leaders once they have used their "capital" are able to gain some or all of it back. At the beginning of their tenure, all presidents have a honeymoon period and possess an initial amount of capital. Kennedy clearly depleted if not exhausted his supply by the end of his presidency, having cashed in whatever was left and more in the course of the playing out of the audit affair. However large a stack of chips Kennedy had before the controversy, they clearly ran out as a result. Had this disaster happened earlier in his presidency he might have survived to live another day. Arguably, Kennedy did not have a lot of choice once events began to unfold. However, when there is a choice and the chips are limited, the question for the leader then becomes when best to cash them in and when to hold them. James Duderstadt claims that three to four times every year his presidency at Michigan was on the line. When these occasions arose, his choice was whether to fight at that moment or to finesse in such a way as to be able to pursue a grander (and more long-term, if sufficiently smart and lucky) agenda and to engage in more important battles.[13]

On the other side of the coin, Stephen Trachtenberg believes longevity can actually work to provide presidents with additional "capital." He contends that the act of simply "being in a place for a while, developing a relationship with the external community, internal community," produces the ability to "say to any one constituency, 'Look, you're going to have trust me on this one,' and have enough plausibility in your tenure so that once in a while they'll give you" a break.[14] It is not a stretch to ponder whether the lengthy tenures of the "giants" were not in part due to the fact that endurance itself is a sustaining force. That is, if a leader has been around sufficiently long, people will know when and how to trust that leader. In Trachtenberg's view, a president's expertise in how to get things done, how to work with competing, maybe even warring, constituencies on and off campus, is an asset that a new, less experienced leader simply would not have.

Rob Oden agrees that leaders are able to use the constant development of trust as a tool to replenish capital even while expending it. He believes two things enable presidents to gain capital in the eyes of constituents. One is to display to the best degree humanly possible adequate preparation for what lies ahead for the institution, thus anticipating the future. This foresight and stewardship convinces members of the community that the president is looking out for their interests and is able to provide a sense of security.

The second is for leaders to show a willingness to rely on the abilities and expertise of others. This too increases the feeling of investment by constituents and thereby their support for the president. Oden makes it a point to be a "student" as he approaches new posts, to become an expert, a historian of sorts about the institution. This enables him to discern the "time" in which a decision might have to be made or an initiative launched. "I study some of what has been done in the past and try to figure out as I look what's coming up whether this is in the category of spending those chips now," and while all this is going on, Oden tries "to think of where I am in my own time."[15]

There are three questions that link considerations about "capital" to those about longevity: How long has the leader been in the post? How much personal credibility may have been earned or expended? What are the leader's plans and aspirations for the institution? These questions hint at the relationship between decision making and the spending and the re-amassing of capital. Oden highlights this critical part of a leader's responsibility: "If it's a matter of integrity or decency or honesty or what's right," you must not hold decisions hostage to worries about timing or personal preference.[16] The point is clear: nothing erodes a leader's credibility and capital more rapidly than poor decision making, including failure or unwillingness to act when constituents demand responses and answers.

Oden's primary tool is the use of process to share ideas and explore possibilities as he navigates these decisions about what to do, what needs to be done, and when it is practical to make a move. With the imprimatur of the presidency in mind, his model is to work earnestly, "to get a group to see that what you think is the right way to go is the right way to go." However, in practice, this approach "doesn't work anything like that all the time, and then you have to say, 'OK, maybe they're right.'" While such a strategy is largely old-fashioned politics, Oden claims: "The biggest reason you put groups into [decision making] is not the political reasons but because of all those brains out there." At this point if the group recommends a different direction or decision, the president is able to acknowledge either that "they're right. I was wrong," or that "this is the way they feel. I don't think they're right, but they've got enough of an argument where the stakes are such that I think it's just the right thing to do."[17]

A Carleton tradition Oden inherited, but one in which he delights, is an example of this collaborative approach. Carleton's governance includes a presidential advisory body, the College Council, a cross-sectional committee with representation from all sectors of the campus community. While it is only one of many groups with which Oden regularly meets and works, the College Council is special because the president creates and suggests to the council an annual theme for its consideration every academic year. For example, Oden placed the topic of affirmative action on the table and the group then formulated the direction for the year's discussion, its members bringing their varied perspectives and other resources to bear in the conversation.

Oden uses the council as a forum to float ideas, to discuss policy matters, and to consider presidential and college decisions. As a leadership vehicle, the council is a structure that permits constituencies the opportunity to react to and to redirect Oden's thinking. Rhodes underscores this balancing act, inherent in presidential decision making, between what the leader wants and what the followers will accept, as the "business of making yourself available and being open, and yet having ideals and goals that are transparent," which is "enormously important as part of leadership."[18]

College presidents are very visible figures, and their images are readily exposed to their campus communities. This is another way in which their leadership positions are substantively different, and more difficult, than those of corporate CEOs, who are able to be more detached, as their constituencies and communities are much more dispersed and have lower expectations about the direct "presence" of their leaders. Given the imprint and impact of presidents, John Sexton views the relationship between presidents and campus communities in the academy as critical.

To Sexton, the role of president goes beyond the idea "of the first among equals to a person that has a particular role in the process of both forcing the process and then saying to people, 'Here is what I hear you saying. Have I got it yet?'"

The reality of this interchange, played out over time and not about a single issue, is that "if the people say something that the president doesn't find in his or her soul, then that's the time to stop being president and have somebody be in there."[19] The growing complexity of life in the university in recent times leads Sexton to assume that campus constituencies are looking now and will in the future look for presidents "to have more input into the processes of defining the excellence of the university."

However, there is an attendant danger for presidents. As they become increasingly expected to lay out definitive positions, there will be an increase in differences of opinion, if not outright disagreements, between presidents and other key constituencies of the university about what truly are the primary concerns and "first principles" for the university and its future. If greater contention is to be avoided as presidents are expected to stake out specific positions about directions and aspirations for the university, they will need to be even more transparently consultative, not merely offering the appearance, or worse the charade, of taking reactions and discussion seriously.

The accessibility of presidents to students and faculty can be a major bone of contention. Rhodes intentionally structured his calendar, work, and activities in order to maintain reasonable and productive access to the many constituencies and subgroups comprising the massive Cornell community. However, today the reality on many campuses is that faculty report and lament the infrequency of meetings and of interactions with presidents other than on formal occasions such as faculty meetings.

Sexton fashions the regular duties of the office in ways that enable him to reach out, in particular, to faculty. Prior to becoming president, a colleague at the Law School remarked about Sexton's leadership that as dean he was able to alter what some believe to be almost universal in academic cultures: "There is a poisonousness in academic life, and a degree of back-biting and professorial whining that are absent here." He continues: "John's genius is creating opportunities for the faculty that take the edge off this tendency. He can take energies that can easily turn into mutual recrimination, energies that have done so in other places, and manage to make them productive. NYU is the least bitter institution I've worked at. There's a mutuality of purposiveness here."[20]

Like most presidents, Sexton has a senior staff of "direct reports." Such senior groups normally consist of vice presidential level administrators including the provost; the dean of the faculty; the vice presidents for finance, external relations including alumni affairs, development, and campus and student life; and often the president's executive assistant. Uniquely, Sexton convenes this group almost daily to engage in a continuing "core conversation" about the institution. Because of the regularity of their contact and the big picture agenda that he puts in front of them, Sexton believes that discrete and seemingly separate issues such as faculty recruitment and allocation of institutional resources (to name just two) tend to "conflate" (and he seems to believe should conflate) at this senior level.

Sexton conceives the notion of the "core" and the conversation as derived from principles of "academic conscience" and from the "ratio studiorum" of the university, the latter being at the foundation of his concept of a university.[21] He challenges this senior group to engage in a continuing comprehensive conversation about NYU. He wants this cabinet to focus on matters primary to the university's mission and purposes rather than falling prey to the distractions that inevitably creep into the running of an institution. With the exception of major crises in the university's life, Sexton believes distractions should be handled at lower, delegated levels.[22] This way he maintains an efficiency and economy of focus on core purposes, deploying his energies and those of his staff in a concentrated fashion to the critical tasks connected to NYU's future.

Given the range and intensity of demands on their time, maintaining substantive contact with faculty members is not an easy task for presidents. Rhodes was enormously disciplined, meeting with academic departments one per week on a three-year cycle to accommodate the 90 departments at Cornell. These sessions provided a structured opportunity to hear faculty concerns and, maybe simpler and more important, let them see him. Sexton uses innovative ways to address contact with faculty and to remain aware of their problems and needs.

To keep his pulse on faculty activities, scholarship, ideas, and interests, Sexton dedicates one to two Saturdays each month for one-on-one and group meetings with professors. Generally these sessions last two hours each, with one or more faculty members in each block. Interested faculty members put their names on a list and are picked for appointments by lottery. Each Saturday eight slots are set aside, six for full-time and two for part-time faculty members. Faculty members exclusively control the agenda for these discussions. As a rule Sexton does not even know ahead of time the nature of the issues and concerns to be discussed. He is willing to discuss anything that is on participants' minds, so these discussions range from professional concerns, such as university support for research and laboratory space, and professors' scholarly agendas, to concerns about human resources, benefits, and faculty morale. As in his conversations with the "core" administrative leadership team, the rationale for these discussions is "what do we want our university to be? How can we make this university be better?"[23] Sexton is essentially running a series of ongoing seminars, continuing conversations about what NYU is and what it might become.

Another aspect of Sexton's presidential style deserving attention is his philosophy and tactics in faculty recruitment and hiring. The concept of "the Enterprise," or more specifically "the faculty as common enterprise," initiated while Sexton was dean of the Law School, has continued in his presidency. Sexton believes faculty members and academician-scholars of today increasingly constitute "a world of independent contractors." In place of this model he wants to substitute one "where you and I are going to be obligated to each other. Where you're not going to be an independent contractor, and I am not going to be an independent contractor, but you are going to get the benefit of the social contract by virtue of a tax on yourself."[24]

Sexton's strategy in hiring and recruiting faculty members is based on nothing more sophisticated than rudimentary assumptions of social contract. Adopting the practice begun as Law School dean and now used university-wide, Sexton willingly trades support for the specific interests of a professor he wishes to recruit for that professor's reasonably long-term commitment to the university. If a candidate wants on the order of $100,000 a year to build a program on a subject at the core of the candidate's work, Sexton will "look [the person] in the eye and I say, you're coming here for life?" And if the person says yes, "I say, now I want you to give me something that will help me recruit the next guy, that's going to impress our donors and other things. You'll get the $100,000 a year for the incentive, but I want you to sign an agreement that says if you leave NYU within 10 years that you will [personally] repay the money with interest."[25] This leverage works because each faculty member recruited realizes that others will be sold on NYU because of assurances about the similar commitments made by recently arrived and highly reputed colleagues.

Judith Rodin's story at Penn in the 1990s through the early years of the twenty-first century became and to a great extent remains Penn's story of that time (though Rodin would clearly acknowledge that as leader she stood and built on Penn's historical stature and foundation). Like Sexton, Rodin led a major research university in a major urban center at a time when new leadership that would reestablish the heritage and visibility of the university, supply a new vision, and assert strategic principles to guide decisions was crucial to the future of the institution.

Rodin defines the challenge of leadership in such settings: "The best part of leadership is to create shared goals. You can't lead if you can't engage people together, believing that they have a piece of the action, that they share in those goals and, therefore, they'll benefit from the outcomes."[26] Rodin used this style beginning with her inauguration and the opening days of her presidency. She had a strong vision for Penn, in part derived from her upbringing in Philadelphia and its public schools (she was raised not far from the Penn campus) and as an undergraduate there. However, the bulk of her agenda was hatched during the search process as she began to articulate with the trustees and others involved what she would subsequently declare publicly about the university's direction.

Offering a behind-the-scenes view, Rodin describes the process she followed: "It was not the typical university bottoms-up approach, getting numerous committees and making sure everybody buys in. It was really the top leadership doing it together." After the senior leadership team developed the broad sketch, "we took it to relevant faculty and student committees, but literally only for buy-in." However, this step was sufficiently consultative as not to be viewed as merely a charade. From these planning steps, Rodin and the Penn community "came out of that with a really important and shared strategic vision and a set of annual benchmarks."[27]

The resulting strategic plan, the "Agenda for Excellence," guided the university throughout her tenure. The plan incorporated six major priorities: "Health

Science, Technology and Policy, American and Comparative Democratic and Legal Institutions, The Role of Race, Gender and Ethnicity in Democratic Participation, The Humanities—Meaning in the 21st Century, The Urban Agenda—Penn in Philadelphia, Information Science, Technology and Society."[28] Annually Rodin kept the university community informed about progress on these targets so that they were able "to expect that every year I would with my senior leadership team lay out for their approval what we would do against the strategic plan. And every year we would critically evaluate ourselves against what we had promised a year earlier to do." She invested "a lot of time trying to bring people, not to consensus, but to embracing a set of shared goals" in this continuing process and with regard to different aspects of the plan.[29]

As an example of this ongoing effort, "The Urban Agenda" section of the plan broadly outlines a reshaping of Penn's role and relationship with its surrounding neighborhoods and the City of Philadelphia. It appears beginning with her candidacy during the search process, this was a problem area that Rodin viewed as a grave threat to the present health and a constraint on the future of the university.

"The Urban Agenda" produced community initiatives and partnerships, one of which was a public school Penn conceived, founded, and assumed full responsibility to fund, staff, administer, and manage. "The school was the most difficult thing we did," underscoring her responsibility and that of the university; "it wasn't to try to give everybody a vote, it was to try to give everybody a vision and a set of ideas that they could share and embrace even if we didn't always agree on the means." "A lot of what I did was use the presidency and the prestige and the platform that it created to get people to do things that they hadn't done before and once they did them [they] thought, why didn't we ever do this before," Rodin declares about her presidential pulpit.[30]

Rodin was meticulous and dogged in adhering to the strategic plan. She used the plan to match Penn's needs to its available resources, resisting deviations from this approach in an effort to succeed in implementation of the interconnected aspects of the plan. Not surprisingly, this led to some political battles. But Rodin steered Penn's course by the intentions of the plan and indicates there were those in the community who were surprised that the plan was not, like many, going to sit "on the shelf."[31] Rather the strategic plan and the process of its implementation helped Rodin and Penn to avoid diversions from the direction it provided for Penn's future.

In these brief stories about the style and substance of presidents, one theme emerges: the value of and the desirability for presidents to possess a central, core, and defining purpose about the conduct of the affairs of the office and of the university. This does not mean doing only one thing. Rather, navigating by a core purpose involves developing a constellation of principles and ideals to guide decisions, and to shape presidential leadership and the meaning and message of presidents' ideas to constituencies. These reflections from various presidential vantage points contribute color to the picture we are able to develop of the office and its conduct. We turn now to further prophecy and predictions from today's presidents about the future of the presidency.

NOTES

1. Robert Oden, president, Carleton College, interview by author, August 26, 2003.

2. Frank Rhodes, "The Art of the Presidency," *The Presidency*, Spring 1998, p. 5.

3. Ibid., pp. 5–6.

4. Frank Rhodes, former president, Cornell University, interview by author, July 22, 2003.

5. John DiBiaggio, former president, Tufts University, interview by author, August 12, 2003. The story that unfolds and the quotations that follow are from this interview.

6. Nannerl Keohane, president, Duke University, interview by author, June 2, 2003.

7. Ibid.

8. Johnnetta Cole, president, Bennett College, and former president, Spelman College, interview by author, June 2, 2003.

9. Ibid.

10. Kennedy, *The Last of Your Springs*, pp. 200–201.

11. Ibid., p. 202.

12. Ibid.

13. James Duderstadt, president, University of Michigan, interview by author, March 6, 1995.

14. Stephen Joel Trachtenberg, president, George Washington University, interview by author, May 7, 2003.

15. Robert Oden, interview by author.

16. Ibid.

17. Ibid.

18. Frank Rhodes, interview by author.

19. John Sexton, president, New York University, interview by author, June 29, 2004.

20. Steven Englund, "John Sexton: Seizing the Mile," *Lifestyles* 27, no. 160 (pre-spring 1999): pp. 16c-17a.

21. John Sexton, interview with author. Specifically the core includes four items, first: "to make sure that the university was stabilized in its financial situation so that it had an accurate picture of itself that could be used for strategic decision making...and that the level of excellence we'd achieved was secure and permanent, so if we're an A/A-university...we're never going back." Sexton continues: "[T]he second thing...is dramatically advancing the quality of student life," especially to catch up with the enormous enrollment increases of the 1990s. The third item on Sexton's list is the process itself and that is "to create an administration that is capable of seamlessly enhancing things." And finally, again the theme of the conversation itself, that is, creating an environment where the faculty and others are engaged in "this iterative conversation...making us first and foremost a university that's constantly [engaged] in that."

22. Ibid.

23. Ibid. Sexton also notes, like Rhodes, that he meets weekly with approximately 40 students similarly selected by lottery to attend and express their opinions.

24. Ibid.

25. Ibid.

26. Judith Rodin, former president, University of Pennsylvania, interview by author, August 16, 2004.

27. Ibid.

28. Judith Rodin, "The Agenda for Excellence, Six University Academic Priorities," September 24, 1996, http://www.upenn.edu/president/rodin/agenda96.html.

29. Judith Rodin, interview by author.

30. Ibid.

31. Ibid. She provided a number of examples where she held fast to the intentions and priorities of the plan in the face of faculty and other pressure to diverge in pursuit of a short-term narrow interest. These actions early in the process convinced members of the Penn community of her seriousness and her convictions about the direction the plan harbored for Penn's future.

CHAPTER 10

The Future Presidency: Guardian of the Soul of the University

The university is an institution of unprecedented longevity and resilience. Over centuries, first in Europe, then exported to America first in the form of the Colonial colleges and subsequently as research universities, colleges and universities have been a fundamental force in increasing knowledge, making discoveries, seeking truths, and educating students for meaningful lives and contributions as citizens of the nation and world. College and university presidents have stood at the center of this academy, armed with leadership, with visions for campus and society, and with arguments to shape the history and direct the future of this vital institution: the university.

We can debate endlessly whether presidents of today shrink in comparison to their predecessors of previous eras, whether we label them as "giants" or simply the large, many of them founding, figures they were. I believe the case can be made that presidents have been and remain enormously influential even into recent decades and the present day.

Today's presidents have to vie for visibility in the public eye, their stature and rhetoric easily overlooked by the glitz and fads of the contemporary "sound byte" culture. However, despite these problems that can at times make presidents appear minuscule and silent, they still wield vast authority, influence, and power. The vitality and efficacy of the presidency remains crucially and profoundly intertwined with the vigor and health of the university. The personal imprint of presidents is crucial and essential in the work to make colleges and universities what they are, aspiring to have them thrive not just survive, and to shape change while upholding the core traditions and values of the academy. This is a continuing battle between principles and values, and the demands of an ever-changing world. Presidents are the guides, the navigators who are depended on to juggle this fragile, essential balance so that the university can be the university.

At the conclusion of *Shakespeare, Einstein, and the Bottom Line,* David Kirp raises a nagging global question about the future of the university: "Can the public be persuaded that universities represent something as ineffable as the common good—more specifically, that higher education contributes to the development of knowledgeable and responsible citizens, encourages social cohesion, promotes and spreads knowledge, increases social mobility, and stimulates the economy?"[1] His concern is the future of the academy. Though Kirp attests to the value of the university as an institution, he provides evidence that paints the university as collapsing under the weight of market pressures. One result he alleges and is very real is that in reacting to market forces, the university is losing or has already lost its historic and traditional bearings about its meaning and purpose.

While focusing on the university as an institution, Kirp uses the leadership of presidents as a lens to view what is happening, and to show how and in what ways it might be different. Kirp extols by name presidents on the contemporary landscape such as John Sexton at NYU and William Durden at Dickinson College. They are featured because of their reputation for putting a sizable imprint of their personae on their respective institutions. He does not compare them to the "giants" of the academic presidency per se, but he presents them as in a league that might pass muster for inclusion in that club.

However, Kirp more generically paints in broad strokes an image of presidents as no longer able to establish themselves and their institutions with sufficient stature to answer affirmatively his question about the future of the university: does it represent the "common good" and does it make the contributions to society that historically have been its distinctive calling? He also depicts the environments in which presidents have to work both inside and outside the gates as hostile toward the mission of the university. Stripped to its basics, Kirp's prophecy about the outcome of these questions is not in the slightest bit hopeful.

His coup de grâce question about the presidency and its capacity to maintain the traditional values of the academy, and whither its future, is telling: "With university presidents consumed by the Sisyphean burdens of fund-raising and the placating of multiple constituencies, it's not clear who will take on this task. Lacking such a principled defense, though," Kirp assuming this to be in the lap of presidents, "the university may degenerate into something far less palatable than the house of learning 'better attuned to the business character of the nation' demanded by Yale's nineteenth-century critics—the transformation that has in fact taken place since the 1970s."

Could the university's future be even worse than the outcome some thought certain during the debate sparked by the *Yale Report of 1828* nearly two centuries ago? Or do fears about the president's ability to lead and the academy's direction simply run in circles? Kirp offers a precise warning about what could be the end of the university: "It might conceivably evolve into just another business, the metaphor of the higher education 'industry' brought to life in a holding company that could be called Universitas, Inc." In this scenario, the high-sounding values and principles presidents must possess to undergird the bully pulpit and to exercise the influence of their office go out the window.

The future of the university is based on the role of traditional, fundamental values. These ideals are required to guide it in the "right" way, to place it on an even keel in maintaining its historical basis and identity as a distinctive institution in society. Absent these principles, the future of the university and the presidency would be jeopardized and possibly irrevocably compromised. Kirp concludes with the challenge facing the presidency today and for the future, and couples it with the future of the university: "If there is a less dystopian future, one that revives the soul of this old institution, who is to advance it—and if not now, then when?"[2]

What concerns then are paramount about the future of the college and university presidency and about how the nature of presidential leadership is tied to that future of the academy? What are the major aspects of the presidency that should be fortified and protected in ways that promise a continuation of valued traditions of respect and esteem for the office? How will succeeding generations of presidents likewise ensure the tried customs of autonomy, scholarly inquiry, and freedom, and the basic and fundamental values of the college and university as founded in America, and as the heir of an Old World heritage? What do we want our presidents to be? What do we want the colleges and universities they lead to be?

Contemporary presidents bear firsthand witness to the office of president in its present form, and possess informed experience and standpoints to suggest ideas about the future of the presidency and the leadership that will be demanded into the opening decades of the twenty-first century. They have a unique grasp of the office, shaped by looking over their shoulders at their predecessors. They know well the pushes and pulls at the center of the presidency and the university. They hold interesting thoughts about who will succeed as the next generation of college and university presidents. What can and should we expect of that generation? What are the thoughts of these presidents about the connection between the future of the presidency and of the university?

Public thought and debate is critical to the shape of the presidency of the future. To a degree, this is a game of perceptions that in turn drive expectations with both immediate and longer term effects on who will be at the presidential helm of universities. Decisions about who are in the pipeline to become presidents should not be left to chance or to a self-fulfilling prophecy created by an invisible hand permitted in the absence of authoritative voices to dictate the traits and characteristics presumed to be required. For example, there exists a nearly universally assumed emphasis on fund-raising and development as critical presidential capacities. If these qualities are viewed as *the* primary, maybe even the only, tangible ability presidents should possess, then they become the major, nearly exclusive, leadership quality presumed to be required in today's presidents. The ambition to display a fund-raising capacity then becomes even more amplified as critical in the minds of presidential aspirants and of those—trustees and governing boards and influential stakeholders—who select them. This tautology then both describes and prescribes how the preparation and caliber of candidates will be discerned and the fate of their appointments determined.

The bottom line, and it is not rocket science, is that colleges and universities get as their presidents those whom they seek and probably likewise deserve. While it is not necessarily an "either or" proposition, if the tilt in presidential searches is overly toward fund-raisers, money managers, and bureaucrats, then these criteria will hold sway when presidents are selected. Further, and more tellingly, the emphasis on money raising and financial management characterizing the culture of presidential searches will have a direct impact on the calculus in the thinking of those who wish to become presidents. However, the converse is equally true. If the qualities emphasized in presidential searches are the historic and traditional values of the university—to speak wisely and with assurance in the public square on and off campus, and to provide Trachtenberg's "balance wheel," to be willing to see themselves at the heart of the "messy middle"—then presidential selection will lean more in this direction in the future.

One aspect of presidential public visibility during the era of the giants was the tendency for presidents to be invited and to serve on major national bodies both for the educational community and for the nation, and on government agencies and assignments. While some bemoan the passing of this aspect, it has by no means disappeared, and in recent years there has been a comeback in presidential participation on such bodies. For example, Tom Kean, president of Drew University, cochaired the 9/11 Commission; Bob Kerrey, former senator and now president of The New School, was a member of that commission; and Richard Levin, president of Yale, was a member of The President's Commission on the Intelligence of the United States Regarding Weapons of Mass Destruction. Certainly Ted Hesburgh is one of the most visible and legendary presidents of the twentieth century due to his governmental and other service off the Notre Dame campus.

Not surprisingly, in assessing the future of the presidency, Hesburgh urges a return to this tradition as a way college presidents can make more prominent the image of their office and reestablish the presidency as a leadership platform of importance outside as well as inside the gates. Hesburgh believes that if presidents were called on with greater regularity and frequency for national and in this global age possibly even international service, the result would be to expand and enrich the profile of the office. This would have a positive effect on the stature of the individuals interested in becoming presidents and would increase the likelihood that those appointed would garner even greater consideration for high-profile public service.

There is also a practical, *realpolitik* angle to Hesburgh's intuition. Johnnetta Cole confirms that her decision to move from being a Board of Trustees' member to becoming president of the United Way of America was the lure of becoming the first ever African American to chair that board in its over one hundred years of existence. Cole recognizes that aspiring to such a commitment transcends personal capacities and choices. She knows this public service carries value in her role as president and adds stature to Bennett College's institutional visibility as well. Cole notes previous college presidents, including people like Benjamin Mays at Morehouse and Willa Player even at small, in many ways unheralded Bennett, as people with "complex agendas. They were not just presidents....they were deeply engaged in civic affairs. They had to be fund-raisers and they also sure stood up and spoke as public intellectuals and as moral forces."[3]

Hesburgh also connects the prospect of presidents being called upon more frequently for civic duty and engagement to the matter of the length of their tenure. Having served well over three decades, Hesburgh is undoubtedly perplexed at the vastly shorter tenure of so many of today's presidents. His informed guess is that the higher the visibility and profile of presidents, the greater the likelihood they will remain in any one slot, thus benefiting from the mutual reinforcement of enhancement of their credibility and reputation and duration in office.

Estimates of today's tenures range from three to four years to not much more than maybe seven to eight years on average. For reasons of relative institutional stability and status, tenures tend to be slightly longer at more elite colleges and universities than at those less in the elite club.[4] Regardless of precisely how long they are, Hesburgh argues that brief tenures create a situation where "you can't become known to the American public" sufficiently to acquire the profile and the recognition that would lead to a major governmental or other "volunteer" appointment to a commission, agency, or association.[5] Cole arrives on the United Way Board and is able to aspire to be its chair for a number of reasons. One is her visibility as a result of dues paid for many decades as a college president.

Neil Rudenstine elaborates on the implications of the increasingly brief tenure of today's presidents. His worry confirms Mark Edwards's thoughts about the near impossibility of remaining long in a presidency due to the spotlight being placed on a few minor weaknesses rather than numerous strengths, and to the idea that the most minor weaknesses inevitably grow in perception to be sufficiently severe that they lead to the downfall and early exit from office of otherwise successful presidents.

Rudenstine agrees that this is one reason for foreshortened tenures, claiming that "presidents leave not because they've decided it's time for them to leave and they'd like to leave, but because somebody else has decided it's time for them to leave."[6] He does not naively think we might see a return of the 20- to 40-year tenure of people like President Eliot at Harvard. However, Rudenstine believes it would be in everyone's interest to counter the increasing tendency for brief tenures and suggests a connection between the length of tenure to the larger picture of who are in the pipeline to become presidents. He emphasizes that American higher education is "a large system and therefore" in a game of numbers "finding that many leaders who are really excellent is hard."[7] If some individuals who are qualified to be and capable of being excellent presidents end up being prematurely spit out of the system after only a few years of service, the number of openings increases and the quality of candidates for appointment becomes more watered down.

Another major cause Rudenstine cites for shortened tenures is a generally accepted assumption about the environment in higher education, maybe mirrored in other professions and in society as a whole. He believes it is a "rough system," shot through with politics. This reality creates a set of forces presidents must manage, and Rudenstine points to a theme, particularly corrosive at public universities, where "boards of regents are elected by constituencies and they feel more obligation to the people who elected them than they do to the university"; in the vernacular, these are constituencies "that can just saw a university president in half."

Rudenstine's presidency overlapped with that of James Duderstadt of the University of Michigan. More than likely he knew Duderstadt personally and undoubtedly has him in mind in this emphasis on the rough and tumble of politics in presidential tenures. Whether he is providing a romantic vision of bygone days or an accurate assessment of the current state of affairs, Rudenstine argues that part of this problem is due to an erosion of the belief during the previous era in colleges and universities as institutions "that people respect, where you feel that most of the time they're going to be understanding of the university's values and be on your side defending the institution."[8] This heightened cynicism and suspicion about the academy as an institution and about its leaders leaves presidents more exposed and vulnerable, particularly during crises and controversies.

Rudenstine's "solution" goes to the heart of problems and pressures concerning the contemporary presidency, in this case focusing on forces that provide stability and those that contribute to destabilizing the presidency. Earlier, I suggested a shift in expectations about the duties of the presidential office as one "answer" to Edwards's dilemma about presidential weaknesses readily outflanking their strengths. The long list of tasks and responsibilities that few, if any, mortals could possibly meet should be replaced by a much shorter, more focused list: What is at the core of the institution and its saga, and how does it stand in the context of the university writ large? What are the principal and essential values crucial to the university's future? What are the requirements that a president must be capable of meeting and can be reasonably expected to meet? These questions, if agreed as starting points, could then fashion fairer criteria on which to judge presidential performance.

This is what Rudenstine has in mind—returning to a main theme about the life of the academy. To regain and to develop respect for colleges and universities as institutions, and to make the office of president more manageable and esteemed, Rudenstine contends, "You've got to get people back on the core mission and the core values rather than the idea that somehow taking a lot of big, strong, political stances is going to help these institutions." Echoing his posture about the presidential pulpit, he notes: "That doesn't mean you have to be neutral, but what you have to do," as president, "is to worry about the values [of the university]. It's not easy to defend those values, but those are the ones to defend."[9] While not fail-safe antidotes to brevity of tenure, these steps could create an environment that would better promote presidential survival.

Concern about length of tenure is essential in considerations about the presidency in the future. What steps could be taken to retain good presidents for longer terms in office? Is it possible to mitigate the factors creating the pressure on presidents that the most critical plans must be accomplished in the near term while they have the necessary capital, or they will simply not be accomplished at all? Are there arbitrary and artificial definitions of "too long," beyond which time there is no point in staying in a presidency? Realizing that "politics" is and always has been part of the territory for college presidents (as for any leaders), are there ways to reduce the adverse and corrosive effects of political arguments and games?

Certainly there are numerous reasons why the job of president appears to foster increasingly brief tenures. First, there is the simple wear and tear of relentless 80-hour-plus, seven-day weeks on even the most energetic and enthusiastic soul. A second reality is that campus communities often readily tire of one person's voice and vision, and thus begin to long for new creativity and vitality in leadership. A third reason is the increasing emphasis on fund-raising, which leads to a desire to synchronize the timing of major capital campaigns with the tenure of presidents. The recurrent and inexorable cycle of these major campaigns with their seemingly endless stages—planning, often preceded by the obligatory strategic assessment, the "who are we and why are we here" stage, followed by the public phase of the fund-raising itself—has become its own grinding and loaded expectation on the shoulders of presidents. The total process from planning to completion of major campaigns often lasts nearly 10 years and this means few presidents will remain in office for more than one cycle of these prodigious investments of time and energy. It should be no surprise then that if the fundraising cycle lasts 10 years and no one president is likely to stay for more than one cycle, then tenures are likewise often 10 years or less.

Though almost any college or university could be substituted, Brown University provides an instructive and well-duplicated example. Arriving at Brown in 1989, Vartan Gregorian was immediately confronted with the need to undertake a major campaign. It was launched and concluded successfully between about 1990 and 1996, and by 1997 Gregorian completed his presidency. Ruth Simmons succeeded to the Brown presidency in 2001 and embarked on a major campaign in 2005 (probably a year later than originally hoped because of the economic downturn caused by the September 11th attacks two months into her presidency), a campaign that will run through the first decade of the twenty-first century and maybe slightly beyond. On assuming the presidency, Simmons indicated she fully expected this to be her last major job and that she would therefore serve 10-plus years. "Her" campaign will conclude around her tenth anniversary or shortly thereafter.

Furthermore, as public universities now mimic their private counterparts, as Coleman accurately points out, in the development race this synchronicity of presidential tenures and major campaigns will even more frequently be the case.

Simultaneously, public institution presidents have to maintain the confidence of citizens and legislators in order to keep public funding flowing, and when this capacity is called into question, the added pressure could well result in even shorter tenures.

If the primary responsibilities presidents must address and meet, and for which they are held accountable, are to be kept in approximate balance, then there must be a counterweight to the claims of fund-raising pressures, Kirp's "Sisyphean burdens," extracted from presidents. Johnnetta Cole has two presidencies under her belt. She has a considerable, nationally known public persona and profile, and is well reputed in the higher education community as a forceful leader. She is recognized as able to tend to financial stability, as evidenced both by her work at Spelman, where she was enormously successful in this, and by the fact that she has come out of presidential "retirement" to rescue and bring order to the fiscal house of more-struggling Bennett College.

Fund-raising and sound fiscal management pressures create demands on presidents that lead to an inherent tension with other essential presidential duties. Cole believes successful presidencies do not develop "without the ability to be the moral voice when it is called for and to be the astute business woman." Presidents, in short, need to be "sterling in this way as a leader, as a visionary, as a voice of conscience but also very, very efficient and successful" in the development and management tasks.[10]

In the face of pressures to meet the fiscal, the public profile, and the broad institutional leadership demands of the office, could presidents' development duties be reconceived as John Sexton contends is possible? That is, conceiving the president's role as promoting the institution and relying on other senior administrators and staff members to capitalize on the fund-raising that develops from broadly constructed presidential spadework. Hesburgh points to the fact that he raised enormous sums of money for Notre Dame despite (and maybe partially because of) his significant public and private sector involvements.[11]

To a degree, Sexton copies Hesburgh's model: raise the profile of the university to a level sufficient to create a larger and more persuasive raison d'être for financial giving. The Sexton approach argues that presidents (and those who select and sustain them in office) should put greater premium on the "job" as more centrally focused on the stewardship and creation of the institutional saga; on promoting and promulgating the true purposes of the university as well as the unique mission inside and outside the gates; and on using the office wisely as a platform to make a difference in the larger society. This more "out-of-the-box" thinking shows how a different construct of presidential expectations and responsibilities could result in making the job more doable, less the seeming impossibility that Edwards contends it is, and less prone to a nearly exclusive focus on fund raising as Kirp fears.

Asked about where the presidency is headed in the future, John DiBiaggio hedges his analysis by quoting Casey Stengal: "Never make predictions, particularly about the future." DiBiaggio firmly believes that "if the job were not desirable, there wouldn't be so many people who want it." He notes that even with all the problems and demands, moments like the matriculation of an incoming class and the graduation of those same students four or so years later is one of the great rewards. "What more wonderful thing to do in life than to be a part of assuring this person is going to have the kind of experience which is going to assure that they're going to have a life of contribution and equality because of education," DiBiaggio testifies, based on his own roots as a first-generation college graduate.[12]

DiBiaggio also takes a stab at the notion that the presidency is an impossible job because no matter how great the strengths presidents possess, their weaknesses will eventually be their undoing. DiBiaggio acknowledges that everyone has weaknesses, but argues that success in college presidency is dependent on a couple of critical traits. His advice is simple, nothing more than a classic leadership suggestion to delegate and delegate wisely. But he combines this advice with the essential ingredient of reliance on sufficient self-awareness and insight into one's limits, which can be, at least partially, compensated for by staff selection and support. "It's what their [president's] attitudes are and how they approach the position and how they perceive of themselves in that role and how much they recognize that we all have our limitations," DiBiaggio asserts. Presidents "who are successful are those who recognize in themselves" things they do well and things they do not, and say, "All right, I'm going to use my skills to the maximum, try to improve in those areas where I have deficiencies, and above all, surround myself with people who can do some of the things that I can't do and give them the responsibility, but the authority to go with the responsibility, of carrying out those tasks."[13]

Debates about the profile of the "ideal" college president are emblematic of the battles about desirable traits fought on a larger scale within and about colleges and universities. Arguments abound about the applicability, or lack thereof, of business leadership and models to higher education. Certainly sometime after World War II, though critics such as Veblen contend much earlier in the century, pressure to fill presidencies with business and corporate leaders loomed large at many colleges and universities. This trend reached its zenith between the late 1970s and the early 1990s. Much of this pressure for business and corporate leadership of colleges developed in reaction to two primary and connected fiscal concerns.

One cause of concern was the fact that colleges and universities suffered a series of financial "hits" from a combination of bad press and low morale among alumni and key stakeholders as a result of the disruptions of the 1960s. A second and related problem was the faltering economy of the middle to late 1970s and early 1980s, exacerbated by dramatic increases in energy prices, an expense that colleges and universities could not avoid and could not address overnight. In addition, business leaders were assumed to be conservative and thus able to stand up to the liberal forces viewed as fomenting the upheavals on campuses in the demand for social and political change. Corporate figures appointed to presidencies were most primarily expected to staunch and stabilize budgets that were running in the "red."

Brown's appointment of James Hornig as president in 1972, from his position as CFO in the senior leadership at Kodak, and Dartmouth's 1981 appointment as president of David McLaughlin, former CEO of both Champion Paper and the Toro Corporation, are just two examples of corporate leaders as college presidents. Hornig stabilized a budget spiraling out of control at Brown, turning a tide that would have eroded the university's critically important discretionary endowment by the end of the 1970s if it had not been for his necessarily heavy hand. McLaughlin's appointment was an attempt to assuage and bring back into the fold conservative Dartmouth alumni. This group had been persistently upset about the "progressive" initiatives of the 1960s and early 1970s at Dartmouth, including coeducation, the aggressive recruiting of minorities, and specific admissions efforts and commitments to Native American applicants and students (ironically fulfilling a long-ignored and unmet part of the college's charter). McLaughlin's record was less of a marked success than Hornig's. But the two with their corporate backgrounds are emblematic of the leadership to which a number of colleges and universities turned during the 1970s and 1980s, a leadership that some campuses and their boards and governing bodies continue to pursue today.

DiBiaggio straightforwardly reacts to this business emphasis and its continuing influence in the leadership of the academy. He is concerned about its effect on the membership of governing boards (though the recruitment of wealthy individuals, often with close ties to business, as essential and influential members of trustee bodies, has to some extent always been the case). Acknowledging that "universities have to be businesslike because there's a business aspect to them," DiBiaggio adds the caveat, "but we're not businesses." Speaking euphemistically, he replays the types of conversations that readily occurred with business people on his boards: "They're sitting here saying, 'Oh, we just do it this way.' And I say, 'We don't do it that way.'"

This interaction between the business approach and the forces for the purely educational view in the leadership and decision-making of the academy could spark a healthy dialogue about how to handle policy and program issues. But DiBiaggio suggests such battles can have a harmful effect on the future of the presidency.

In the short run, business pressure often leads to battles over whose judgment should prevail in governing the institution. In the longer run, the business mindset can produce intrusive micromanagement of decision making and thus compromise presidential leadership. Such an impingement on presidential authority would be "a terrible situation, especially when you have [business] people who see it [decision making] very simplistically," when it clearly is not.[14] There is also an unspoken but clear fear that intrusive board involvement can have the further adverse affect of discouraging potentially outstanding presidential candidates from even wanting to enter the arena.

Nan Keohane believes there is a telling difference between the elite and less elite class of institutions in terms of the types of presidents they seek. She deems less elite schools as understandably more prone to need presidents with proven corporate and business capability and the ability to meet expectations related to basic institutional needs, especially the requirement of being able to control the force of external political and public relations pressures. Her worry about this tendency is that when "commitments are less clear and where the board may not fully understand" the cornerstone foundations of the academy, these institutions will capitulate to "more and more pressure to have a pure business type in office." The danger for these institutions is that they quite accurately and appropriately view themselves as needing to select presidents who are institution builders, and this leads automatically to a tilt toward the business and corporate sector as the breeding ground of such leaders. "I think," Keohane concludes, "that would be a very great mistake. But I can see that that might happen."[15]

By contrast, in Keohane's opinion, elite colleges and universities have a bit more leeway, given their sagas, stability, and generally high profiles and positive reputations, to lean toward seeking and selecting as president "someone who has a strong academic background, speaks the language, has the credibility of the faculty." Also those in positions to direct the future of these schools can see "what happens on campus after campus," she adds, alluding to the use of business-type leaders "where the [that type of] leadership just doesn't work."[16]

As a coda, the emphasis on recruiting business leaders as college and university presidents has significantly ebbed in favor of a return (and these never really left the scene) of the academician, scholar, and public intellectual in the contemporary cadre of presidents. Examples include the successor generation to that we have been featuring, presidents of intellectual weight and gravitas such as Amy Gutmann at Penn, Susan Hockfield at the Massachusetts Institute of Technology, Richard Brodhead at Duke, Shirley Tilghman at Princeton, and Larry Summers, despite his self-inflicted foreshortened tenure, and now Drew Gilpin Faust as his successor at Harvard. This group is not coincidentally marked by a significant influx of outstanding women in this leadership generation.

Donald Kennedy concurs with DiBiaggio about the quality of today's presidents. Not without bias, he singles out the presidential generation of which he was a part—Rhodes, Bok, Hesburgh, and Shapiro to name just a few—as a "strong" and impressive group."[17] If Kennedy's perception is correct, maybe the "giants" are in actuality only the most recent generation of presidents, not some vanished breed of many years ago. However, turning that interpretation on its head, Frank Rhodes believes there may be too much of a tendency to revere the generation of presidents just past.[18] Rhodes is interested in clearing a path for current presidents to be able to develop legacies less cluttered by images, judgments, and comparisons with predecessors. Indeed, many of today's presidents are shaping comparable imprints on their colleges and universities and in society to those of bygone eras.

This does not mean today's presidents are or should be beyond scrutiny and criticism. For example, Rhodes believes that generally very good people are being appointed to presidencies, while Kennedy characterizes the current generation as "pretty good managers" but believes that "very few of them take strong positions on issues of broader interest than their own campuses." In part this constriction of their voice "emerged from a growing caution on the part of boards of trustees about what their presidents ought to do." However, Kennedy also self-critically remarks that there were those on his Stanford board "who were a little unhappy at how outspoken I was at times, and I'm absolutely certain that they wanted more restraint." Defending the way he conducted himself as president, Kennedy rationalizes: "I worried about the sort of disappearance of the president as public intellectual."[19] Part of Kennedy's concern is that public image has become a growing and governing force in the academy to the extent that as priorities the pursuit of positive public relations coupled with fear of a negative press can easily crowd out aspirations for courageous public stands by today's presidents.

Kennedy's "solution" to this problem about public relations is a plea to trustees and governing boards simply that "boards need to develop a stronger sense that publicity isn't always bad, that they shouldn't shrink from *edgy people*, and that in the long run, *it will do the institution more good to have a president with views that he or she is not afraid to express than to have very good managers that are hushed at critical moments about things*" (italics mine).[20] Judith Rodin underscores this crucial point, which also goes to the heart of what we want and will get in our presidents, arguing that "you have to have a board convinced that they're willing to take the risk of [the institution's] name being out there. And the better the name, the more risk averse in a way the institution becomes and that's a problem."[21]

Rodin also chose a particular strategic approach to make sure that there would be a public voice at Penn, an approach that reveals notions about sharing leadership and leadership burdens: the strategy was to recruit and support faculty who would be public intellectuals at Penn and on the local and national scene. Though originally her idea, she enlisted Penn's board to endorse this approach. "We did that intentionally because I said I shouldn't speak out on every issue." As president, Rodin believes her responsibility was to "create a group [of faculty] who are brave and out there in the public writing op-ed pieces, speaking out on important social issues, who are challenging the body politic and the general public." Elaborating further and displaying the collaboration this required, Rodin adds that "my role as president in that is to support [the faculty] and to get my board to be brave enough to believe and not worry about having such people at Penn. And, again, that was part of the strategy that I talked to the board about."[22]

Gazing into the future, Kennedy is also very concerned about the state of public universities and the impact of a changing institutional ethos on their presidents. These "public institutions have become disturbingly crippled both by the economic straits" created, Kennedy believes, primarily by Republican-controlled states and state legislatures, coupled with "the very bad governance systems that they have."[23] He cites in particular, and probably with the downfall of James Duderstadt as Michigan's president in mind, the statewide elections for the regents of the University of Michigan, elections increasingly marked and marred by litmus-test campaigns to identify slates of candidates.[24] This trend has been especially enforced from the right of the political spectrum, pushing candidates to embrace right-to-life and other conservative views in order to create opposition within university governance to still liberal, progressive initiatives, to limit research in specific areas (for example, stem cells), and to eliminate and resist policies antithetical to the right-wing agenda such as gay and lesbian partner benefits.

Kennedy and Rodin offer glimpses of the not surprising struggles in the minds of presidents as well as the pushes and pulls of their boards and trustees about the public voice of presidents and their institutions. Good people will disagree on the best approach for presidential action and behavior, and the ways the reputation of a college or university can be promoted, defended, and enlarged. Certainly trustees cannot duck the fact that they are charged with the duty to preserve and protect the foundation and future of their institutions.

But the "problem" of reputation is all the more pronounced because society's and the higher education community's hope and expectation is that institutions with the highest profile and greatest repute should be the ones that are leading voices. If Rodin and Kennedy are correct that those institutions and their presidents with the greater reputations may shrink from public notoriety in controversies and conflicts precisely because of their stature and an aspiration to protect it, then the challenge to presidents of these schools is even greater if their voices are to be heard in the public square.

This is clearly a stance more easily talked about than taken, and Harvard's "experiment" with Larry Summers certainly puts it to the test. Summers stretched the limits of Kennedy's notion of "edgy." In this case the key point not to be overlooked is that presidents have reasonable but not absolute discretion in the conduct of their office. Decisions about the use of the bully pulpit are made in light of a range of factors that presidents must wisely consider in exerting their voices in the public square.

Kennedy's concern is that the challenge of risking the public voice is readily quashed by a countertendency of presidents, matched by their boards, to place too large a premium on public relations and the search for positive spin. Looking at both the present and the future we must recognize that those who aspire to college and university presidencies, and the hopes they have for what they are able to accomplish by being in these offices, will inevitably be shaped by the way the ethos of the academy is publicly perceived. The president of the future will be of a certain type if there is at least room for "edgy" people in the office. Presidents will be wholly different if those who want to speak out in the public square, taking risks in times of controversy and conflict, preselect out of the running for these positions, convinced a priori that they would be unlikely to be selected or successful as presidents.

Harold Shapiro seconds this desire for greater bravery from his presidential colleagues and their boards, and the tolerance of a degree of "edginess" when leaders—whether presidents or others—noted as outspoken are incorporated into the life of the academy. Shapiro suggests that the real or romanticized view of the "giants" among presidents as "lone" bravehearts regularly summoning the courage of their convictions and commitment to argue positions in the public square is a risky way to conceive the presidency today and in the future. Presidents need political "cover" and must be able to rely on support from core constituencies—boards and also faculty—for at least a modicum of protection from critics of presidential and university positions.

Shapiro raises a series of rhetorical questions to press his point: "Where do they get support? Where do they find the energy and sustaining support to get people to think, to take unpopular positions, to take on things that are a little troubling?" His answer is that it should primarily be the trustees' responsibility and that "we" (former and current presidents, faculty, other concerned parties) have failed in "the mobilization of trustees with the right kind of focus and intensity of purpose."[25]

During Shapiro's presidency at Princeton, one of its highly publicly visible faculty members, Peter Singer, was taken to task by an equally high-profile university board member, Steve Forbes. Forbes took moral exception to Singer's comments about euthanasia and ideas about the end of life of elderly and disabled people. He publicly pronounced that he would not further support the university unless and until they fired Singer. Shapiro knew this was an issue of academic freedom for Singer who was speaking and writing from the context of his field and that Forbes was out of line. He urged the board to discipline Forbes and to distance themselves from him. For board members to take this step, especially against one of their own, was "something they never imagined in their wildest dreams that they would ever do." With a touch of humor but more than a bit of truth, Shapiro closes this story by commenting that presidents do not generally enlist board members in this way. In most cases, boards "aren't mobilized. They are used in the least important ways—that is, to raise money."[26] In this case the Princeton board refused to accede to Forbes's demand, effectively isolating him as a member, and thus sustaining the academic freedom of faculty members threatened by his attack on Singer.

Contemplating the qualities desirable in presidents, Rhodes believes that in the best of worlds they should have strong academic credentials (read PhDs) in an academic discipline and have taught at least somewhere along the line, even if years ago in the case of those who climb the career president ladder. This type of academic pedigree is critical to establish and maintain high credibility with faculty. In addition, presidents need a personal orientation and sense of commitment to education. Rhodes contends that they must possess beliefs and commitments about their work and a gut-level inspiration that that work truly matters. To Rhodes, "if you don't believe in the business you're in, if you don't believe the situation matters, if you don't believe that education is the most important civic undertaking there is, you're going to find all the endless routine a very wearisome business because a successful presidency is very hard work."

From the standpoint of those who select presidents and of those who aspire to these positions, Rhodes elaborates a bit further: "Commitment to the world of knowledge, to the significance of knowledge ultimately in human betterment is something that's profoundly important in selecting leaders." Rhodes adds that he thinks institutions today are doing a very good job in this regard, in terms of who we are getting as presidents.[27]

This foundation leads Rhodes to an assumption at the core of his construction of a vision for the future of the college and university presidency: that it is a "sacred trust."[28] He makes two points to underscore this contention.

One is the importance of former presidents, like Rhodes, remaining involved in explaining the university and its purposes to a wider public and being available for consultation with today's leaders. The cadre of retired and emeritus presidents is a source of experience and perspective, and this resource should be used, though cautiously making certain that it not become a meddlesome force. Major foundations and other higher education associations and organizations could enlarge models such as the ACE Fellows Program, expand publications that would provide a voice for former presidents, and establish presidents as more prominent in public discourse.

Rhodes's second point is that while it is important for presidents to hold scholarly credentials, there is a danger: "Being brought up in that world of scholarship, you tend to underestimate the power of the presidency. It's not direct power in the sense of being a corporate CEO, but the power of influence for good is immense, and taking hold of that and using it responsibly is a wonderful opportunity."[29] The track from the professorate and the world of scholarship to a presidency can be significant and important, but Rhodes cautions that the qualities of professors and scholars not be overemphasized at the expense of neglecting the value of intuition, and the capacity and willingness to use the *realpolitik* power and influence of their office.

Rhodes, Keohane, and DiBiaggio feel that the current cadre of presidents is strong and that this bodes well for the future. Judith Rodin does not disagree, but further advocates that in the present and the future "we need to reembolden university presidents." The reason for this push is the "sense, I think accurate, that many presidents fear speaking out on important issues."[30] The current political climate is one factor that compels Rodin to push in this direction, but the same conditions bear warning flags that signal caution to presidents as well.

The social and political context within which higher education must function today, Rodin fears, is more resistant to messages about the value of the university and its mission than it was in the experience of previous generations. She is particularly concerned about attacks in three areas of the life of the academy: "For the research that's done here and the ideas that are expressed here and also because of the expense of coming [attending]."[31] This causes Rodin to desire even a greater resolve that presidents not be silent, because the vacuum of their silence risks opening the floodgates to more intense criticism and opposition with regard to these fundamental principles of the academy.

Thus she wants the next generation of presidents to be "much more direct and much more open and much braver." However, Rodin also notes that even in the face of this challenge, "I think it's very important to choose those issues to be ones on which you really have some stature and some legitimacy by virtue of your professional training." Though less than sanguine about whether and to what extent this will be the future, Rodin hopes that current and future presidents will "take bold stands both for their institutions but also on important social and political issues on which they have standing."[32]

Johnnetta Cole, certainly no shrinking violet given her pronounced national profile inside and outside the world of the academy, concurs, though acknowledging that at times she has tempered her message. "Today I find myself in a very, very troubling place where in my view it's become very difficult to speak in not necessarily critical but even questioning tones about many things that are going on now," Cole declares. Increasingly she tries to use nuance in expressing her views: "I tend not to hold back, but I do try to think carefully as to how to phrase what it is that I will say."[33] Cole acknowledges that, "no matter how many disclaimers I make, I am the president of Bennett College." She also knows that in a polemical climate and time she must do everything possible to be clear in her positions, "because many, not all, of the very individual organizations, corporations from whom we need support," may well be in "disagreement with views that I may hold."[34]

Care in presidential speech should not be underestimated. Presidents must be clear in their public utterances if they are to succeed in shaping discussion on the many issues that confront their offices and in engaging constituents on controversial issues. Otherwise, arguments about presidents and their public stances will distract from the core purposes they need to be pursuing. The bottom line, and few even of the "giants" would deny they functioned any differently, is that the presidency demands great political skills. These skills must be applied inside and outside the gates, with faculty members and academics as well as with trustees, key donors, politicians, and other outside individuals and organizations on which the academy depends.

These issues, especially those regarding the primary role of research and inquiry in the world of ideas at the center of the university, are tied to the problems Kennedy underscores at the crux of governance problems, and to board and trustee member litmus tests particularly at public universities such as Michigan. In such cases the voices of presidents become even more decisive, because "we need to regain public confidence and we need to take on as presidents that obligation in assuming the presidency." Rodin's advocacy that presidents be more outspoken is directly connected to the role their image and actions play in public perceptions of the university. Her advice about what is required is that presidents "can't be insular. We can't just worry about our campus." Staying in the orbit of one's campus is "not just enough because" as president you "lose the public trust if you aren't...willing to engage the public at large about the power of ideas and the importance of what we do."[35]

This leads Rodin to suggest a collaborative, even if not fully unified, voice of college presidents on behalf of the affairs of the academy. In Rodin's opinion, *all* presidents of both public and private, especially elite and highly reputed, universities or colleges have to engage in public debate and dialogue to address criticisms, whether well founded or more like witch-hunts, of the academy. Presidents need to act and make decisions from the starting point that when one is attacked, all are attacked. Such an alliance would enable the academy to present an even stronger front in the face of criticisms about research, free speech, and freedom of expression. Rodin pushes the argument further, asserting that it is even more important for presidents of private universities like the University of Pennsylvania to involve their institutions in public discussion. This is because these colleges and universities have significant influence and thus are precisely the ones that critics of higher education hope will stay on the sidelines in an effort to avoid threats to their status and image.

Scanning the present political and cultural times, Rodin says that while endorsement of the worth of education is "apple pie and motherhood," "there isn't as much consensus on the power of debate, on the benefit of diversity, of the power of many voices, and all of the things we stand for that are about fairness and equity and opportunity." The problem therefore is that "we need to convince a much more skeptical general public of the importance of those values and of the importance of what we do here." In order to assert more determined leadership on behalf of the higher education community, Rodin is convinced that major national educational organizations need a dose of bravery and less risk aversion in their public stances as well, similar to that required of presidents, their offices, institutions, and boards. Though this is not an impossible task, Rodin fears "both for the institution of higher education and for its leadership if we don't take that on."[36]

Neil Rudenstine further assesses the present and future of the presidency, pivoting his view on the watchwords of "integrity and values" as qualities presidents must have and must embody in the institutions they lead. Rudenstine probes three components critical to expectations and thoughts about the presidency. But the overarching theme in his ideas is a creed that urges the presidency and the university back to basics, and that repeatedly returns to commitments and beliefs about the fundamental principles and values of the academy.

First, he believes "the only thing" higher education in general, individual institutions and the public "understand or fall by in the end is academic quality and integrity."[37] He believes this is matched by the "human qualities" of our colleges and universities "that we hope [express the need for] human dignity." In assessing the world-renowned and revered system of higher education in the United States, clearly the envy of much of the globe, Rudenstine contends: "The one reason why we are where we are is because people have not been afraid to think hard and to take appropriate risks and to invest a lot in constantly advancing the quality of the institutions." He humorously though accurately adds: "We didn't get here by accident." The quality of the academic life and the integrity of colleges and universities are values "any president has to deliver on."

Rudenstine's second point, accomplished simultaneously, is "the quality and integrity of the individuals in the office," who the presidents are as people, and the appointments they in turn make. Rudenstine highly valued his appointments, whether administrative or faculty, and made them not solely based on merit and excellence in an individual's field or area of specialty but on the basis of "confidence that that person was not going to let the reputation of the institution slip in terms of its integrity in any way." Even institutions as large as Harvard are made up of the resources of their people. While not using the throwback notion of "character," Rudenstine substitutes the nearly interchangeable "values" to contend that with appointments, "You just have to trust them and you have to build relationships with them and that means you have to choose them for those values." To Rudenstine the connection is clear: "If the values aren't there, the whole institution quickly gets in trouble."

Lastly, Rudenstine notes a sometimes-overlooked quality in presidents. He believes an "insider's" perspective and sense of loyalty to an institution developed over time is a critical feature in presidential selection, and can bear on the potential for success or failure. He connects these qualities to aspects of presidential preparation and tenure. One reason for the increasingly briefer tenures of today's presidents is the lengthy process of preparation that they must undertake and that more often than not is expected and required. Rudenstine's personal journey typifies this sketch of prepresidential background: nearly 20 years in upper level administrative positions—all at one institution, Princeton—prior to the presidency. Building such essential qualifications on an apprenticeship model is more and more de rigueur.

Trustees and corporation members who select and appoint presidents demand candidates with proven track records and demonstrated ability in areas crucial to the duties of presidents. Given the years required to meet these expectations, candidates are often well into their late forties or even their early to middle fifties before their first presidential appointment. Beginning a presidency at such an age in life makes it difficult reasonably to expect tenures much beyond 10 years, if even that long. Rudenstine adds the desirability of a degree of long-term affiliation with and working knowledge of an institution as an asset to a successful presidency. Rudenstine's counsel highlights the contrast with the brief tenures and almost nonexistent institutional affection and loyalty of what he calls "frequent flyer" presidents, his description of career presidents who simply move about from one presidency to another.

Rudenstine's idea that presidential candidates should possess more limited and specific institutional experience, that is, having spent the bulk of their careers at one or two institutions, is not in the mainstream of thinking about preparation for presidencies. His experience—Harvard as an undergraduate and Princeton for graduate work and a 20-year career as an administrator—leads Rudenstine to this notion. However, he is not that far out in left field. There are numerous examples of presidents in the 1960s, 1970s, 1980s, and into the present, such as Kemeny and James Wright at Dartmouth, Kennedy at Stanford, Edward Malloy at Notre Dame, and Duderstadt at Michigan to name just a few, who rose to successful presidencies through the ranks of the professorate coupled in most cases with upper level administrative experience at their "home" institution. Judith Rodin acknowledges a sense of coming home and the value of familiarity upon returning as president to the roots of her undergraduate days at the University of Pennsylvania and of her childhood and youth in the city. Though Rudenstine suggests that greater familiarity is an attractive feature, he would also acknowledge that as always the correct "match" must be the overriding concern in presidential appointments.

Another question facing colleges and universities in the development of candidates and the caliber of presidential search pools is the reality of the people in the presidential pipeline. For example, Cole is critical of the higher education community for not planning sufficiently for turnover and for failing to "incubate" and "create" the next generation of presidents. A balance and a range of leadership capacities are needed in the presidency. Cole notes that regarding the range of these essential skills, "if indeed what is required is a combination, then we better discover how to find it or at least how to help to begin to create it."[38]

Harold Shapiro is likewise concerned that colleges and universities have not done a good job developing future leadership for presidencies, as well as for upper level administrative positions that serve as breeding grounds. A large part of the problem is that there are few incentives and that the terms of appointments for department chairs and other faculty leadership positions are normally too brief—usually two to three years maximum—to offer sufficient time for good faculty leaders to gain adequate experience and to couple that with a sense of satisfaction and accomplishment.[39] The American Council on Education's Fellows Program is highly visible and successful in attracting prominent faculty and administrators, often fast-tracking them to presidencies. However, it alone is not sufficient to meet the need to enlarge the pipeline of highly qualified candidates.

Frank Rhodes adds that colleges and universities need more intentionally to nurture campus leadership in order to contribute to the development of presidents for the future. He focuses on department chair positions as potential launching pads that could be utilized much more fully than is currently the case. Rhodes charges that "perhaps the weakest link in the chain of institutional responsibility is that of the department chair. Too many department chairs serve reluctantly and ineffectively. If colleges and universities are to prosper in hard times, they need to redesign the position of chair by redefining the role, improving the selection process, providing training, and creating new incentives, support, and recognition for those who occupy this crucial position." It is the task of presidents to view this as their job and responsibility: "The president and the provost need to work with deans to correct the present weakness."[40]

Undoubtedly a barrier for some potential candidates is reluctance to be pushed onto the unavoidable public stage of the presidency with its microscopic scrutiny of style, behavior, and actions to which presidents must subject themselves. Little can be done about the personal sacrifices extracted from those who serve, or who are at the point of considering service, as presidents. Those who become presidents will be "read" in numerous ways. They have some, but in actuality limited, control over these judgments: who they are as people, the diverse expectations and projections of constituents, and the ordinary to extraordinary situations in which their leadership is demanded.

This leads to an additional leadership characteristic that must be considered: the role and potential importance of personal vulnerability in the presidency. One of the ironies of this consideration is that in many ways, the more of an imprint presidents put down, the more outspoken they are, and the longer they serve, the more vulnerable they are likely to become in the public eye. However, John Sexton believes that now and in the future, college and university presidents need to be prepared to reveal this vulnerability in the exercise of leadership.

Prior to being appointed as president of New York University, Sexton cut his leadership teeth as dean of the university's Law School. Early in his deanship and in an effort to map the school's future, Sexton single-handedly produced a lengthy "diagnosis and aspirational statement" and shared it with a senior administrative colleague at the university. The advice he got was, "People who will not oppose you at step one because they don't know where you're going, if they see where you're going to be at step 10, they'll start opposing you."[41] His colleague's advice was that you want to succeed, and if you release this document you run the risk of being judged a failure before you even get started.

But Sexton had a counterintuitive sense of how to proceed. His reaction was "look, first of all, those people might be saving me from a misstep. And secondly, none of us succeeds completely." Sexton decided to follow his gut and widely distributed the specifics of his assessment and plans to the Law School community. "What happened at the Law School, by virtue of the community reacting to the statement, dwarfs what was in that statement itself. What was in it was trivial compared to what happened," Sexton reports with pleasure but still some surprise. He hastens to add the coda that getting this type of outcome "requires a willingness to make yourself vulnerable."[42]

Sexton brought a personal style to the deanship, but this and similar experiences convinced him that vulnerability was a cornerstone of leadership. So on the occasion of his presidential inaugural address, Sexton publicly unveiled his personal philosophy of leadership. In his speech he laid out the expectations of himself as president, his aspirations for the engagement of the university community in discussion about its future, and his hopes for that future.

The speech is a portrait of his leadership philosophy, but in more broad brush strokes contains contentions about the future of the presidency. Arguing for the importance of a reliance on first principles, Sexton claims that "the University I envision is that we will place a new demand on ourselves, one that insists that we be able at any given time to articulate our institutional mission—what might be called our ratio studiorum. And we must ask how each move we make advances our overarching goal." New York University is a massive place, "a community of more than 100,000 persons and we take pride even in our differences of opinion." To make such a large and diverse place and organization work, Sexton's formula is "that if we hold ourselves to a standard of accountability, require ourselves to listen to all viewpoints in a serious way, and then set out the basis of our decisions, this community will embrace them, and," ever the rationalist, "even those in the community who disagree with them ultimately will understand them." He sums up a philosophy based on the claim that "this first feature of the university is a matter of process—process with an essential purpose—one that must permeate the entire institution from top to bottom. It is an inherent part of the category change, because in the rapidly changing context of higher education today, nothing short of a highly inclusive form of leadership," a style he pledged to provide, "will produce the appropriate blend of conservation and adaptation."[43]

Sexton knows this plea for the "listener-leader," establishing a consultative and collaborative approach to the college and university presidency, can easily be turned on its head. He is aware that the context of the life of the university continues to include an inevitable and influential business mentality among decision makers, that is, boards and other key stakeholders. It is no secret that nearly all college and university boards are liberally sprinkled with business and corporate leaders, and being located in the corporate center of power and influence of New York, Sexton is well attuned to this pressure.

Though by nature optimistic, Sexton is not sanguine, certainly less sanguine than some of his colleagues, about the tilt in the pushes and pulls between the corporate CEO versus the academician scholar in the selection of future presidents. His fear is that corporate and business-oriented pressures, especially if left unchecked and un-countered, could overwhelm the forces that he believes are more fundamental as qualities essential in the coming generation of presidents. Sexton believes corporate leaders on college and university boards tend to push for leaders who are more autocratic than the those with the "listener-leader" style that he sees as the "ideal" in leadership. "The danger is that we will see the corporatization of universities and we will see university presidents moving in the direction of the CEO," Sexton warns.[44]

Scanning the array of men and women in presidencies, Sexton contends there may be a handful who, despite their "pompousness," are "people who are so gifted and so intelligent that they have the answer that no one else sees." These are "strong philosopher kings and there will be examples of people capable of that, but they will be as rare as Einsteins."[45] Though he wishes they would behave otherwise, Sexton knows these presidents do not need to listen to or collaborate with others, and are sufficiently correct in their assessments and judgments that followers often defer to them. The existence of these few leaders in the academy, combined with a perception that the business world is loaded with similar leaders, makes this model the feature in some presidential searches. Pushing back, Sexton notes that the danger for the academy in this pressure for more autocratic leaders is that there are not "very many people capable on a CEO model of capturing the complexity and fullness of the academic side of the house."[46]

To Sexton the danger of falling for the seductions of the corporate model in both the selection of presidents and the shape of the university's culture puts at risk the very being of the academy. His concern is that when "boards of trustees are comprised principally of very successful businessmen," they tend to reduce education to the "business side of the enterprise." When this pressure and this emphasis go unchecked, "we will lose the soul of the university that is its enduring strength." The resulting fear is that "we will bring universities into the realm of the ordinary, and that route should be cause for great lamentation."[47] Sexton's hope is that among the three major alternative possibilities—the corporate model, the "philosopher kings," and the leader-listeners—that he envisions as outcomes, the vast majority of successful presidents in the future will be drawn from the leader-listener category.

There is no absolutely "correct" or "best" path to the college presidency. The skills and abilities demanded of presidents are wide and diverse. The people who aspire to these positions are, after all, people. They are human and need to be, even if the jobs themselves seem at times almost to transcend human capabilities and the energy and resources of mere mortals. As has long been the case, high-profile and trend-setting colleges and universities will be the major force determining the style and substance that will dominate presidential appointments. But in most ways, college presidents to this day still "have no equal," and that probably will forever be the case. What will these appointments of the future look like? Who will be the presidents and what might be the pathways to the office in that future?

Will there be appointments like Dartmouth's appointment of John Kemeny in 1970 when "all" he had done administratively was to chair a modest-sized math department for a couple of years prior to the presidency? Will we see more appointments such as those of Donald Kennedy at Stanford, James Duderstadt at Michigan, or John Sexton at NYU, where lengthy, dues-paying service to the institution as faculty members and senior administrators leads to a clear internal choice that readily receives the imprimatur of upper level administrative teammates? Might we see more of the Rudenstine example of a decade or more of developing administrative experience in increasingly responsible positions at one or more institutions, in some cases concluding in multiple but not "frequent flyer" presidencies? Examples of this "type" abound, including Ruth Simmons at Brown after a presidency at Smith, Mary Sue Coleman at Michigan following a presidency at Iowa, Shapiro at Iowa and Princeton, and Jim Freedman at Iowa and Dartmouth.

Or might we see more appointments such as those of Larry Summers at Harvard or Vartan Gregorian at Brown, in which an academic faculty or administrative career is interrupted by other leadership service—governmental or other nonprofit sector—prior to a presidency? Is the appointment of Amy Gutmann at the University of Pennsylvania, certainly with her share of administrative experience—though briefer than some of these other examples—but with far more noteworthiness and acclaim as a scholar, writer, and thinker, truly a public intellectual, thus a bellwether with regard to a "new" breed of presidents to come?

More than likely we will see combinations of these choices, no one predominating, but all in the mix. The corporate, business CEO will likely remain alive and well and will be the desired type, especially for certain types of institutions. Certainly this is often the case in for-profit university leadership, a sector where the "business model" of organization and leadership certainly obtains. Indeed these institutions do not hide and often are quite proud of and readily broadcast their profit orientation and business mindsets. But one of the major influences will be the overriding emphasis, especially at elite colleges and universities, of the consistent historical feature, returning again into favor, of presidents · selected because they are bona fide academicians and scholars, that is, having true faculty and professorial experience. In most cases, this fundamental requirement will continue to be complemented, as has been the case for the last half-century or more, by demonstration of sufficient administrative experience prior to the presidency.

An overriding theme in the voices of these presidents is the essential connection that must exist and persist for presidents as leaders between the historical import of their office including the platform of the presidential pulpit, and the philosophies they personally hold about the fundamental historic and timeless creeds and traditions of the academy. Those fundamental beliefs and the principles and values derived from them are the foundation of the university and of the office of president. They include, though they are not necessarily limited to, the following: the value and pursuit of knowledge and search for "truth," the importance of learning, the requirements of academic freedom and free inquiry along with responsible speech, the value of education for the betterment of the individual and for society, the transmission of the best of culture from one generation to the next, and a commitment to meritocracy and basic tenets of human dignity and equality. Wandering away from or ignoring these core principles places the university at peril. The continued platform of these values, beliefs, and creeds will not remain firmly in place or well understood without constant attention and defense in almost catechetical, though clearly not dogmatic, fashion.

Presidents are the prime guardians of this foundation and these principles. They must see this as a foremost duty and responsibility. Ponderings about who the presidents of the future will be must begin with the assumption that they will be fully capable of securing the gates of the academy from threats within and without, lest the university as we have known it cease to exist.

This affirmation applies equally and universally to the most elite and famous of the major public and private universities and the finest liberal arts colleges, as well as to public colleges, including the numerous, critical for the important niche they fill, community colleges. At their core they all adhere, even in varying degrees and with diverse traditions and sagas, to these basic principles of the academy. Sexton is correct that the soul of the university is lost if it is permitted through neglect or folly to turn into just another institution in society premised on business ideas and motivations, and to end up with leaders who follow suit.

But the soul of the university is equally at peril if its foundational and fundamental principles are not watched over on a regular and continuing basis. We conclude with further thoughts about these crucial criteria at the center of the academic presidency and at the core of the academy.

NOTES

1. Kirp, *Shakespeare, Einstein, and the Bottom Line*, p. 263.
2. Ibid.
3. Johnnetta Cole, president, Bennett College, and former president, Spelman College, interview by the author, June 2, 2003.
4. An unscientific but reasonably accurate calculation with regard to a handful of Ivy League schools indicates that even at these institutions, presidential tenures have been averaging only about 10 years, especially over the last four decades or so. For example, Brown University is now served by its 18th president in slightly more than 235 years, but had 10 presidents in the 100 years of the twentieth century, averaging a decade each, and is on its sixth in the last period of less than 40 years, about a seven-year average. Dartmouth College's current president is its 16th president in a slightly longer history, but it is currently on its fourth in 35 years, and Harvard University, the oldest college in the country, and the clear standard to which so many compare themselves, has had 27 presidents in just over 270 years, an average of 10 years each. While some of the "giants" did serve, like Hesburgh, for three to four decades (Nicholas Murray Butler at Columbia serving some 44 years, from 1901 to 1945), there were clearly many with much more "average" tenures.
5. The Reverend Theodore Hesburgh, former president, University of Notre Dame, interview by author, June 26, 2003.
6. Neil Rudenstine, former president, Harvard University, interview by author, April 10, 2003.
7. Ibid.
8. Ibid.
9. Ibid.
10. Johnnetta Cole, interview by author, June 2, 2003.
11. The Reverend Theodore Hesburgh, interview by author.
12. John DiBiaggio, former president, Tufts University, interview by author, August 12, 2003. Underscoring what a superb opportunity it is to serve as a president, DiBiaggio juxtaposes an interesting encounter at a national meeting of presidents and other higher education leaders: "I was getting on an elevator, and hearing one of my colleagues say to a new president colleague, 'Well, I don't know whether I should congratulate you or commiserate....' And I wanted to say to that person, 'Why are you in the job?'" For DiBiaggio, if a president does not truly enjoy the position, there is no reason to be in it and he would likely go so far as to urge that the person get out of the post.
13. Ibid.
14. Ibid. Expanding on this last point about the great complexity in the life of the academy in contrast to the corporate sector, DiBiaggio exclaims, "A lot of times, they [corporate leaders] don't understand this. 'Why don't you just do this?' 'Because we don't do things that way, and besides that, we're educating students not just in the classroom,

but in all of our efforts. We're teaching them. It's the moments, and you have to let [students] learn. You might have to let them make mistakes, you have to let them. You can't just criticize; it's so simple.'"

15. Nannerl Keohane, president, Duke University, interview by author, June 2, 2003.

16. Ibid.

17. Donald Kennedy, former president, Stanford University, interview by author, August 29, 2003.

18. Frank Rhodes, former president, Cornell University, interview by author, July 22, 2003.

19. Ibid.

20. Ibid.

21. Judith Rodin, former president, University of Pennsylvania, interview by author, August 16, 2004.

22. Ibid.

23. Ibid.

24. Duderstadt was forced to resign by the Michigan Board of Regents when they learned of his attempted collaboration with then Governor John Engler to change the regents' selection process from citizen election to gubernatorial appointment. Showing his colors, Kennedy characterizes these conservative forces and their efforts and initiatives as "Banana Republic stuff."

25. Harold Shapiro, former president, University of Michigan and Princeton University, interview by author, July 8, 2003.

26. Ibid.

27. Frank Rhodes, interview by author.

28. Ibid.

29. Ibid. His coda to this statement is an enthusiastic, "It's a great life."

30. Judith Rodin, interview by author.

31. Ibid. We noted previously Oden's concern about the third of these, primarily its role as part of a broader criticism of poor management and handling of finances in the academy. Robert Oden, president, Carleton College, interview by author, August 26, 2003.

32. Judith Rodin, interview by author.

33. Johnnetta Cole, interview by author. In making this comment, Cole mentions her feelings about the current war in Iraq, but extends this sense of the landscape to other major political issues such as affirmative action.

34. Ibid.

35. Ibid.

36. Ibid.

37. Neil Rudenstine, interview by author. The points that follow are from the interview.

38. Johnnetta Cole, interview by author.

39. Harold Shapiro, interview by author.

40. Rhodes, "The Art of the Presidency," p. 4.

41. John Sexton, president, New York University, interview by author, June 29, 2004.

42. Ibid.

43. John Sexton, "Address of John Sexton on the Occasion of His Installation as the Fifteenth President of New York University," September 26, 2002, President's Office, New York University.

44. Ibid.

45. John Sexton, interview by author. Sexton estimates there to be three or four such people in presidencies today, but leaves their possible identities to our imagination.

46. Ibid.

47. Ibid.

A CODA: CREEDS AND CHARACTER

I n recent years there has been an explosion of books about leaders and leadership. These range from autobiographical, personal accounts of corporate
executives to self-help applications of leadership skills in everyday life hand-
books. Regardless of the genre, rarely do more than a few pages in any book about
leadership go by before the reader confronts the word "vision." Throughout the
history of leaders and leadership, even before President George H. W. Bush made
it famous, or infamous, by admitting that he was not good at the "vision thing,"
the concept of vision has always been important.

For college and university presidents and those responsible for their selection,
the desire to focus heavily on the "vision thing" is dangerous because it is not
exclusively or even primarily the most important personal asset of the president
as leader. College presidents certainly cannot lack "vision," but in the context of
the academy, their vision is and must be joined seamlessly and symbiotically to
the basic foundations of the university. The values, beliefs, and principles of that
foundation constitute the core vision for the academy and for the presidents who
lead it.

Historically this relationship between presidential philosophy and aspiration
and the principles at the core of the university has been the case from the very
first imprints of the founder-presidents of the Colonial colleges. As the story of
today's presidents reveals, the foundation provided by the basic tenets and values
of the university—its creed and character—is directly connected, and must be
seen as so, to the "vision," to the grounding, and to the pulpit of presidents—their
creeds and character. This reality is more critical and pronounced in the contemporary era than at any preceding time. The arguable reason for this actuality

is the greater need today for transcendent principles and values as a rationale to counter ideological and brazenly political pressures that, if left unchecked, will reshape the academy into a vastly different and unrecognizable form at odds with its historical contours and traditions.

Presidents are prime architects of the formation and reformation of the institutional saga. They make imprints on the future of their individual colleges and universities, and influence society's conception and understanding of the university writ large. Every new president inherits the best (and the worst, for sure) of an institution's fundamental beliefs, values, and principles, in their own ways broadly reflective of those associated with the larger idea and concept of the university. Certainly choices about leaders are determined *in situ*, dictated by recent institutional history, saga, temperament, and needs. However, a president should not have to search very far or have great difficulty in locating the foundation of the college or university, though there are moments and opportunities for traditions and saga to be re-mined and resurrected. This much of the "vision" of any college is in place, even if it needs to be dusted off and reinterpreted in order to be more visible, valuable, and meaningful in the contemporary world.

Our contention is that once selected, presidents have the major responsibility and duty to locate and propose to their various constituencies a "center" of the university that will "hold." Presidents, and no one else, are the guardians, the leaders who must sustain and protect the critical fundamental concepts at the foundation of the academy. Using these underpinnings, presidents are then able to identify what needs to be said from their pulpits about the connection of these principles and values to a "center" that will hold for their diverse communities. Presidents must put forward their vision by locating, crafting, and shaping the "center" for the university and college, no mean feat in the heat of the political correctness and ideological pressures of today's academy.

The academy has a creed and the best among presidents understand and stress the critical role of this creed, even if called by other names, in the leadership of their office. The creed of the university is simply constituted: freedom of thought and inquiry, freedom of academic and scholarly expression, respect for divergent and diverse opinions, commitment to civility in discourse and behavior; the belief that education passes the best of culture from one generation to another, the belief in human equality and progress, and the belief in the tenets of meritocracy. These creedal principles are at the crux of the academy and they bear heavily on the complexities of successfully navigating the presidential office in the contemporary culture of the academy.

The reality for today's presidents and the challenge distinguishing them from their predecessors, the "giants," is that they unavoidably face the necessity to argue for the reestablishment of this creed. This means separating actual principles about the creed of the academy and beliefs based on those principles from simple lip service generated from vague notions of what the creed stands for. By contrast, this creed in the "giants'" era was much more universally assumed and accepted, as a result of greater authority in that bygone time. To succeed in watching over this core of the university, presidents must creatively use this creed as the fundamental starting point in the identification and articulation of a center for the university, the location of common ground and of commonality of purpose sufficient to create a center that will hold. This task was simply of immeasurably less concern to the "giants" because of the vastly more homogenous culture of their day.

The responsibility to tend to these joined foundations, the basic creed of the university and the need to hold the center, must arguably be viewed as a major distinguishing feature in a contemporary examination of the role of presidents. In more homogenous bygone eras, the basic principles of the academy were more taken for granted, and thus did not have to be repeatedly uttered, underscored, and embraced. The center was once commonly assumed and held, not contested as it is today by the competing, and corrosive to the foundations of the academy, voices of political correctness and an unrestrained ideological drumbeat.

Pursuing the twin goals of reestablishing the creed of the academy and locating a center requires a relentless focus on foundational principles that today's presidents must bring to their work. This disciplined and concentrated focus is decisive for the defense of the academy in the face of the regular and relentless diversions of political correctness and ideological battles. However, the exercise of these duties exacts a toll. Thus the importance of Frank Rhodes's advice that presidents must in their heart of hearts be committed to these basic values of the university and truly want to do this work.

More importantly, by concentrating on the core principles of the academy and on developing a center that can hold, presidents strengthen their hands in battling politically correct and ideologically driven thinking about the university. Presidents need to defend the university, to let the university be the university. Fixated as they are on their particular agenda, the forces of political correctness and ideology care little, if at all, about the historical foundation and image of the university. Unchecked, the devices, thinking, and demand for change of these political forces in and outside the academy could willy-nilly produce an evolution of the university that would be the fin de siècle Minogue warned of. That is, absent the tending of its foundations, the university could easily turn into just another social, political, or other—business, economic, commercial—institution in society. Presidents need to ensure that Minogue's worst-case scenario is not the future of the university. They must defend the gates of the academy against assaults from within and without.

Along with that of the academy, presidents too have creeds. Their creeds are born of personal educational and professional—professorial, scholarly, and administrative—experience, philosophies of education and of the university, ethical and moral values, and religious or transcendent beliefs or both. These constitute the moral compass of presidents and shape the way they navigate leadership and the fortunes and futures of the university. The key in presidential searches is to match the creed of the university or college, as discretely fashioned, to the creed of the president. Presidents are not obliged to possess a vision as much as they ought to possess a creed. In office, presidents should pay attention to making the core values and beliefs of the university the ground of their tenure and then, and only then, contribute personal vision and aspiration to form an imprint they can hope to leave behind.

In addition, presidents need to be the architects of shaping a center that is able to hold. Of course college presidents have egos; no one aspires to leadership positions of this level of prestige and influence without enormous ego-strength and self-confidence. However, their presidential role must not be confused or conflated with personal ego and a cult of personality. For the president as leader, the life of the academy is not about the president as an individual. It is about the college or university, its saga, and the demands of its future. Presidents should use their creeds to fashion legacies that stand on the shoulders of predecessors and that, engaged with colleague faculty, administrators, and trustees, strengthen the institution's saga and fortunes.

The pressures of political correctness and the ideological battleground will remain very much in play, as they always have, in the academy and will exert force from outside the walls as well. The challenge for presidents is to avoid capitulation to these forces, and to create an ethos and ethic of dialogue and debate framed in the broadest definition possible of the "middle." Stephen Joel Trachtenberg provides a practical "how to" for presidents to meet this challenge by "constantly searching for equilibrium," and through his perception of the president's responsibility "as a balance wheel in an institution which has strong passions, made up of individuals who wish to steer it in any one of various worthwhile and even noble directions." This is a leadership duty far exceeding that of the average corporate CEO. Trachtenberg adds that "my passion is to allow all those passions to play out in the name of a healthier academic community, but also in a healthier society in general."[1]

A distinct vehicle and avenue for presidents with its strong heritage, and present as well as future possibility, is the expectation that they possess and fully use the bully pulpit. But the very thought that presidents have pulpits and that they might use them to make utterances about core values and principles can trip alarm bells in and out of the academy. At least two major dangers prevent, or at least constrain, presidents from speaking out on issues and concerns of the day.

The first, and to some the most obvious, is where we began our story: the relentless fund-raising pressure on presidents—the era now of the almost continuous "campaign"—and the fear of losing major donors, especially in reaction to "hot button" issues. The fleeting nature of fund-raising, a business in which timing can be everything, can make presidents reticent about what they say and how they might be quoted. Most presidents will acknowledge that in practice they err on the side of caution and nuance in what they have to say, wisely avoiding utterances that might offend a major donor, potential or otherwise, or any keystone constituency of the university.

While this pressure may be more myth than reality, it still makes presidents wary. Former Brown University President Vartan Gregorian's warning bears repeating: presidents need "tact and diplomacy" and should act ever mindful of Lord Chesterfield's advice "that wisdom is like carrying a watch. Unless asked, you don't have to tell everybody what time it is." Some colleges have refused gifts because of an overt or implied quid pro quo. However, the quest for gifts does not have to compromise the presidential voice. Nan Keohane maintained a vigorous bully pulpit all the while running and concluding a highly success- ful billion-dollars-plus campaign. Neil Rudenstine pushed controversial issues to the forefront even as he attracted enormous gifts for Harvard from alumni and other donors. There is a fair bit of talk about how fund-raising pressure constrains the voice of presidents, but it is clear that this burden by itself does not prevent presidents from speaking out publicly.

However, a second danger lurks as a potential area of constraint within which presidents must maneuver: the ideological battleground of political correctness. This is a much more insidious problem for the presidential voice and for the future of the university. The peril is that presidents, seeking rightly to defend the turf of the university from critics, generally on the right, are characterized instantly by those same critics as therefore on the side of "progressive" academics, generally on the left, who like their right-wing opponents want to use the univer- sity to achieve their own set of overt and covert social and political goals.

The intentions and machinations of these politically motivated faculty members and other supporters inside and outside the gates ironically confirm and provide a steady stream of fodder for the critiques the Right trumpets in the public square: the university is no longer a place of objectivity and of the unbridled search for truth. Paradoxically, these left-leaning faculty and their "progressive" allies, often found in administrative ranks, set on pushing political agendas, contrib- ute, largely unintentionally but nonetheless harmfully, to the undermining of the very principles of free and open inquiry, of the search for truth, of debate and dialogue—fundamental hallmarks of the university—that they should be defend- ing. This leaves it to presidents, often operating alone in Oden's "messy middle" between the factions of Left and Right, to guard and protect the heritage and values of the academy regardless of who gets crossed and offended in the process.

John Sexton's voice is exemplary with regard to what is required of today's presidents and those of the future. His notion of "the university as sanctuary" is a profound idea that ought to be a clarion call for the times. Sexton's ideas about the contemporary threats to the university and what leaders must do to secure the university's future are of value to all colleague presidents and to those involved— primarily trustees and faculty—in presidential selection. Joining Sexton, univer- sities and their presidents need to accept the challenge of the "powerful evidence that the quality of dialogue in much of our society increasingly is impoverished— that, just when there is a need for more nuanced reflection and discussion, civil discourse seems ever less able to deliver it." We need to heed Sexton's advice, warning that "it is ironic that at the time when sustaining the university as sanc- tuary is so important to society at large, society itself has unleashed forces which threaten the vitality if not the existence of that sacred space."[2]

Sexton aptly concludes that "simply put, the polarization and oversimplification of civic discourse have been accompanied by a simultaneous attempt to
capture the space inside the university for the external battle. This trend does
not arise from one political side or another, but from a tendency to enlist the
university not for its wisdom but for its symbolic value as a vehicle to ratify
a received vision."[3] The greater the university's perceived value and stature, the
more attractive it is as an institution that can provide critical support of agendas
and beliefs. When those agendas are antithetical to the principles of the academy, irretrievable and lasting damage can quickly result. Ironically, then, the very
image and esteem accorded the university can be its undoing.

This threat is very real and must not be understated or underestimated. What
can and should presidents do to face it? First, the challenge needs to be viewed as
a primary responsibility of the office. If not presidents, who would have a voice
powerful enough to be heard as defender and protector of the fundamental values
of the academy?

Second, as guardians of the gates, preservers of the "sanctuary," presidents must
steer a middle course in the ideological battleground. Some might find such an
approach too tentative, further compromising the bully pulpit of the presidency.
I contend, rather, that the challenge of Trachtenberg's "balance wheel" is actually the major and crucial way that presidents exercise courage. Leading from the
"middle" is where their moral authority is most needed. The challenge of being
"balance wheels" is greater than anything that was expected of the "giants" of
previous and bygone eras. It is a task critical to prevent the muzzling and changing of the true spirit of the academy and thereby the academy itself. Presidents
need to be voices ensuring that the university not be turned into something used
"for its symbolic value as a vehicle to ratify a received vision."[4] In short, presidents are called upon to do nothing less than use their voices and pulpits to let
the university be the university. The future, as is always the case, will judge their
success or failure in this important work and mission.

The challenge then is for today's presidents simultaneously and seamlessly to
embrace the fundamental principles of the university, acting as "balance wheels"
to defend and maintain those values while crafting a common core and center
that will hold for the campus and its varied constituents. This has historically
been the task of presidents, but the complexities of the present environment—
political correctness and ideological thinking often to the exclusion of all other
ideas and methods—make this demand more difficult to meet than in previous
eras. We have painted a picture of how presidents cope with this challenge, how
they meet and address it, in many cases with great success. A concluding series of
conceptual ideas serves as a framework to understand this presidential work and
to comprehend the presidency in the contemporary era and for years to come.[5]

The centerpiece of these ideas is that presidents are called upon to understand and interpret a civil religion of the academy, analogous to the civil religion or religion of the Republic of the American nation.[6] There are numerous
common threads tying together these two religious notions for the nation and

for the academy, not the least being that both are "experiments" and feature core democratic values and principles at their center. The civil religion of the academy serves its culture and ethos and is tangentially but yet importantly connected to the core of the religion of the Republic in its beliefs about the destiny of the nation, its creedal foundations in the Declaration of Independence, the Constitution, and the Bill of Rights, and its theology of the hand of a deity in the affairs of state.

However, there are great similarities, joined in the spirit of Tocqueville's focus on the tensions between individualism and community, between freedom and liberty in the quest for coherent governance, and between pluralism and commonly agreed central, unifying principles and values. Both civil religions, that of the academy and that of the Republic, are constituted of commonly held secular yet transcendent beliefs and values. The specific role of a deity per se is not directly in the mix of the civil religion of the academy, except in the case of church-related and religiously affiliated colleges and universities. However, transcendent values and ideas are in play, even if they often remain sub rosa. That is, though the speech and commentary of college presidents often reflect general references to higher principles, mores, and claims on human endeavor, as a rule, their voice is not punctuated with religiously particularistic transcendent language and references.

I have suggested that college and university presidents are high priests of an ever-evolving civil religion in the academy bearing a striking resemblance to that of the American nation. The notion of "priests" is heavily reminiscent of bygone eras of minister- and priest-presidents at the many religiously founded and affiliated colleges and universities. It is an idea rooted in patriarchal imagery that must be reinterpreted for the contemporary era. Despite the danger of misinterpretation and the baggage of the connotations of "priests," there are suggestive elements of the clerical tradition worthy of consideration as we examine the future of the presidency. For example, we might think of college and university presidents as theologians, that is, thinkers about transcendent ideas, including those deemed broadly "religious" in nature, about schools of thought and systems of belief, of a civil religion of the academy. If the term theologian is too high-handed, at the least presidents might be thought of as advocates and philosophers of this civil religion of the academy.

College presidents have historically used the authority of their office to stress the need for agreement on common values in social and civic life. This duty is undiminished, though arguably more difficult to accomplish in the contemporary era. Much of the reason for this vast complexity today, as Harold Shapiro reminds us, is the problems that befall us if "the age of tolerance ushered in by the ideals of the Enlightenment" leads us to "succumb to the idea that all values are equally acceptable and, thus, deny the existence of any absolute values."[7] Juxtaposed to this is Burton Clark's definition of the institutional saga as "[A]n organizational legend (or saga), located between ideology and religion, partak[ing of] an appealing logic on one hand and sentiments similar to the spiritual on the other."[8] It is this close linkage "between ideology and religion" of these "spiritual" assumptions at the basis of its relationship to the saga and our understanding of the university that needs to be explored and debated and discussed. It is this task that presidents face and must confront.

There are first-rate arguments in the academy about whether there are absolute values, whether there are spiritual sentiments, but even these deliberations are in part Shapiro's point. The academy should have that ongoing debate. Presidents are responsible for leading in that dialogue, because of its connection to locating the center and of its role in clarifying the transcendent values and purposes in the culture of colleges and universities.

The claim here is that one guidepost for contemporary presidents in this task of establishing and expressing a common core, not without its own fragility, is to rely on a civil religion. A part of that undertaking requires that presidents be about the business of creating language applicable for civil discussion and of establishing the ethos in which that dialogue can take place. A couple of examples are Sexton's call that the university be understood as a "sanctuary" and Trachtenberg's use of Abraham and the "Abrahamic tradition" as a uniting theological idea for Christian, Jewish, and Muslim members of his and other university communities, especially in a post–September 11th era.[9]

Presidential rhetoric can underscore concern for diversity and the need for tolerance, equal opportunity, and racial and ethnic fairness and sensitivity. What is needed, and what is much more difficult to do, primarily because religion is not viewed as it should be as a feature of diversity, is to create and use language fitting for a secular, transcendent set of values and beliefs in the presidential pulpit. Presidents understandably fear that they could easily be misinterpreted if their utterances began to be interpreted as in some fashion religious. However, rather than running from the challenge to the use of such language in the presidential pulpit, presidents ought actively to embrace the possibility that there are transcendent yet uniting forms of language and ideas that can be risked in the dialogue of the academy. A fitting starting point is for presidents to use voices tailored to and consistent with the multireligious and multifaith aspects of today's diversity era and agenda.

The leadership of today's presidents is crucial in developing the common agreements essential to guide and govern the university. This quest requires delicate balance. Presidents must be careful not to impose values on their communities. But the establishment of ethical norms need not be reduced to a choice between either the norms and interests of campus communities or the visions and voices of their leaders. In the democracy of the academy, presidents must respond to the collective wisdom of constituents without limiting their bully pulpit or reducing their influence. That pulpit can be the place for testing and shaping Shapiro's "working hypotheses," and this charge demands a different style than merely the exertion of authoritarian power.[10]

However, the dangers of a collapse of commonly agreed values in the contemporary climate of the academy are equally inescapable. The pressure applied by ideologies and their advocates, less concerned about the common good and the larger importance of the university qua the university than about their particular agendas, makes agreement on common principles more difficult, if not impossible. The challenge of overcoming these centripetal forces is enormously complex. To do so, presidents have to answer questions about what will comprise and constitute the ethical, civic, and social—civil religious—working hypotheses they can use as platforms and as propositions in public utterances to their constituencies. This duty that they must not shirk requires presidents to use their voice, at times in uncompromising ways, to suggest unifying hypotheses and to argue the common principles at the heart and soul of the university. It also demands that college and university presidents use their essential personal character to exert the courageous leadership required by this crucial undertaking.

The future of presidential leadership pivots largely on Shapiro's major contention: moral discourse rests on common agreement that in the free interchange of ideas, all sides of an argument are of value. This is a fundamental principle of the academy, the absence of which would produce a dramatic change in the nature of academic discourse and thereby the nature of the academy. Underlying this contention is the basic question: can the center any longer hold? The basic conundrum of the academy, like that of a democratic society, is embedded in the reality that the social compact based on commonly agreed secular beliefs, a civil religion, is always at risk because of individualism. In more pronounced and probably more difficult ways than in the society surrounding it, the academy must hold in tension the spirit of the individual—freedom, choice, and action—with those elements held in common essential to a community of scholars—inquiry, intellectual discourse, and toleration of opposing points of view. We come full circle, for these are surely the fundamental values and beliefs of the university.

The challenge to presidents and their leadership could not be more profound. Some commentators have described the affairs and ethos of the academy as a battle for the heart and soul of the college and university.[11] Trachtenberg, for one, saw this danger early on, warning of the "new ideological edge...often called a 'search for values'...[but more likely] a longing for authority and discipline."[12] Though Trachtenberg might not go so far as to call it a conspiracy, he decries critics of higher education who use the promotion of values to divert attention from their real goal of implanting a specific orthodoxy. A. Bartlett Giamatti, then president of Yale, expressed similar fears about the breakdown of consensus in the academy. Giamatti contended that the university could not afford to abandon the pursuit of consensus, no matter how difficult or lengthy the process, for the ease and simplicity, but finally corrosive impact on the academy, of codification to resolve disputes and differences of opinion. Doing so would surely result not only in a failure to resolve differences, but worse, exacerbate and magnify divisions and controversies.[13]

Presidents, even in the face of secularity and pluralism, can make clear statements about the ideals of the academy. Their leadership is strongly rooted in a unique American tradition combining democratic principles and liberal education.

A starting point for renewing this alliance—an alliance that answers, at least in part, Shapiro's concern about the center holding—is for presidents to ground their voice in the fundamental beliefs and values of the college, and in the uniquely American educational experiment at the heart and soul of the nation's colleges and universities. These ideals stand importantly as a counterpoint to the tyranny of political correctness and ideological shibboleths within the gates of the university and outside in society. This liberal democratic ideal is what leads to notions of leadership in the "messy middle," more than likely an abiding reality for the presidents of the twenty-first century. If true, the better presidents are able to negotiate and navigate the "messy middle," the more successful, and likely in the process more visible, they will be as leaders on campus and in society.

The optimistic prospect is that democratic principles and liberal education—an education that seeks to liberate and inspire the mind—will continue to be the foundation of colleges and universities and of presidential leadership. The compass for presidents in navigating the course of these challenges resides in the history and tradition of their leadership and office. In the future as in the past, debate about education, the nature of the university, and its role in society will best be shaped and informed by the leadership that, in many ways, presidents alone can and must provide.

NOTES

1. Stephen Joel Trachtenberg, president, George Washington University, interview by author, May 7, 2003.

2. John Sexton, "The University as Sanctuary," speech delivered at Fordham University, February 17, 2004, p. 5.

3. Ibid.

4. Ibid.

5. In different and less extended form, the ideas that follow were originally presented in Nelson, "College Presidents: Voices of Civic Virtue and the Common Good of Democracy," pp. 24–26.

6. Harold Shapiro supplies a historical context as follows:

> The founding "fathers" settled for the inevitable uneasy compromise between a belief in moral certainties—largely Calvinistic Protestantism—and the belief in the desirability of change and progress. Their solution could be described as a secular regime buttressed in important ways by a civil religion.
>
> The role of this civil religion was to provide a set of background values and commitments that would balance the general interest against the weight of private interests and to provide the necessary moral meaning to our individual and joint efforts. The official theology was that such a "secular" religion could be embodied in our civil laws. What was not fully appreciated, then or now, was the basic fragility of such an arrangement and how much the harmony of liberty and religion (our joint moral code) depended on religious uniformity. Tocqueville himself, noting that individual freedom weakens political ties and, therefore, increases the need for moral ties, concluded that Christianity was integral to representative democracy.

Shapiro, "Ethics in America—Who Is Responsible?" pp. 4–5.

7. Shapiro, *Tradition and Change*, p. 35.

8. Clark, *The Distinctive College*, p. 235.

9. Stephen Joel Trachtenberg, interview by author. In a speech, "Abraham's Children," Trachtenberg goes into great exegetical detail about the family heritage of Abraham. He raises the question of whether what we are really looking at today is "what some scholars have called a 'clash of civilizations,' with the obvious undertone of inevitability? Are we looking at an intractable enmity that was ancient and preordained?" He concludes, "Genesis tells us otherwise," and that "[I]n fact, during most of their history, Jews and Muslims were not at each other's throats." Does this, then, mean that "any 'clash' is more virtual than real"? Indeed, does it have "less to do with the way one group worships as compared to another or with their interpretations of God's will and intentions than with the problems of being family?" http://www.gwu.edu/-gwpres/speeches_abraham.html, p. 3.

10. Shapiro, "Ethics in America—Who Is Responsible?"

11. Among those making this argument are Bill Readings, *The University in Ruins* (Cambridge, MA: Harvard University Press, 1996); and Bruce Wilshire, *The Moral Collapse of the University: Professionalism, Purity, and Alienation* (Albany: SUNY Press, 1990).

12. Stephen Joel Trachtenberg, "Presidents Can Establish a Moral Tone on Campus," p. 9.

13. Giamatti, *The University and the Public Interest*, pp. 181–82.

BIBLIOGRAPHY

Bowen, William, and Derek Bok. *The Shape of the River: Long-Term Consequences of Considering Race in College Admissions*. Princeton, NJ: Princeton University Press, 1998.

Brodhead, Richard H. *The Good of This Place*. New Haven, CT: Yale University Press, 2004.

Clark, Burton. *The Distinctive College: Antioch, Reed, and Swarthmore*. Chicago: Aldine, 1970.

Cole, Johnnetta. Interview by author. June 2, 2003.

Coleman, Mary Sue. "Coleman Statement." November 7, 2002. http://www.umich.edu/~newsinfo/Releases/2002/Nov02/r11070a.html.

———. "Comments from University Leaders." News Service, University of Michigan. June 23, 2003. http://www.umich.edu/news/Releases/2003/Jun03/comments.html.

———. Interview by author. July 23, 2003.

———. "Letter to the Campus Community." University of Michigan. October 1, 2002. http://www.umich.edu/~urecord/0102/sept30_02/coleman-1tr.html.

———. "President's Day Talk." Detroit Athletic Club. November 18, 2002.

DiBiaggio, John. Interview by author. August 12, 2003.

Dim, Joan Marans, and Nancy Murphy Cricco. *The Miracle on Washington Square: New York University*. Lanham, MD: Lexington Books, 2001.

Duderstadt, James. Interview by author. March 6, 1995.

Edwards, Mark. Personal communication. June 7, 2005.

Englund, Steven. "John Sexton: Seizing the Mile." *Lifestyles* 27, no. 160 (pre-spring 1999): 16c-17a.

Fanelli, Alexander. *John Kemeny Speaks*. Hanover, NH: Dartmouth College, 1999.

Gerety, Thomas. Interview by author. July 27, 1994.

Giamatti, A. Bartlett. *The University and the Public Interest*. New York: Atheneum, 1981.

Gulley, Stuart F. *The Academic President as Moral Leader*. Macon, GA: Mercer University Press, 2001.

Herrnstein, Richard J. and Charles Murray. *The Bell Curve: Intelligence and Class Structure in American Life*. New York: Free Press Paperbacks, 1994.

Hesburgh, Theodore. "The Future of Liberal Education." February 9, 1980. University of Notre Dame Archives.

———. Interview by author. June 26, 2003.

———. "The Moral Dimensions of Higher Education." October 13, 1983. University of Notre Dame Archives.

———. "The University in the World of Change." Fourth Annual Meeting of the Council of Graduate Schools. December 10, 1964. University of Notre Dame Archives.

Hirsch, Werner Zvi, and Luc E. Weber. *Challenges Facing Higher Education*. Phoenix, AZ: Oryx Press, 1999.

Honan, William H. "At the Top of the Ivory Tower the Watchword Is Silence." *New York Times*, July 24, 1994, sec. 4, 5.

Kemeny, Jean. *It's Different at Dartmouth*. Brattleboro, VT: Stephen Greene Press, 1979.

Kennedy, Donald. *Academic Duty*. Cambridge, MA: Harvard University Press, 1997.

———. Interview by author. August 29, 2003.

———. Interview with Anne Flatte. http://becoming.stanford.edu/interview/donaldken nedy/html.

———. *The Last of Your Springs*. Stanford, CA: Stanford Historical Society, 1998.

———. "The Lost Art of Teaching." *Stanford Magazine*, January/February 1998, 1–6.

———. "Universities: Costs and Benefits on the Academic Frontier." Stanford University.

Keohane, Nannerl. Interview by author. June 2, 2003.

———. "The Public Role of the University." Duke University. October 24, 2002. http:// www.dukenews.edu/news/opinion.asp?id=843&catid=2,45&cpg=opinion.aslp.

Kerr, Clark. *The Uses of the University*. 5th ed. Cambridge, MA: Harvard University Press, 2001.

Kirp, David L. *Shakespeare, Einstein, and the Bottom Line*. Cambridge, MA: Harvard University Press, 2003.

Laney, James. *The Education of the Heart: Selected Speeches of James T. Laney*. Atlanta, GA: Emory University Press, 1994.

———. Interview by author. April 27, 2003.

Leading Out. Producer James Ault. James Ault Productions, Northampton, MA, 1994.

Lind, Bill. "The Origins of Political Correctness." Accuracy in Academia Conference, 2000. http://www.academia.org/lectures/lind1.html.

Massey, Walter. Interview by author. May 25, 2004.

———. "A More Excellent Way: Realizing the Academic Village at Morehouse College." Convocation Address. September 18, 2003.

Minogue, Kenneth. *The Concept of the University*. Berkeley: University of California Press, 1973.

Nelson, Stephen, J. "A Study of the Moral Voice of the College President." University of Connecticut, 1996.

———. "College Presidents: Voices of Civic Virtue and the Common Good of Democracy." *Journal of Leadership Studies* 8, no. 3 (winter 2002): 11–28.

———. *Leaders in the Crucible: The Moral Voice of College Presidents*. Westport, CT: Bergin and Garvey, 2000.

———. "Presidential Profiles." March 2001. www.collegevalues.org.

Newman, John Henry. *The Idea of the University*. Oxford: Clarendon Press, 1976.

Oden, Robert A., Jr. "Affirmative Action and the Michigan Cases." *The Carletonian*, February 21, 2003, 6.

———. "Inaugural Convocation Address." October 25, 2002. http://www.carleton.edu/ inauguration/speeches.php3?id=2.

———. Interview by author. August 26, 2003.

———. "Presidential Profiles." March 22, 2002. www.collegesvalues.org.

———. "The Time Famine of the 1990s." Kenyon College. August 19, 1999.

Pelikan, Jaroslav. *The Idea of the University: A Reexamination*. New Haven, CT: Yale University Press, 1992.

Readings, Bill. *The University in Ruins*. Cambridge, MA: Harvard University Press, 1996.

Rhodes, Frank. "The Art of the Presidency." *The Presidency*, spring 1998, 5.

———. Interview by author. July 22, 2003.

———. "Interview with Harry Kreisler." Institute of International Studies, University of California, Berkeley. March 31, 1999. http://globetrotter.Berkeley.edu/people/ Rhodes-con2.html.

———. "Reinventing the University." In *Reinventing the Research University*, ed. Luc E. Weber and James J. Duderstadt. London: Economica, 2004.

———. "Thoughts on the American University at the Dawn of the Third Millennium." Office of President Emeritus, Cornell University. December 7, 1999.

Rodin, Judith. "The Agenda for Excellence, Six University Academic Priorities." September 24, 1996. http://www.upenn.edu/president/rodin/agenda96.html.

———. Interview by author. August 16, 2004.

———. "The University and Civil Society." October 12, 1999. http://www.upenn.edu/ president/rodin/civil_society.html.

Rudenstine, Neil. Interview by author. April 10, 2003.

———. *Pointing Our Thoughts*. Cambridge, MA: Harvard University, 2001.

Rudenstine, Neil, and William Bowen. "Race-Sensitive Admissions: Back to Basics." *Chronicle of Higher Education*, February 7, 2003, B7.

Rupp, George. Inaugural Address. October 4, 1993.

Sexton, John. "Address of John Sexton on the Occasion of his Installation as the Fifteenth President of New York University." President's Office, New York University. September 26, 2002.

———. "Inaugural Address." President's Office, New York University. September 26, 2002.

———. Interview by author. June 29, 2004.

———. "The Role of Faculty in the Common Enterprise University." Northwestern University's President's Teaching Series. President's Office, New York University. May 6, 2004.

———. "The University as Sanctuary." Speech. Fordham University. New York. February 17, 2004. A fuller version is available as a draft paper, President's Office, New York University.

Shapiro, Harold. "American Higher Education: A Special Tradition Faces a Special Challenge." May 22, 1986. Bentley Historical Library, University of Michigan.

———. "Ethics in America—Who Is Responsible?" *New York Times*. Presidential Forum, December 1, 1987.

———. Interview by author. July 8, 2003.

Shapiro, Harold. *A Larger Sense of Purpose: Higher Education and Society.* Princeton, NJ: Princeton University Press, 2005.

———. "Is Taking Sides a Good Idea for Universities?" *SCIENCE* (American Association for the Advancement of Science) 225, no. 4657 (July 1984): 19.

———. "Thoughts on the American University at the Dawn of the Third Millennium." Office of the President Emeritus, Cornell University. December 7, 1999.

———. *Tradition and Change: Perspectives on Education and Public Policy.* Ann Arbor: University of Michigan Press, 1987.

———. "Tradition, Continuity, Discovery, and Change: A Conversation with Princeton's Past." President's Office, Princeton University. January 8, 1988.

Trachtenberg, Stephen Joel. "All Abraham's Children." September 26, 2002. http://www.gwu.edu/~gwpres/speeches_abraham.html.

———. "Healing with Words and Acts on Campus." Annual Meeting of the Jewish Social Services Agency. October 2, 2002. http://www.gwu.edu/~gwpres/speeches_healing.html.

———. Interview by author. May 7, 2003.

———. "Presidents Can Establish a Moral Tone on Campus." *Educational Record* 70, no. 2 (spring 1989).

———. "President's Preoccupations." Address. President's Office, George Washington University.

———. *Reflections on Higher Education.* Westport, CT: Oryx Press, 2002.

"U-M Responds to NCAA Decision." University of Michigan News Service. May 8, 2003. http://www.umich.edu/~new/Releases/2003/May03/r050803a.html.

Will, Katherine Haley. "Alma Mater as Big Brother." *Washington Post,* March 29, 2005, A15.

———. "The Voices of Gettysburg." Inaugural Address. President's Office, Gettysburg College. October 17, 2004.

Wilshire, Bruce. *The Moral Collapse of the University: Professionalism, Purity, and Alienation.* Albany: SUNY Press, 1990.

INDEX

About the Author

STEPHEN J. NELSON is Assistant Professor of Educational Leadership at Bridgewater State College (MA) and is a Senior Scholar in the Leadership Alliance at Brown University. He holds a Ph.D. in Professional Higher Education Administration from the University of Connecticut, and is the author of *Leaders in the Crucible: The Moral Voice of College Presidents* (2000). He received a Kellogg Foundation grant to conduct the further research about college and university presidents that led to this book. Dr. Nelson holds a B.A. degree in history from Gettysburg College, an MS in Religious Studies from the Harford Seminary, and a Masters of Divinity from Andover Newton Theological School.